Essentials of
Elementary Social Studies

Essentials of
Elementary Social Studies

Third Edition

Thomas N. Turner
University of Tennessee, Knoxville

Boston   New York   San Francisco
Mexico City   Montreal   Toronto   London   Madrid   Munich   Paris
Hong Kong   Singapore   Tokyo   Cape Town   Sydney

Executive Editor: Traci Mueller
Editorial Assistant: Krista E. Price
Marketing Manager: Elizabeth Fogarty
Editorial Production Service: Whitney Acres Editorial
Manufacturing Buyer: Andrew Turso
Cover Administrator: Kristina Mose-Libon
Electronic Composition: Omegatype Typography, Inc.

For related titles and support materials, visit our online catalog
at www. ablongman.com.

Between the time Website information is gathered and then published, some sites
may have closed. Also, the transcription of URLs can result in typographical
errors. The publisher would appreciate being notified of any problems with URLs
so that they may be corrected in subsequent editions.

Library of Congress Cataloging-in-Publication Data

Turner, Thomas N.
    Essentials of elementary social studies / Thomas N. Turner.—3rd ed.
        p. cm.
    Includes bibliographical references and index.
    ISBN 0-205-40266-6 (pbk.)
        1. Social sciences—Study and teaching (Elementary)—United States. I. Title.

    LB1584.T87 2004
    372.83—dc21

                                                                                2003051873

Printed in the United States of America

10 9 8 7 6 5 4 3 2 1   08 07 06 05 04 03

Contents

Preface

I keep learning new things and how to do old things better. That is the best explanation that I can give for this third edition. Events of recent years have changed the social studies. The terrible news of Columbine, as well as other killings and gun incidents involving students, and the subsequent development of zero tolerance policies in schools have changed how we view schools. The tragedies of 9/11 and the subsequent worldwide "war on terrorism" have given Americans and peoples of all ethnicities and religions different perceptions of the world and of personal safety. President Clinton's "Goals 2000" program and President Bush's "No Child Left Behind" Program have had pervasive influence on assessment. The standards movement, begun late in the twentieth century has become increasingly pervasive and its influence is felt on every level of social studies instruction (Chapter 3). If anything, our concern for assessment (Chapter 5) and character education (Chapter 9) have grown stronger. The use of technology in the social studies classroom grows incrementally so even greater stress is given to the subject (Chapter 6). I have also attempted to incorporate my own concern for multiculturalism and give greater attention to how children learn. Lastly, I received so many comments and ideas about the chapter on drama (Chapter 10) that I have tried to strengthen and add to it.

Social studies today is for children who will live in a world that is far different from the one their teachers and parents grew up in and from the one that they are living in right now. We simply cannot stand pat. I hope that this book helps younger teachers to grow, to be ever more creative, and to fully involve, with care and excitement, the children whose lives they touch.

Writing past the first edition does not come easily. It takes a lot of gentle prodding, encouraging, and reminding for me to reconceptualize and rewrite, following essentially the same battle plan. I can be encouraged, but not bullied; urged, but not forced. Fortunately people who are very good at this have abounded in my life. I want to thank my chief encourager, my wife, Nancy, as well as my secretary, Patti Fagg, who is a gentle critic and a far better proofreader than I am. To them especially I dedicate this book. I also appreciate my children, Noelle, Michael, and Nathaniel, for still thinking that I am good in spite of years of evidence to the contrary. I also want to thank Traci Mueller, my very kind editor at Allyn and Bacon, and her assistant Krista Price. They never once yelled at me and were never anything less than extremely nice. I also want to thank the reviewers of the third edition: Jay Monson, Utah State University, Emeritus; and June Slobodian, Ohio University-Lancaster.

CHAPTER

1 Today's Elementary Social Studies Classrooms

LOOKING AHEAD

The purposes of this chapter are to help you see why social studies is needed in the elementary school and to suggest an overall approach to curriculum and teaching it. If you are to achieve these goals, you need to understand what social studies is and how it springs out of a need in society.

To understand social studies, you must first understand the purpose that it serves in the total school curriculum. That purpose, stated in simple form, is to develop good citizens for the democratic society in which we live. Becoming a good citizen is sometimes referred to as developing civic virtue, and there is, of course, a wide interpretation of exactly what either term really means. Even so, we can say that we want children to feel positive about themselves and have a desire to be positively contributing members of the various communities of which they are a part. It also means that children will develop the desire and the ability to be economically independent, to be informed about and involved in the decision making that goes on in those communities, and be aware of and knowledgeable about the world about them. We want them to be free from prejudice and be fair minded in dealing with others, to believe in a system of justice and law, to take leadership roles where they can and should, and give reasoned, fair support to legitimately appointed or elected leaders.

Since society is changing rapidly, teaching social studies is even more of a challenge today than it was in the past. Teachers really need to think about different approaches to teaching the social studies. They need to work more effectively with students who have different cultural backgrounds than themselves. They need to teach in ways that involve active

1

learning, and to find approaches which focus on solving *problems.* The final section of this chapter addresses the goals of social studies as perceived by different groups. Social studies itself, is a product of the changing society, prevailing approaches to its teaching, and the varying conception that social studies teachers have of its goals.

CAN YOU? DO YOU?

Can You

- Describe how the social studies have changed since you were in elementary school?

- Tell how the social studies have remained the same?

Do You

- Have some understanding of what might be meant by "a problems approach" to teaching the social studies?

- Have some idea of what a teacher needs to know about the social studies?

- Think of the social studies simply as history and geography?

- Know what the goals of the social studies should be?

CHANGE IN SOCIETY AND CHANGE IN THE SOCIAL STUDIES

There is no doubt about it—elementary social studies just has to be something different in today's society than it was even a decade ago. Society has changed. Schools have changed. Children's lives keep changing. Even the problems that children face are different. For example, there has been a constant increase in the number of latchkey children, in child abuse, in divorce in families with children, in domestic violence, in gangs, in the use of drugs and other substance abuse among children, in the number of single parent homes, and in crimes involving juveniles, and in reported child abuse. The world of work that schools are preparing students for is changing rapidly and the demand for workers is very different in kind and amount than it was (Boutwell, 1997). Though less negative, there have been changes that influence children's present and future lives in other ways. There has been a dynamic, complex revolution in technology, information, and communication. There have been major shifts in society including sweeping changes related to sex roles and ethnic and cultural relationships. There have also been major changes in the governmental and economic make up of American and world society.

In a world in which change has become the norm and we have to constantly face dilemmas for which there is no precedent, the social studies needs more than ever to help children learn to deal with problems. Teachers need to take a problems approach. Though the word *problems* may be defined in many ways, we are going to use it to mean any task or situation for which a solution is required or desired and for which a method of solution is not provided or immediately apparent. But problem solving is more than the situation itself. Often problems involve moral dilemmas or difficulties, dangers, or curiosities for which there is no verifiable solution. Problems require that existing knowledge be retrieved and used to resolve new or different difficulties. Most importantly, intrinsic to problem solving is the ability to deal with failure and with the inability to identify easy or quick solutions in constructive ways.

Problem-solving ability is, perhaps, the most pervasive of skills from a curricular standpoint and the one skill most needed throughout life. Almost all of the situations we face as a society and nearly all of the decisions demanding personal events may be best described as problems. If children (and teachers) can develop the requisite mindset, attitudes, and skills of problem solvers, they are equipped to meet the future. If they do not, their education becomes obsolete almost before it is complete. Problem-solving ability is the essential skill for each of the disciplines. That is, a person with a problem-solving mindset will be a more successful student. This is one ability that teachers need to emphasize if ever children are to become independent learners. Problem-solving ability is also the essential survival skill for school. Each teacher, each class, each other student, each school day, each assignment presents a unique intricacy of circumstances and demands. It would not be an overstatement to say that the essential life role is problem solving.

OBSERVING THE PROBLEMS APPROACH IN OPERATION
IN A PRIMARY CLASSROOM

The primary teacher who uses the problems approach is going to be constantly asking questions, trying to arouse curiosity, and having the children make decisions. The teacher will be encouraging children's questions and helping them to find ways of seeking answers. The entire environment of the classroom becomes fixed on learning how to learn. Children's awareness of problems and their ability to generate alternative solutions is heightened in this kind of environment.

Perhaps the best way to look at how the problems approach works is to look at how one primary teacher used this approach as she entered into a study of community. The teacher started her first graders into their study of the community by reading Dr. Suess's *Horton Hears a Who.* She soon had them thinking and talking about the perils and dangers faced by the people of the tiny world in the story. The point of the story, of course, is that everybody in a community needs to work together to solve the problems, and of course these children thought themselves very clever when they figured it out.

The teacher would not let them rest on that, though. Soon she had them talking about how we come to recognize problems and different ways that the "Whos" could have solved their problem once they discovered it. One of the questions that she asked was how different television characters might have solved the problem. (Both cartoon characters and prime time heroes were suggested.) She also got them thinking about how important they were in their own community and how they could not help unless they knew more about their community and its own particular dangers and problems.

The next day, the teacher took the children on a walking field trip of their community. They went only a few blocks, but as they went they began looking for different problems in their own community. Sometimes the teacher had to make suggestions and probe with questions, but always, she let the children decide if something was a problem. When they got back to the classroom they began making a list of the problems they had seen. The list included some things that were dangers and some others that just seemed to give people difficulties. Different types of garbage and litter were among the most common things that the children noticed, but the teacher tried to shift their attention to other kinds of problems. This all started to sound somewhat negative, so they also started making a list of the good things they knew about or had seen in their community.

That day the children went home with the assignment of asking their parents and others about problems in their community as well as what the adults liked about the community. The next day, in school, the children added to their lists, taking a little time to talk about the ideas that were brought in. The teacher put all the ideas on large pieces of paper, but she had left lots of room. When the list was finished she passed out scissors and old magazines and newspapers. The children worked in pairs, each pair trying to find a picture that showed one of the ideas. If they could not find a magazine picture that they thought was appropriate, the teacher encouraged the children to draw a picture. (The pictures later helped serve as reminders to these mostly nonreading children of what each sentence said.)

Later, the children built a box community on a large table. They got to decide what went into a community like theirs and to design their own buildings. The teacher and a parent volunteer helped them label their buildings. One of the questions they had been asking was, "Why was there so much litter in the community?" To help them understand, the teacher covered the completed scene with a tablecloth. Each day for a week, every child put a single small piece of scrap paper under the tablecloth. When they removed the cover, everyone was surprised at how much trash had accumulated on the streets of their community.

The box community was used to study other community problems as well. The children had tried to follow the layout of their own community in designing it. Therefore, they were able to look at such problems as traffic congestion and sidewalk hazards through their own model.

Soon the children decided that they needed a map of the community, and they began making one. The teacher started them thinking about the problems of making a map; for example, things like accuracy, relative size, symbols, and orientation.

There was a natural flow in every transition. Each situation led to a new set of questions and curiosities. Though there were some places where some children seemed to be lost for a few minutes, most often due to a lack of verbal memory, the presence of the problems was so pervasive that attention was never lost for long. The children kept wanting to be back with "the program."

OBSERVING THE PROBLEMS APPROACH IN OPERATION IN AN INTERMEDIATE CLASSROOM

In the intermediate classroom, the focus is shifting toward independence. Students can deal with problems and content that are much more distant and removed from their own experience. These students need to be more involved in the systematic development of questions and problems. Because they have more skills, knowledge, and experience, the students can be involved in a greater variety of research activities. They are more peer oriented and less teacher oriented, so group problem solving can be structured into the activities. The emphasis remains on an environment where curiosity is encouraged and stimulated. The teacher in such an environment is going to be constantly leading children to events and ideas that will set them thinking. The student in this setting is going to be "on the learn."

Looking again at a particular classroom, this time we will focus on an upper intermediate grade teacher who has launched into a study of the medieval period in European history. The teacher began by trying to get the students to systematically examine their existing concepts of the period. They talked about movies and television programs that they had seen as well as some things that had been picked up from cartoons, comic books, and games. Some of the children also had some knowledge that came from children's literature. There was as much, if not more, fantasy as reality in what they thought they knew about the period.

At about this time, the class was surprised by a visit from two people in medieval clothing. One of these men told the children that he was an architect and that he was involved in designing and building castles. The other man said that he was a knight. The men described a situation they were involved in on the coast of England near the Welsh border. King Edward had sent them there to build a castle. Now they had to decide exactly where to build it, but it was not all that easy. While the men were in the classroom, they talked with the children about the reasons for castle building, about all the problems that might be involved, and about the rudiments of castle defense.

By the time the men left, an idea had evolved. Soon the children had developed a hypothetical map of what the region would be like. At the teacher's insistence the map was quite large. In addition, the children were urged to orient their map to some real area on the English coast. The map itself was not altogether fiction because the children did some reading about the geography and geology of the area. The completed map showed a seacoast, the Welsh border, three villages for which the children made up names, and a monastery. It also showed a river, some fens or swampy land, a forest area, and a few roads. Other features were added as the children continued to read and discuss. They learned something about feudal land division and tried to reflect it in the map. Other landmarks, including a ruined castle and some churches, were added. The villages themselves began to take on detail and show differences in size and complexity. As the children researched, they decided that there had to be a feudal manor or two in the area with some kind of fortifications; these were added.

The people came last. The children's research began to reveal the different roles and social statuses that the various people at the monastery and in the villages would have had in all likelihood. The class developed a set of characters, each of whom they tried to describe in some detail. They gave them names and described where they lived, what they did and how they did it, how they dressed, and what their lives were like. They were particularly fascinated by the diet of the common people during this period. The study of daily life, clothing, and customs evolved through group work over about a week.

The students then drew names so that each could "become" one of the characters. Once more in groups, this time according to where they "lived," they continued researching their character. The groups also began talking about where they wanted the king's castle to be built. They looked into the dangers and fears that faced the lives of the people of this period.

Nearly three weeks after their first visit the two medieval men returned. For this visit, the children had planned and worn costumes of their own and the questions were almost unstoppable. The children eagerly told the visitors what they had been doing. Then each group made a presentation in which they introduced themselves in their medieval roles. The groups each made a case for one particular site for the king's castle. Some of the groups, especially the one representing the monastery, did not want the castle built right in their area. Others had noticed not only the protection that the castle offered, but the commercial possibilities that a garrison of soldiers would have for the nearest town. When the groups were finished, the architect and the knight explained where they thought the king's castle should be built. Most importantly, they showed that they had listened to the children's reasoning as they presented their own case.

This was the beginning rather than the end. The study went on into the actual building of the castle and to several follow-up activities. However, this beginning had laid a foundation of interest and reason for research, on which the teacher could continue to build. While the children were creating a scenario and story line as well as a setting of their own, nearly every major theme and concept of medieval life was explored.

GOALS OF THE SOCIAL STUDIES

What do you need to know about the social studies? The answer probably seems to be more than you do know or can learn. It is certainly more than you will be able to get from any textbook. As a teacher, you owe it to the generations of children that you teach to become mindfully, curiously, purposefully alive to them, to their world, to history as a thick endless blanket of stories about people and events, and to the values and rules needed for people to live together. So the real answer to the question, "What do you need to know about the social studies?" is, "As much as you can learn about history, geography, political science, sociology, anthropology, economics, psychology, and, yes, about religion, too."

Social studies in the elementary school has most often been regarded as an area that should be taught, but only if there were time. Priority time in the school day, of course, has to be given to the basic skill areas of reading, mathematics, and language. It has not been that the social studies are considered unimportant, but that the basic skill areas are seen by society, by administrators, and by elementary teachers as "basics" or "fundamentals" that have to be learned first. Important as language and mathematics skills may be, they are taught only because the children will need them to live in the social world.

The "back to basics" years of the 1970s and early 1980s had a strong adverse influence on elementary social studies. Separate studies by Gross (1977) and Hahn (1977) affirmed that the social studies were disappearing in the early grades. If anything, that trend continues in the presence of the whole-language movement (Hahn, 1985; Goodlad, 1984). Many would argue that the social studies are, after all, embedded in curriculum. This curriculum involves an emphasis on reading stories, poems, and plays, all of which have extensive social studies content. Then too, the school day itself consists of a rich and complex series of social situations and problems, ranging from homeroom to recess to lunchroom to school bus. Social studies specialists would argue that the focus in these programs is still largely on skill and that language, not social development, is the focus.

Educators and politicians may soon have to wake up to the fact that the social studies are basic and fundamental in the earliest schooling. Educational reform has not had any real impact on achievement in the basic skill areas and schools have about run out of time to take from other areas. Children simply are not likely to improve their learning attitudes. There simply has to be more attention given to help children learn about themselves and their place in and responsibility to society. The National Council for the Social Studies Task Force on Early Childhood/Elementary Social Studies (1989) has described a major purpose for the social studies as equipping children with "the knowledge and understanding of the past necessary for coping with the present and planning for the future. . . ." The Task Force went on to say that the social studies enable children to "participate in their world" by helping them understand their relationship to other people and to social, economic, and political institutions.

Barth (1993) has said that one of our most basic beliefs is that "Social Studies is citizenship education." Hartoonan (1993) has added that "our work should be to illuminate the essential connection between social studies learning and democratic values" and thus be a "liberating force in the lives of citizens." Put another way, the two primary jobs of schools are to help the society by producing effective, contributing citizens and to help the children lead happy lives in which they are enabled to achieve their potential. That is what the social studies are all about, and it is also why they are so needed in the elementary school.

Though social studies specialists disagree as to priorities, the following list identifies those purposes that are most often associated with social studies programs:

- Preparing responsible citizens for the nation, the state, and the local area.

- Preparing students who have the knowledge and skills in social studies needed for college.

- Developing awareness and understanding of contemporary social issues.

- Developing healthy self-concepts.

- Teaching the methods of social scientists.

- Motivating students to want to learn about the social studies.

- Developing the ability to solve problems and make decisions.

- Dveloping "global" citizens with a world vision.

Whatever we do as teachers is certainly done for the present, but it has to be done with an eye to the future.

In trying to help you become good social studies teachers, or good teachers of anything for that matter, it is important to get you to look at what happens if you succeed as teachers. The children you teach will, in due course, become adults themselves. They will obviously be living in a different kind of society, one that teachers must try to anticipate and prepare them for. But, beyond that, the kind of impact that teachers will have had on them and the kind of people they become are critical outcomes of education. Following are just a few of the areas where we, as teachers of elementary social studies, will have had an impact when the children we teach become adults:

- The jobs they have and the way they do their jobs

- The way they feel about themselves

- The way they handle responsibility

- The way they treat other people

- How they meet and resolve problems and difficulties

- Their motivation and overall attitudes

- What they value and how they treat the things they value

- How they relate to their heritage

- How they relate to their environment

- How they relate to and deal with people of other cultures, nationalities, and ethnic groups

In each of these and in other areas where teachers influence children, I think that it is safe to say that most of us would happily accept a broad variety of outcomes and still feel that we had been a positive force. The question is, "Just how much in each area can we expect of ourselves?" That is not a question that can be left unanswered. I like the analogy of putting together a jigsaw puzzle. It is always easier to do if we have a picture of what it is going to look like when we get it all together. The same holds true for teaching. From an attitudinal standpoint, I have always found it useful to envision my students 10 or 15 years into the future, and imagine them in the most positive light I can. It gives me an idea of what I am working for.

Goals and objectives should be the first and most important concerns of any teacher, especially any social studies teacher. They complement one another. Goals are distant, unmeasurable, and even unattainable. They give direction to our efforts and, if we are goal oriented and goal driven, we constantly work toward them, yet never reach a point when they are achieved. How can one reach the goal of becoming an effective problem solver, for example, or the even broader goal of being a good citizen? The essence of goals is that they describe the person we are constantly in the process of becoming (Moore, 1989).

Objectives, on the other hand, are short term, attainable, often measurable, and very specific. We can know when we achieve them, so they become for us milestones and markers of our progress. Goals determine the directions we want to go, but the accomplishment of objectives lets us know that we are getting there.

In education, we generally begin planning by defining our goals. Once goals are set, we try to describe the specific teaching and learning outcomes for short periods of instruction that will move students toward the goals. Goals without objectives remain as only dreams. Objectives without relationship to goals are purposeless. Objectives for the social studies tend to be decided on the basis of the specific content being taught and the group to which it is being taught. (Social studies objectives will be discussed in more detail in Chapter 2.) The broadest goals for the field have been centrally determined and defined in the United States by various groups, given authority by still larger organizations. Regardless of the group, throughout this century social studies has invariably been linked to goals of citizenship education (Jarolimek 1990). The frameworks developed in the reports of the various commissions, task forces, and committees have served as models for textbook curricula and for those developed for state and local school districts.

Among the most recent of these reports, three will probably influence the direction of elementary school social studies in the 1990s and on into the twenty-first century. These are the National Council for the Social Studies Task Force on Scope and Sequence (1984), the National Council for the Social Studies Task Force on Early Childhood/Elementary Social Studies (1989), and the Curriculum Task Force of the National Commission on the Social Studies in the School (1989).

The introductory, summarizing statement of the goals section of the report of the NCSS Task Force on Scope and Sequence set a problem-solving focus for the social studies and emphasized thinking skills. The Task Force said, "Social studies programs have a responsibility to prepare young people to identify, understand, and work to solve problems that face our increasingly diverse nation and interdependent world" (NCSS Task Force, 1984, 251). The report went on to say that the social studies derive goals from the nature of citizenship and then organizes those goals into the broad categories of knowledge, democratic values, and beliefs and skills.

The NCSS Task Force on Early Childhood/Elementary Social Studies (1989) echoed much of the same tone and similar organization in its report. The goals focused on cooperative problem solving, claiming that basic skills in reading, writing, and computing were necessary but not sufficient if children are to survive in today's world. Critical thinking and the development of positive attitudes toward self and others were given priority in this report.

The Task Force of the National Commission on the Social Studies was funded by the Carnegie Foundation, the Rockefeller Foundation, the MacArthur Foundation, and the National Geographic Society. It enjoyed the sponsorship of the National Council for the Social Studies and the American Historical Association. Over two years in preparation, the Task Force's report, titled *Charting a Course: Social Studies for the 21st Century* (1989), formulated the following goals that the social studies curriculum should enable students to develop:

1. Civic responsibility and active civic participation

2. Perspectives on their own life experiences so they see themselves as part of the larger human adventure in time and place

3. A critical understanding of the history, geography, economic, political, and social institutions, traditions, and values of the United States as expressed in both their unity and diversity

4. An understanding of other peoples and of the unity and diversity of world history, geography institutions, traditions, and values

5. Critical attitudes and analytical perspectives appropriate to analysis of the human condition

LOOKING BACK

Social studies has been throughout most of the last half of the twentieth century and will continue to be into the twenty-first century reformist in nature; that is, the curriculum has been and will be in flux. This is due, in part, to the constant changes in the social world.

The one educational need that remains constant in a world of change is that children need to learn how to solve problems. When teachers take a problems approach in social studies, they work at enabling students to deal with situations where their experience and knowledge offer no ready answers. Problem solving is, perhaps, the most pervasive of all skills.

In spite of growing concern that the social studies may be disappearing, at least from primary classrooms, the two main jobs of the school continue to be producing effective, contributing citizens and helping children lead happy lives. Social studies programs have a variety of purposes which relate to these two jobs. Among the most important of these are preparing students to be responsible, aware of contemporary issues, and to have a world vision. In some cases, elementary social studies teachers have to be concerned about preparing students for college and even for careers in the social sciences. If they are to be successful at all, though, teachers must develop both the love of learning and the ability to solve problems.

Goals and objectives should be major concerns of teachers of the social studies. Goals are distant and unattainable, but they give direction to teaching. Objectives, on the other hand, are short term and obtainable. Objectives are the building blocks toward goals.

The National Council for the Social Studies, as the organization of teachers most concerned with social education, has constantly examined and reexamined the goals of the social studies. Recent task forces of that organization have particularly emphasized problem solving and thinking skills.

SELF-TEST

1. How would you characterize the problems approach to the social studies?

2. Why was the map-creation exercise so critical in the class where they were studying medieval history?

3. In what areas are teachers of the social studies going to have impact?

4. In what ways did the two NCSS task force groups referred to in the chapter stress the role of thinking skills in the social studies?

REFERENCES

Barth, J. L. (1993). Social studies: There is a history, there is a body, but is it worth saving. *Social Education, 57*(2), 56–57.

Boutwell, C. E. (1997). *Phi Delta Kappan, 79*(October), 104–111.

Geisel, T. (1954). *Horton hears a Who.* New York: Putnam, 1954.

Goodlad, J. (1984). *A place called school.* New York: McGraw-Hill.

Gross, R. E. (1977). The status of the social studies in the public schools of the United States. *Social Education, 41* (November/December), 194–200, 205.

Hahn, C. W. (1977). Research in the diffusion of social studies innovations. In Hunkins, F. P. (Ed.), *Review of research in social studies education: 1970–75.* Washington, DC: National Council for the Social Studies, and Boulder, CO: ERIC Clearing House for Social Studies/Social Science Education Consortium, pp. 137–177.

Hahn, C. W. (1985). The status of the social studies in the public schools of the United States: Another look. *Social Education, 49* (January), 220–223.

Hartoonan, M. (1993). A guide for redefining the social studies. *Social Education, 57*(2), 59–60.

Jarolimek, J. J. (1990). *Social studies in elementary education.* New York: Macmillan.

Moore, C. et al. (1989). Mental terms and the development of certainty. *Child Development,* 60 (February), 167–171.

NCSS Task Force on Early Childhood/Elementary Social Studies. (1989). Social studies for early childhood and elementary school children—preparing for the 21st Century. *Social Education,* 53 (January), 14–23.

NCSS Task Force on Scope and Sequence. (1984). In search of a scope and sequence in the social studies. *Social Education,* 48 (April), 249–262.

Task Force of the National Commission on the Social Studies in the Schools. (1989). *Charting a course: Social studies for the 21st century.* Washington, DC: The National Commission on the Social Studies in the Schools.

SUGGESTED READING

Edelman, M. W. (1992). The challenges of the 90's: Saving our children. *Social Education,* 56 (April/May), 240–243.

Longstreet, W. (1989). Education for citizenship: New dimensions. *Social Education,* 53 (January), 41–45.

McArthur, J. R. (2002). The Why, What, and How of teaching children social skills. *The Social Studies,* 93(4) (July/August), 183–185.

Pratt, F., Laney, J. D., and Couper, D. (2002). A multipurpose guide to teaching the ten thematic strands of social studies through life span education. *The Social Studies,* 93(4) (July/August), 170–175.

Sewell, A. M., Fuller, S., Murphy, R. C. (2002). Creative problem solving: A means to authentic and purposeful social studies. *The Social Studies,* 93(4) (July/August), 176–179.

Turner, T. N. (2000). What to do when you burn out. *Tennessee Association of Middle Schools Journal,* 26, 1–2.

Woodward, A., Elliott, D. L., and Nagel, K. (1986). Beyond textbooks in elementary social studies. *Social Education,* 50 (January), 50–53.

2 Making Plans to Teach

LOOKING AHEAD

The purpose of this chapter is to help you become a better planner. To do this, we begin with the problems that teachers have in planning. We then move to the structures of different teaching plans. As you read the chapter you need to consider these questions:

- What are your strengths and weaknesses as a planner?

- What do you need to be able to do in order to plan a teaching unit?

- Are you likely to need to rely heavily on a textbook?

- What purposes do other teaching plans serve?

- Are you planning to meet the needs of all of your students, including those with special learning needs and those whose cultural background is different from your own?

Effective planning is a necessary, though not sufficient, ingredient of good teaching. In other words, although good teachers are good planners, it does not follow that even the most thorough, imaginative focused planning automatically makes anyone an effective teacher. Obviously, there is more to teaching than planning, but imagine a teacher who does not plan at all. Such a teacher has no sense of what is to go on in the classroom and quickly loses efficacy and impact. Fortunately, few teachers fail to do at least some planning, but many do far too little. Too often, teaching plans consist of cryptic notes in lesson-plan books referring to pages in the text-book. These kinds of plans can hardly lead to exciting, creative classrooms.

CAN YOU? DO YOU?

Can You

- Plan an instructional unit?

- Identify and describe different types of units? Write objectives?

- Establish "set" in a lesson?
- Identify the steps in a case study?

Do You

- Have experience in collaborative planning?
- Know how to go about choosing a unit topic?
- Know how much freedom teachers have about what they teach?
- Know what is meant by the term *webbing* when referring to planning?
- Have an understanding of the concept of instructional objectives?

FOCUS ACTIVITY

Before reading this chapter, you might try this activity as a class.

SOCIAL STUDIES PLANNING: PEOPLE SCAVENGE

You may remember going on a scavenger hunt as a youngster. You were given a list of often strange items to bring back. Probably you competed in teams within a time limit. A people scavenge is very similar to the familiar scavenger hunt. The major differences are that (1) instead of objects, you are searching for people with certain experiences or knowledge; and (2) the whole activity is done in the classroom. Following are the rules for a people scavenge:

1. Your job is to get the initials of someone in each blank on the list that follows. You find out who has the knowledge or experience named simply by asking questions of each classmate.

2. Everyone in the classroom (including yourself) is eligible, but you can use each person for only two items. Find someone who:

   - _____ Has a social studies topic that they have studied as a hobby
   - _____ Knows the difference between a goal and an objective
   - _____ Can tell the difference between a teacher activity and a lesson
   - _____ Can identify the greatest planning problems of social studies teachers
   - _____ Has made a lesson plan and taught from it
   - _____ Knows what a unit is

- _____ Can name five sources of social studies plans on the Internet
- _____ Has looked through at least one copy of a journal for social studies teachers
- _____ Knows the names of five journals or magazines for teachers in which teaching plans are found
- _____ Has helped a teacher prepare a unit
- _____ Can give three reasons for planning what you teach
- _____ Can remember three social studies units from his or her own elementary school days
- _____ Carries and regularly uses a pocket calendar or palm pilot for planning
- _____ Can name two publishers who publish a series of social studies textbooks with good teacher's editions
- _____ Can give three excuses teachers might have for not spending enough time planning
- _____ Can tell the difference between a resource unit and a teaching unit
- _____ Has observed a well-planned social studies lesson being taught in the last year
- _____ Makes "to do" lists and checks off items as completed

After the instructor ends the search, discuss the list. This people scavenge technique can also be used with elementary school children with almost any topic as (1) an icebreaker, (2) a way of assessing readiness or background on a topic, or (3) a way of grouping.

WHY IS PLANNING IMPORTANT?

Planning has special importance in broad content areas like the social studies where there is so much information. Because of the breadth of the field, even the best and most experienced teachers cannot have sufficient knowledge. All teachers need to use numerous resources. The resource possibilities are constantly growing. The Internet and a growing variety of computer software packages alone have increased the possibilities astronomically. One of the major elements in good planning is finding and collecting the best resources and organizing them in a purposeful way.

With the exception of those working at kindergarten and perhaps first grade levels, most beginning teachers are likely to start their planning with a textbook. Some will find their best, or even required, assistance and direction for planning in a curriculum guide provided by the school district

(Woodward, Elliott, & Nagel, 1986). New teachers may also get help from mentor teachers in some schools, or from a team leader, a department chair, or an entire group of grade level colleagues. Because state governments are legally responsible for the schools there may also be state guidelines containing frameworks, rules, and regulations regarding what is taught. National teacher organizations also provide input about what should go on in the social studies. (NCSS, the Association for Supervision and Curriculum Development, and the National Education Association are among the largest of these organizations. The NCSS alone publishes two useful journals, *Social Education* and *Social Studies and the Young Learner.*)

One problem with having all these resources, and, remember, these are only the beginning points for planning, is that they end up as mountains of pages of print telling the young teacher what to do, more than he or she can cope with. By its very size, the accumulation of resource guides, instead of helping, intimidates and confuses new teachers. Novice teachers feel they can only retreat to the safety of that first one, the textbook. Staying strictly with that safe resource soon becomes a comfortable, safe pattern and that is where they may stay for the rest of their careers. It is a natural thing to do. It reduces uncertainty and confusion, and leaves the difficult decisions of planning to the so-called experts. However, it prevents these teachers from reaching their own potential.

There are some good reasons why long-term total reliance on textbooks is not the best course: (1) Following this route means that the teacher, the social studies, and the classroom are not likely to be very exciting, interesting, or enjoyable for the children. If the whole point of schooling is to produce involved, independent learners, and I think that it is, this is surely the last kind of atmosphere one would want to create. (2) "Read and answer the question" social studies, which is the type of teaching the textbook approach is likely to produce, is not likely to be very meaningful or seem very purposeful to students. Though it is almost a corollary to reason #1, not only are students not going to enjoy this kind of approach, they are not going to learn from it or understand why they are doing it. (3) There is little teacher satisfaction gained from such an approach. What makes teaching exciting is seeing what you have planned come alive in the classroom and seeing student learning result from your plans. When you repeatedly use a "canned" plan, teaching soon becomes boring and unrewarding. No wonder teacher burnout has become a national epidemic in our schools (Turner, 2000).

SETTING THE STAGE: CREATING THE ENVIRONMENT

How do you begin to plan, if you are the kind of teacher who wants to avoid the textbook pitfall? Curiously, both the planning process and the actual planning product that flows out of this process involve a good deal of scene setting. Doing social studies in the classroom is almost like doing theater. We are trying to create a dramatic climate, one with just the right kind of tension and sufficient excitement for learning to occur. With effective planning in the social studies, that climate is there and it can be identified by some predictable hallmarks (Brophy & Good, 1978).

These include:

1. A sense of anticipation or expectancy on the part of the student audience: They know that something special is going to happen and they have a fairly good idea of what it is, with just enough uncertainty for the sake of anticipation and suspense.

2. A feeling of purpose and direction: Students know why they are there and what the class is all about.

3. An awareness that is more than knowledge of continuity: What is done today relates to yesterday as well as to tomorrow. Not only are there connections that give lots of satisfied "Aha!" moments, but there is a wholism that in itself adds to the meaning.

4. An atmosphere of involvement or participation in the planning process itself and how the plans flow into the doing: There is a sense of community or even family that acknowledges that "we are in this together."

5. An awareness of leadership: To a degree, this seals off or at least pulls the reins to control conflict. It keeps a sense of urgency, allowing flexibility, but keeps at the job.

WHY TEACHERS DO NOT PLAN

It may seem negative to approach planning from a "why don't teachers (even the experienced ones) do it?" perspective, but if we look at some of the reasons teachers don't plan or at least don't plan well, you may see why planning is so difficult yet so important. This may be helpful when we examine some of the planning tools that are used in the social studies. First, we have to recognize that we must deal with teachers' perceptions of their reasons as the reasons themselves. How teachers feel about what they do and do not do and how they look at themselves is very important. There is a growing belief that time management is an area in which simply understanding the problems and deterrents may help the teacher in overcoming them. Here, then, are a number of reasonable conclusions about the factors involved in teachers' failure to plan.

1. Not enough time: Teachers have crowded days often filled with unavoidable trivialities, both planned and unplanned. Clerical tasks, children demanding attention, classroom accidents, discipline situations, paper grading, and many others compete to more than fill every minute.

2. Failure to set time priorities or give priority to planning: Because teaching is time intensive, teachers must be very careful to choose what they do and do not give priority to.

3. Depending on previous material: Once teachers have taught a topic a few times, they begin to accumulate a quantity of "stuff that works." There are obvious advantages to this and the old adage, "if it isn't broken, don't fix it," comes to mind. But there are also dangers, including creeping staleness and a tendency to get behind the times.

4. Procrastination: For some of us, the whole problem is reduced to being slow about getting around to things.

5. Failure to communicate: There is a cooperative element even in teacher planning. Good planning means letting involved people (parents, resource people, school officials, other teachers, etc.) know what they need to know and what they need to do in advance.

6. Experience: Experience itself may stand in the way of effective planning. Teachers can develop patterns and habits very quickly that are counterproductive, and these may persist and transfer.

7. Lack of interest or enthusiasm or content fear: Some individuals will say that they do not like the social studies.

8. Low energy: Many teachers say that they just do not have the energy, psychological or physical, to plan.

9. Inability to deal with peer pressure: Teachers want to be approved of and liked by other teachers. They model their behavior on experienced teachers.

There are no easy ways to deal with all these forces that work against planning. Obviously, self-discipline, resolve to plan well, and a firm sense of purpose are qualities that teachers need. But beyond these difficult and elusive acts of will, there are some concrete strategies that teachers can use to improve their planning habits and skills. Not all of the following suggestions will work for everybody, but they are worth a try.

1. Schedule your time to include specifically designated planning time, and stick to the schedule as though a planning time were a meeting with the president.

2. Make lists of planning jobs and prioritize the lists.

3. Examine and change your patterns of behavior to avoid distractions.

4. Do the worst first, meaning, complete that which you most dread and want to put off before you do the easier or more satisfying things.

5. Learn to be rude politely and without feeling guilt, turning off and away those who would interrupt your planning time.

6. Record and celebrate your planning successes in ways that you can remember and then repeat. (If it works, make sure you can do it again.)

TYPES OF PLANNING FOR INSTRUCTIONAL UNITS: WHY DIFFERENT UNITS ARE SUITED TO DIFFERENT KINDS OF INSTRUCTIONAL PLANNING

As I said earlier, textbook teaching is an easy pattern to set and a difficult routine to break. One reason it is so prevalent is that nearly all teachers have to do some of it, particularly early in their teaching. There are some positive ways a teacher can make use of this pattern to take control of their own teaching, though. The simplest of these is to use the textbook that you have relied on as a base, but expand from that textbook. In this section we will look at using and adapting different planning units, beginning with expanded textbook units.

Expanded Textbook Units

Social studies textbook series are structured into units that consist of single chapters or, in many cases, series of two or more chapters. Teachers' editions provide such material as vocabulary lists, activity ideas, day-by-day lesson plans, questions to ask the students, and even lists of additional resources. Publishers may also make available numerous supplementary materials, including such items as blackline masters from which student handouts can be made, project planning procedures, posters, maps, and charts.

Teachers who rely heavily on the textbook for at least part of their social studies program need to be especially concerned about purposeful teaching. A regimen of careful planning with a focus on how to use the textbook creatively can help reduce, if not totally avoid, the pitfalls usually associated with textbook teaching. The following steps might be considered by the less experienced teacher:

1. Try to get the "big picture." Be sure that you understand what the goals of the textbook program are and how each book is organized and fits into the entire series.

2. Roughly map out the entire calendar for the school year in terms of the amount of time you want to give to the various units in the program. As you do this, be sure to consider unequal treatment (giving more time to some topics than others) and omission of some topics.

3. For each unit, use the teachers' edition guide materials judiciously to plan activities to introduce the topic and then to help students achieve the objectives and reach a wholistic understanding of the topic.

4. Maintain a high level of sensitivity to reading difficulties students may encounter and be ready to adjust instruction. (There will be more about avoiding and helping with reading problems in Chapters 3 and 4.)

5. Remember that it is the purpose of the textbook's editors to center on students and teachers using their book, while, to you, that book is only a tool to do the job. If you try to think of alternatives to the textbook's

suggested activities that address the goals and objectives of each unit in a student-centered way, your teaching will be less textbook centered. Try to establish a balance of new versus repeated instructional activities from chapter to chapter. This gives students both the security of being able to learn a set of expectations about how to do things and the motivational freshness of activity variety.

6. Examine evaluation materials provided by the text carefully, and use them only after seeing their relationship to the teaching objectives. This usually means that you see what information, concepts, and basic skills are being assessed. Make sure these do not have errors. (One way of checking is to do tests yourself first, just to see if the answers *are* there.)

Collaborative Units

In many school districts, teachers work in teams to prepare units. The arrangements for doing this vary. In some cases, there are structured formal efforts across entire school districts by appointed groups of teachers. Other formal arrangements may involve a head or coordinating teacher or a mentor teacher relationship in a single school teaming of teachers in a given grade level.

The kind of units produced and the ways that teachers are expected to use them are almost as varied. In most instances, the intent is to combine talents and save individual teachers' planning time while producing some consistency throughout the school or system in the content that is taught. The units may in some instances even be developed to ensure that all teachers will be following exactly the same sequence of activities. It is more common, though, for team planning to produce resource units which can be shared among teachers. Resource units systematically delineate common objectives, identify the most appropriate and useful available resources for teacher and student use, and create and share plans for activities (teaching strategies). Resource units may also include common tests and other evaluation procedures.

Some units that are planned by collaborative effort may be regarded as teaching units. These will not offer the same number and variety of activities as resource units, but they will have specific activity or lesson plans. Only few, if any, alternative activities will be provided. Teachers may be expected to follow such units entirely, or they may have the option of doing the prescribed lessons or developing their own plans.

Teachers who are making a move into a grade level and school where such collaborative units are used may want to consider the following as guidelines:

1. Find out what degree of conformity and collaboration is expected from you as well as the extent to which you are expected to use units already prepared. At this step and all others it is good to establish an advice-seeking relationship with a mentor teacher or the lead teacher

if possible. (At the same time, you can find out how much creativity is encouraged.)

2. Become familiar with available units, paying particular attention to the goals and objectives. (Make sure that you understand and follow the pattern of intent.)

3. See how the collaborative units relate to the textbooks that are in the classroom (if there are any).

4. Browse through the activities looking for the overall motivational and teaching quality as well as particularly outstanding ideas and plans.

5. Look for ways that you can put your own creativity into existing activities. Simply by adding details, embellishing, and improving the focus of activities and lessons in existing collaborative plans you may enliven your own teaching.

6. If the school allows, plan alternative activities and lessons to substitute for those that you see to be weaker.

7. Work through and implement the plans provided. Keep an open mind, but review effectiveness and possible alternatives.

Teacher-Developed Units: Why and When

The word *unit* is used with a lot of different meanings. Basically, a unit includes everything a group of learners does to explore a particular topic. What unifies the study or makes it a unit is the topic itself. This is true whether that topic is a general category type (such as Transportation), a concept (such as Democracy), a time period or event (such as The Age of Exploration), or a question (such as, What can be done to reduce pollution?). When we talk about units in teaching, we are usually talking about the teaching plan for that topic. Such plans vary in length, in amount of detail, and even in their source of creation. A unit may attempt to plan for a week or for six weeks of work. Some people think that children ought to learn more about each topic they do study, while others are convinced that we need to cover more topics. For most teachers, a unit plan will be for three to four weeks, but early primary units tend to be for shorter periods.

A pressing question at any level of experience is when and how teachers should develop their own teaching units. The prevailing pattern, especially in the upper grades, is to stick to the textbook, partially because beginning teachers have the feeling that this is what they are supposed to do and partly because this route is secure and easy. We have already said that textbook teaching is an easy pattern to set and be stuck with. Nearly all teachers, pressured with too much to do and too little time, find it absolutely necessary to use textbook units or some other pre-prepared instructional plans.

As a rule of thumb, I think that teachers should, if they have the option, develop at least one new unit of their own every school year. I believe that teaching is a creative profession and that creative teachers will want to be constantly developing new ideas themselves. However, given the amount of time required to find, adapt, and develop resources, one new unit is probably all that any teacher can do well in even the best year. Of course, this does not mean that there cannot be constant additions, adaptations, and alterations to existing units. The unit developed in any particular year would depend on such factors as (1) current teacher interests and concerns, (2) calendar events occurring in particular years, (3) materials that the teacher discovers, (4) major perceived weaknesses and gaps in the units available, and (5) current interests of children.

Teacher-made units may take practically any form, but whatever form they take is almost certainly going to mean more work for the teacher than simply following a prepared unit plan. The major purpose of doing them is that planning such units will mean better teaching. There are also several arguments supporting the view that teacher-made units are worth the effort. First, there is the contention that the teacher can plan them to fit particular needs and abilities of a particular class. Teacher-made units can take into account resources that are the teacher's personal possessions as well as those that may be part of an individual teacher's classroom collection. Such units can also reflect a teacher's individual abilities, talents, personality, and teaching style. Most important, perhaps, is the argument that planning a teaching unit can be creatively and personally satisfying. It can provide teachers with that sense of accomplishment that is so important for retaining a positive attitude and avoiding burnout in any profession, especially one like teaching.

Individual teaching units have the tailor-made quality of being uniquely suited to achieving what the teacher thinks to be most important in the very ways that seem most suitable for the people most directly involved.

DECIDING ON UNIT TOPICS

Teachers do not usually have total freedom in choosing unit topics. The teacher may be expected to go by a set of curriculum guidelines or a curriculum outline where a course of study is outlined. In some instances, teachers are required to stick to the topics described in these systems or state guides, but sometimes they have the freedom to develop their own interests as well. A second option that teachers may have is to plan in conjunction with other teachers on their team (either grade level or some other configuration) so that all children are exposed to similar topics or themes. In a few cases, teachers have the initiative of doing teacher-guided group planning through which interests, needs, and problems identified by the children are explored.

Whether the teacher is planning the unit him- or herself or helping students to plan, a similar process occurs. Sometimes a wonderful, exciting idea seems to almost jump out. The teacher or the class experiences some stimulating, motivating event that generates enthusiasm and curiosity. For example, something in the news, an event on the calendar, a happening in the neighborhood, or something someone reads or sees on television grabs your attention and makes some topic seem the perfect study for the class. More often though, the teacher may be searching for a topic. For such searches, thinking seems to go through four stages: (1) coming up with a menu of possible topics, (2) narrowing the field and finding a broad focus, (3) identifying a particular topic and refining that selection into a title that adds zest and uniqueness (takes it out of the boring and mundane class), and (4) deciding on the direction and structure that studying that topic ought to take.

The teacher first needs to have an idea of what classes of things are appropriate as unit topics in social studies. It would be true, but not very helpful, to say that the range of topics almost defies description. Looking at one or several textbook series may give some idea of the types of topics that might be appropriate. This is going to provide a limited notion, at best, and probably an unimaginative one. To get a broad picture it might be suggested that, among the classes of things studied as unit topics, the following are typical: countries or groups of countries, regions, civilizations, specific places or types of places, eras, specific time periods, events or series of related events, processes, phenomena, problems, historical figures, historical developments, and issues.

To show how the evolution of selection can take place, it might be useful to take the example of a fourth-grade teacher who has already gone through part of the agony and the indecision, which is exactly what such often frustrating activity is. The first level of decision making has already been passed and the decision is to teach a unit dealing with the Middle East. The topic is timely, but greater focus is needed.

At this point the teacher uses a few resources and perhaps discusses his or her ideas. Eventually, this produces a list of possibilities that vary in quality, focus, usefulness, appropriateness, and appeal. For example, the list might look like this:

Middle Eastern Folk Tales

Islam and the Middle East

Leaders of the Middle East Today

From Mohammad, to Saladin, to Sulieman: People of Influence in Middle Eastern History

European Colonies in the Middle East

The Countries of the Middle East Today

What It Is Like to Live in the Middle East

The Riches and Resources of the Middle East

Cities of the Middle East

Once a satisfactory list is formed, the narrowing process begins. The individual topics are weighed in the balance of questions such as:

- How does this fit in with the other units that are being taught?

- How does this relate to the overall goals and purposes for the class?

- Is this something that this class might really get excited about?

- Is this broad enough (or narrow enough)? Is it too general (or too specific) in the focus it allows?

- Are the right kinds of resources available to teach this?

- How does this approach fit in with the way we are handling other topics in the class?

- How excited could I get about teaching this topic?

Through this narrowing process, our hypothetical teacher may decide that the basic emphasis that he wants is geographic as opposed to historic and that, for a variety of reasons, too specific a topic may limit the directions that children may go with their explorations. After deliberation, he is able to reduce the list to five or six possible titles, and at last to decide on "What it is like to live in the Middle East" as the focus he wants to plan to. It seems provocative, creates curiosity, and yet leaves room for some of the geographic focus he wants. But it is precisely because of that openness that more thought is necessary.

The teacher then starts to flesh out some sense of direction. For example, the teacher may want to deal with areas where children lack accurate knowledge about the Middle East. He may want to identify a series of problems such as the following:

- The belief that the people in the Middle East all have the same culture.

- The belief that all the Middle East is a desert.

- The idea that Middle Easterners all support terrorism.

- Ignorance about how modern Middle Eastern people live.

DEVELOPING THE UNIT PLAN

Once a focus has been found, effort can be directed at developing one of three types of units. The teacher may decide to develop his own resource unit. The kind of work that this involves is mainly creating, collecting, gathering, and ordering materials, teaching ideas and activities, much as a team of teachers would do in developing a collaborative resource unit. One major difference is that the teacher can include personal resources that would not be available to everyone in a collaborative unit. The other two options, sketch units and teaching units, differ from one another most in the extent of development and in the amount of attention that is given to detail. Sketch units are of greatest use to teachers who are trying to form a broad overview of the teaching content, sequence, and activities, and who then use the sketch unit as a basis to gather resources and do more specific planning later on. These outline plans are also useful to teachers who find it convenient to rely heavily on textual materials, but who want to have the control of doing their own basic planning.

Teaching units are more thorough and fleshed out in greater detail. They offer teachers the advantage of a plan of study that needs only calendar and success-failure adjustments as the actual teaching evolves. That is, the teacher has to do very little planning other than to make those adaptations that become necessary when teaching sequences take more or less time than planned or where careful monitoring indicates a need for additional activities.

Whether the teacher is doing a sketch unit or a teaching unit, the next step in planning is to get some kind of clear and specific picture of the desired learning outcomes. This is going to help in at least two ways: It will give directional focus and it will help limit the scope. This targeting tells us what to teach, while, at the same time, it keeps us from the pointless and sometimes frustrating activity of trying to teach everything about often broad unit topics.

There are several ways to attack the problem. The teacher may choose to begin by developing a set of instructional objectives. Another starting place is the content itself. Some teachers prefer to start with a content outline or a content organizational chart in which a list of generalizations serves as headings. A newer idea is a kind of visual representation called a web, which shows the interrelationships of the different concepts and/or elements to be covered in the unit. Let us examine objectives, content outlines, and webs.

INSTRUCTIONAL OBJECTIVES

At some point in planning, a teacher needs to be concerned with the learning outcomes that he or she wants to occur as a result of the instruction. Educators usually refer to these outcomes that are given special focus as objectives. A social studies centered unit will have multiple objectives. In fact, most social studies activities have several objectives in addition to much incidental learning.

Objectives are targeted gains in knowledge or skills or desired changes in affective areas like aspirations, attitudes, values, and feelings. Since they are targets, objectives need to be identified as specifically as possible. A well-stated set of objectives should give clear direction to the teacher and be of help in planning activities. Specific objectives are also helpful to teachers and students in evaluating learning. By clearly identifying what the outcomes should be, everyone can tell when they are achieved.

For this reason, many school systems insist that teachers use what are referred to as behavioral objectives. Behavioral objectives are even more precise. They identify specific acts that students can perform that will show that the desired learning or change has occurred. Such objectives are observable, and the standard of successful achievement is identified.

Language is very important in writing behavioral objectives. Words and terms that suggest that the teacher would have to know what was going on inside a child's mind are simply unacceptable. A properly stated behavioral objective would never suggest that the child would "know" or "understand" something. Following are parallel examples of objectives. In each set, the first objective uses acceptable behavioral objective language while the second does not. It should be noted that behavioral objectives cannot be written simply by referring to some word list of strong specific action verbs. Teachers who do this may fall into the trap of focusing on trivialities or identify activities rather than desired learning outcomes. Words and phrases in isolation may be deceptive. It is the specific identification of an observable action that actually shows a learning that defines an objective as behavioral. It should also be noted that an objective can be very specific, important, and valuable for teaching, yet not be behavioral.

EXAMPLE SET 1
Behavioral: After a study of the maps of Africa, the student will be able to name five countries in Africa.

Nonbehavioral: Students will know that Africa is a continent made up of over 40 nations.

EXAMPLE SET 2
Behavioral: The student will be able to correctly identify areas of high population density on a population map.

Nonbehavioral: Students will understand how to use a population map.

EXAMPLE SET 3
Behavioral: After a study of the Middle Ages in Europe, students will be able to list three provisions of the Magna Carta.

Nonbehavioral: Students will realize the significance of the Magna Carta.

EXAMPLE SET 4
Behavioral: After studying the community and the people who work in it, the students will be able to match pictures of ten community helpers they have studied with their place of work on a pictographic map of the community.

Nonbehavioral: The students will become aware of the workplaces of community helpers.

EXAMPLE SET 5
Behavioral: Given a cup of multiple colored candies, the children will be able to correctly make a graph showing the distribution by color.

Nonbehavioral: The kindergarten children will learn to graph using one criteria.

CONTENT OUTLINES AND FLOWCHARTS

Content outlines help the teacher determine what is most important to teach. They help teachers and students discover the structure of the topic being studied. An outline may be a simple content flowchart such as the following, which identifies the key subtopics in a unit on Egypt and the order in which they will be taught. Such a flowchart not only identifies the areas of study but begins to suggest the order of the teaching itself.

Content Flowchart

Unit Topic: Egypt

Locating Egypt

Physical Features

Cultural Sites

Current Government, Political Situation, and Events in Egypt

Historical Significance and Background

Importance of the Nile River

Ancient and Medieval Civilizations of Egypt

Such a topical flowchart offers little more than broad and general headings. The teacher will undoubtedly want to develop a much more detailed outline before proceeding further if this approach is followed. Nonetheless, as nonspecific as the flowchart may be, it begins to provide the unit with direction. Building at least a mental content flowchart of a unit is an effective way for the teacher to develop a very helpful mental picture or what might be referred to as a *cognitive map* even for textbook-centered teaching.

Those with a strong content orientation might prefer a much more detailed content outline as the beginning point for mapping a unit of studies. Others might prefer a cognitive-elements chart such as the one that follows for a unit on the Middle Ages.

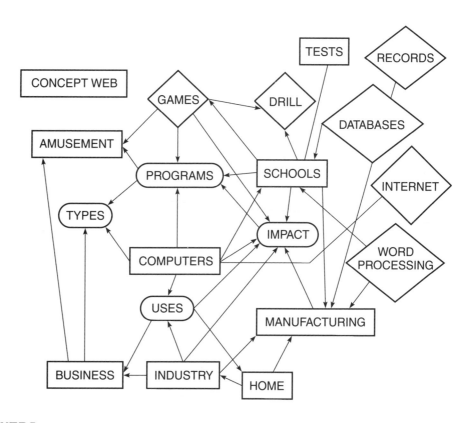

CONCEPT WEBS

A visual device that teachers can use to frame the big picture of a unit is called a web, because its appearance bears a strong resemblance to a spider's work. Basically, a web shows how the various concepts covered in a unit are linked or interrelated. Near the center of the web are the broad topics and most important ideas. Peripheral layers show the subordinate and less important ideas. Unit webs are better evolved in two stages. The first stage is simply brainstorming and choosing topics to study. The second stage arranges these topics according to priorities (importance) and relationships. Webbing is a better tool when the teacher has a comfortable familiarity with the unit topic and therefore knows the content. Because brainstorming is involved, it is a good technique to use in collaborative units or with a mentor or friend. The illustration below shows a web for a unit on computers.

MOVING TOWARD THE DEVELOPMENT OF ACTIVITIES

As the teacher is building toward this mental picture of the unit, a lot of other work and thinking need to be going on simultaneously. One thing that is very important is that the teacher needs to be constantly on the look out for resources. The possibilities can be overwhelming. Among the available resources are such things as books and magazines with good teaching activities, fiction and nonfiction books and stories that children will want to and be able to read, information resources both for the teacher's use and that of the children, films, filmstrips, videotapes, slide sets, pictorial materials, computer programs, music, and artifacts.

The possible tools of teaching often accumulate until there is a problem of selecting the best, most appropriate, and most useful. The resources, along with the overview of the content and the development of the objectives, begin to shape the kind of learning activities that will form the unit itself.

The dramatic element of the classroom was alluded to earlier. The sequencing of the teaching-learning activities in a unit is very much like structuring the drama itself. Much like a play or a movie, if you can imagine a very long drama, the unit unfolds over several days or weeks. Like a drama, the earliest stages of the unit have to grab the students' attention; provide a sense of direction and purpose; create excitement, interest, and suspense; and give a great deal of background information. This is often referred to as the *initiation stage* of the unit, and teachers usually have just one or, at best, two days to accomplish everything I have described. During that time, teachers also have to discover something that dramatists can only guess at when writing plays—what their students already know and what background they are bringing to the study. If a playwright guesses wrong, the show flops. If a teacher misjudges, but remains sensitive and alert to student reactions early on, there is still time for adjustment with a minimum waste of student and teacher time, education's most valuable commodity.

Once the unit is launched, the body of the unit can be built of activities that are aimed at developing the objectives and maintaining and extending interest. These activities, which form the greatest part of the unit, are sometimes referred to collectively as the *developmental phase* of the unit. Most of the research, information gathering and sharing, problem solving, and extension and enrichment of the unit goes on during this developmental period. In other chapters in this book, various types of activities and activity building will be shown. However, the chart on pages 57–60 indicates some of the endless variety of activities that might be part of a unit plan.

The final phase of a unit, called the *culmination phase,* serves multiple functional purposes. At this point, it is fairly obvious that closure is needed, some activity or activities that will give the children a sense that they are finished with this particular study for now at least. Going back to the drama analogy, a unit needs a climax and the culminating activities need to provide this. It may be that the children will show what they have learned by sharing their knowledge with someone else: parents, the principal, other classes, or even each other. So, one type of culmination activity might be a program, a festival or cultural celebration, the making of a videotape by the class, or some similar activity. The culmination of the unit also serves as a summative overview and a drawing together of all that has been learned. It should be, in fact, the time when the teacher helps the children to comprehend the significance of what they have been studying. If the children have been working on a problem or a group of problems, this is the point where solutions are offered and findings and conclusions are reached. Not surprisingly, the culmination of a unit is also the place where the teacher needs to take stock or make the final evaluation of what has been learned. Of course evaluation should be ongoing and present in every activity, but it is again at this culmination level that the teacher needs to make the final assessment. One last set of functions that the culmination of a unit may serve is that of maintaining or even stimulating interest in the topic that has been studied while providing a transition to some new area of study. While it may seem strange to try to create interest just as you are leaving an area of study, this is the very point at which we want to be saying to children, "We've spent all the time we can, but there are a lot more interesting and exciting things for you to learn if you want to go on your own. Now here are some other ideas for you to look into and here are some great resources you can use." The transitional function is equally logical when you think about how children learn. Basically, they understand new experiences by comparing them to things they already know about. So the transitional aspect of the culmination is simply the beginning of showing relationships, similarities, and dissimilarities with the new area of study.

The format of a unit may be developed in many different ways, no single one being *the* correct method. To mention a few of the alternatives, units may be organized as sequenced daily lesson plans with lessons of varying duration each structured around one or more specific objectives; as sets of lessons, each teaching specific concepts, generalizations, or subtopics; or as subsets of activities reflecting the various curricular areas from which the activities are drawn (art, music, language arts, etc.). Regardless of the format that shapes the unit, all unit plans need to show reflection on certain necessary elements. These are shown in the format that follows. A short (one week) unit follows, illustrating how this format may be used.

UNIT ELEMENTS FORMAT

1. Descriptive and identifying information
   A. A title (This may be in the form of a statement, a problem statement, an issue description, or a descriptive and appealing title.)
   B. Grade level(s) of students toward whom the unit is directed
   C. Estimated or allotted duration (the time in weeks with some description of how much time is to be spent each week)

2. Rationale
   A. Overview statement of the importance of the area of study regarding both content and the approaches used

    B. Arguments and assertions regarding the significance and the appropriateness of the topic of study

3. Unit objectives
    A. A list of the most important targeted learning outcomes of the entire unit (These may be categorized in some way, the most common classification being cognitive or knowledge objectives to include facts to be remembered, concepts and generalizations to be understood, etc.; affective objectives to include values and attitudes to be developed, beliefs and aspirations to be gained, appreciations to be cultivated, etc.; and psychomotor or skills objectives.)

4. Content description (This may be embodied in the objectives and not needed as a separate entity.) Content description may be presented in several ways, including the following:
    A. A list of generalizations
    B. A sequenced content outline
    C. A concept web of the unit
    D. A list of concept definitions

5. Activity sequence. Again, there is more than one way to present this area, including the following:
    A. An ordered set of lesson plans with initiating, development, and culminating activities in order
    B. Parties arranged according to the subject area with which the social studies is being integrated (art, music, language arts, etc.)
    C. Unit activities organized into subunits each representing a subtopic, a generalization, a key concept, or some other content heading
    D. Unit organized around key activities with contingency alternatives stemming from each of these
    E. Unit organized into key activities with enrichment activities and skill and background activities plans on a needs basis (Often this will be done in the form of Learning Centers.)

6. Description of the unit evaluation process. Development of the evaluation or assessment design as it is built into individual lessons and activities. Ways of assessing to what extent learning outcomes have been achieved, detailing evaluation strategies, including any unit test(s)

7. Resources. This cataloging effort may take the form of a simple bibliographic listing or a more useful but more time-consuming series of annotated bibliographic entries. One convenient organization pattern for resources is division into teacher-resource and student-resource sections. It is also useful to create subcategories based on resource type (e.g., audiovisual materials, games and computer resources, reference materials, enrichment trade books, etc.).

AN ILLUSTRATIVE PRIMARY GRADE UNIT

Unit Title: Why Do We Have a President and What Does a President Do?

Grade Level: First or second grade

Allotted Time: One to two weeks with follow-up sessions throughout the year

Rationale: It is very important for children in this society to begin learning about the office of the president in the government of the United States. Children constantly hear and see presidential references from parents and other adults, on television and in movies, and even as they look at money and stamps. The president is the most important single figure in the government, and presidential decisions and policies influence everyone's life.

This unit is an introduction to the presidency that will be an aid to understanding in future years. The focus in the initial unit will be on the office itself and the current president. The follow-up to the unit will involve an introduction to the presidents of the past.

Conceptual Areas and Concerns:

> The concept of president
>
> Who the current president is
>
> The president's jobs
>
> The White House as the home of the president

Unit Objectives:

The students will:

- Know who the current president of the United States is and what that person looks and sounds like.
- Learn what the president's jobs are.
- Gain an idea about where the president lives and how the president travels today.
- Learn about the different jobs and the work of the president.
- Know about some of the past presidents.

Activities

Initiating Activity

Objectives

- The students will be able to recognize and identify a picture of the president of the United States and name the president.

- The students will be able to name some of the jobs of the president in the government.

- The students will know that the name of the president's home is the White House and have an idea of its location.

Procedure

Begin by showing the children a series of pictures of the president. In many classes, some children will be able to make an identification at least by title. Make sure that the word *president* and the president's name are mentioned several times as you talk about what the president is and what the president does. If possible, find a recording of "Hail to the Chief." Talk about why the bands play that song sometimes when the president arrives. Play any available videotapes of the president in the news. (Avoid recordings that will be too boring, especially long speeches.) Tapes showing the president signing bills or making official visits will be useful. Talk with children about what they know about the White House. Again show pictures. If you think they are ready to learn about location and to do U.S. map work, ask if the children know where the White House is and show them Washington, D.C., on a map of the United States.

Use a pattern for a stack of four labeled hats, one for each of four specific jobs of the president.

Uncle Sam hat: Chief of State

Army hat: Commander in Chief

Top hat: Director of Foreign Policy

Hard hat: Guardian of the Economy

Have the children color each hat and then practice saying the role and stacking the hats. End the activity by having the children identify the president by name and title and the White House from pictures, and rename the four jobs of the president.

Developmental Activities

1. Make a presidential library in the classroom. This will include a bulletin board, a scrapbook of newspaper and magazine clippings (especially those with pictures). It will also have a browsing table of activities and books about presidents.

2. Look at presidents' pictures on money, stamps, and so on.

3. Show pictures of the First Lady and talk about who she is.

4. Have each child tell what he or she would do if he or she were president.

5. Have children all tell something that they would like to say to the president if the president should come to visit their class.

6. Have each child suggest something they would like to show the president about the school.

7. Let the class try to come up with the following information about the president:

   • How tall is the president?

   • What is the president's favorite food?

   • What food does the president not like?

   • What are the president's hobbies?

   • Where does the president go to vacation or rest?

   • What are the president's favorite sports?

   • Does the president have a favorite movie or television show?

8. Choose two popular cartoon or television characters and have an election for president in the class. Have children try to tell why they think that each would be a good president. Then go through the exercise with written ballots and a voting booth.

9. Show pictures of the Oval Office and talk about it as the president's office. Present a trash can and ask the children to imagine that it is the trash can from that office. Ask them to think about what items might be found in it at the end of a work day for the president.

10. Keep a yarn map showing where the president travels. If possible, show television news showing the president's visits to different places.

Culminating Activity

Assign the children one sentence each about the presidency and have them draw a picture showing their sentence. After all the pictures are drawn, use a camcorder to record the children showing their pictures and telling about them. Show the videotape both to the children and to a gathering of parents.

Sentences

• _____ is the ____ (number) President of the United States.

• The president has many jobs.

• Some of the people who help the president are called the cabinet members.

• The president lives in the White House.

• The White House is in the city of Washington, D.C.

• _____ , the president's wife, is called the First Lady.

- If the president should die, the vice president would take over the job.
- The Secret Service guards the president.
- The president is commander in chief of the Armed Forces.
- The president is the head of the government.
- The president is the chief ambassador to other countries.
- The president likes _____ . (favorite food)
- The president sometimes travels in a plane called Air Force One.
- I like the president because _____ .
- One of the things that the president likes to do is _____ .
- When the president signs bills, they turn into law.
- The president tries to decide what is best for the country.
- George Washington was the first president.

Follow the unit by presenting and talking about one president every week. Keep a cumulative bulletin board with pictures of each president as they are discussed. Each week, have the children try to rename all the presidents that have been previously covered as a group choral exercise.

AN ILLUSTRATIVE INTERMEDIATE GRADE UNIT

Unit Title: The Acquisition of the Louisiana Territory

Grade Level: Fifth grade

Allotted Time: Five 50 minute class periods spread over less than two weeks

Rationale: The unit will deal with the acquisition of the Louisiana Territory by the United States and the subsequent exploration of that territory. Because the class is studying the history of the United States throughout the year, the study of a particular historic episode in more detail is especially useful to show the human side of history. The Lewis and Clark expedition shows the hazards and some of the difficulties faced by pioneers, without violence or sensationalism. The journal of the expedition is a complete and detailed primary resource that the children can read with understanding. The members of the expedition exemplify courage, resourcefulness, a sense of responsibility and duty, and other desirable character traits. The purchase and the exploration of the Louisiana Territory nearly doubled the territorial size of the United States, thus having tremendous impact on the young nation.

Objectives:

The students will

- Be able to identify the importance of the Louisiana Purchase.

- Know the major details of the Purchase.

- Be able to identify purposes for the Lewis and Clark expedition.

- Be able to name several of the difficulties that the expedition encountered.

- Be able to trace the approximate route of the expedition on a map and know about how long Lewis and Clark spent on the trip.

- Be able to make comparisons to other explorations.

Content Outline:

I. Events leading to the purchase
  A. The need of Americans on the western frontier to be able to use the port of New Orleans
  B. The acquisition of Spanish territories by France and the closing of the port of New Orleans
  C. Monroe and Livingston appointed by President Jefferson to go to France
  D. The personality and motivations of Napoleon
    1. Need for money to finance his military efforts
    2. Lack of desire to defend large distant territories against a powerful British navy
  E. The vision and opportunism of Monroe and Livingston to exceed their authorization

II. The Lewis and Clark expedition
  A. Purposes of the expedition
    1. Gathering of scientific information
    2. Contact with the natives
    3. Proving the feasibility of travel
    4. Exploring and mapping
  B. Difficulties and dangers
    1. Environment and weather
    2. Travel hardships and problems (including the danger of being lost)
    3. Possible encounters with hostile natives and wild animals
  C. Impact of the expedition

Activities

Initiating Activity

Objectives

Students will

- Know the events leading up to the Louisiana Purchase and the terms of the Purchase

- Be able to identify the major purposes of the Lewis and Clark expedition

Procedure

Present the background to the Louisiana Purchase as a series of problems in a storytelling context, getting the children to respond.

Problems

If you are in a business, what do you have to do? (Sell the goods or services.)

Now, if you have something to sell and you and your product are one place and the people who want it are hundreds of miles away, what is your problem? (To get it to market as quickly and cheaply as you can. Give the background on the furs and other goods Americans had to take down river to New Orleans.)

Well, what happens when the officials in New Orleans will not let you bring your goods through any longer? (Guide discussion to the eventual involvement of President Jefferson.) What do you think the president will do?

The next step is to lead into a role play activity in which two students portraying James Monroe and Robert Livingston are given their commission by the president and Congress to buy New Orleans and Florida from France for $2,000,000. They meet the Emperor Napoleon who was, so the story goes, in his bath at the time of the interview. (Napoleon should be portrayed by the teacher, another adult, or a very well-coached student.) At the point where Napoleon makes his offer, interrupt the role play to discuss with the class the implications and the reasoning of all parties. Explain to the students that the final terms were worked out, not by Napoleon himself, but by the French Foreign Minister whose name was Talleyrand Périgord and by the Treasury Minister, Barbé-Marbois. Tell them that these two ministers got more money out of the Americans than Napoleon expected. Have students guess how much more money (It was $5 million.) Ask the students about who they think got the better deal. Then bring closure.

Tell the students that at this point Jefferson and the United States had bought "a pig in a poke." Hold up a cloth or leather bag and explain the expression. Tell them that Jefferson knew there was a big river involved (pull a long crooked strip of blue paper out of the bag) and an important port city (pull out a number of Monopoly-type houses and tiny toy ships). But all Jefferson or anyone else knew about the rest of that purchase was that there was a lot of it. (At this point, empty the bag, which is filled with the jigsaw puzzle pieces representing the current states that were eventually carved from the Louisiana Territory.) Tell the students that Jefferson was not the kind of man who would leave something like this alone. Lead into the commissioning of the Lewis and Clark expedition and its purposes.

Close by announcing the objectives of the rest of the unit and then reviewing the details of the purchase, using a large wall map and tracing the expedition's route very quickly.

Developmental Activities

Review the Louisiana Purchase. Tell the children that this amounted to a cost of about 2 cents per acre. Have them figure the number of acres and square miles. Possibly have them figure cost using inflation (about 200-fold).

Explain the purposes of the Lewis and Clark expedition by reading or having children read portions of the Lewis and Clark journals. Discuss the importance of the expedition.

Using the journals and maps, have the students make a carefully measured time line of the 28 month journey. Also have them use string measures (pieces of string cut and marked to fit map scale) to measure various segments of the journey. Discuss the reasons some distances would take longer.

Discuss the hardships, dangers, problems, and difficulties that the students imagine the expedition might have encountered. Then have the students do the following in-basket activity, which is based on actual incidents during the expedition.

UP THE RIVER WITH LEWIS AND CLARK

For the Teacher

Student Objectives

- Students will understand the dangers and difficulties faced by Lewis and Clark.

- Students will be able to recognize differences in significance and urgency among frontier situations, where outside help could not be available.

Have students work in pairs playing the roles of Lewis and Clark. The role-play activity should be done in the following steps:

1. Let students examine a map showing the route of the Lewis and Clark expedition. Explain the reasons and purposes of the expedition.

2. Pass out Student Handout 1. Have students work through the 15 situations prioritizing the need for action and finding solutions. You may want them to write down their solutions. Some will be obvious, others will require some creativity.

3. Discuss the various ways students have ordered the situations and compare solutions.

4. Distribute Student Handout 2 and have students compare their solutions with what Lewis and Clark actually did.

5. Pass out Student Handout 3 and have students discuss how their priorities differ and compare with a historian's views. (Note: You may prefer to use only a teacher copy and present them orally.)

6. Have students discuss what they learned from the activity. You might discuss why most Native Americans were so friendly (this is very different from the picture painted by movies and television), other dangers that might have come up, the length of the journey, and the time it took. Tell students there is, of course, no correct order for the problems to be solved. Then, discuss with them the logic that they used in their own sequencing of the tasks.

As a follow-up activity, give the students a list of other explorations that they might like to read about and study

• The voyages of Columbus

• LaSalle's trip down the Mississippi River

• NASA space explorations, including Neil Armstrong's moon landing

• Leif Eriksson's voyages

Have children discuss how these were like and how they were different from the Lewis and Clark expedition.

Culminating Activity

Have the students put on a program consisting of:

• A reenactment of Jefferson's decision to send emissaries to France and the meeting between Napoleon and Monroe and Livingston

• A Living Time Line in which children costume themselves as events in the Purchase and Lewis and Clark expedition, each describing his or her own event

• A floor-map activity in which guides lead guests along a large floor-map representation, showing guests the route of the expedition

Evaluation

Evaluation is built into every activity in some way. A final unit test might consist of the following questions:

• From what country did the United States purchase the Louisiana Territory and what was the price?

- Name two dangers faced by the Lewis and Clark expedition.

- Give one reason why the Louisiana Purchase was important.

- Give one purpose of the Lewis and Clark expedition.

- On an unlabeled map, trace the route of the Lewis and Clark expedition, naming the rivers they traveled.

Resources

Adams, A. B. (1981). *The disputed lands: A history of the American West.* New York: Putnam.

Barnard, E. S. (1987). *Story of the American West.* Pleasantville, NY: Readers' Digest.

Coit, M. L. and the Editors of *LIFE.* (1963). *The life history of the United States: The growing years.* New York: Time.

DeVoto, B. (Ed.) (1953). *The journals of Lewis and Clark.* New York: Houghton Mifflin.

WHAT MAKES A UNIT PLAN SUITABLE FOR SOCIAL STUDIES?

The utility of any type or format of unit plan in bringing about effective social studies instruction will vary with the teacher and the school situation. Organized, highly structured teachers who are capable of and comfortable with precise, long-in-advance planning and follow-through will probably do well with the daily lesson plan approach to planning. Teachers who want to provide maximum flexibility to adjust to student interest may find this style uncomfortably rigid.

Any type of unit plan is most likely to help bring about effective social studies instruction if it does the following:

- Helps the teacher keep a focus on the intended learning outcomes

- Aids the teacher to gather the best available resources quickly and efficiently

- Aids the teacher in assimilating social studies within the whole of students' learning

- Helps the teacher in building in motivational, creative teaching ideas

- Reduces the time needed for the teacher to plan effectively

FINDING AND USING PREPARED UNITS

Teachers may feel, usually with justification, that they do not have the time, energy, or ingenuity to prepare elaborate and extensive units of their own for the entire school year. At the same time, they may not want to fall into the pattern of teaching directly from the textbook.

There is an alternative available to teachers even if there is no established district or school curriculum guide complete with authorized, already prepared units and even if there is no easy collaborative planning or sharing going on in the school in which they teach. That alternative is to "borrow" premade units from some source outside the school.

The maxim of unit "borrowing" ought to be, "If you are going to 'borrow,' then take the best!" But how does a teacher with little time to search (if you had the time, you would have planned your own unit in the first place) find the best?

Two rules seem to apply here. The first is that the best place to search is among the professionally, even commercially prepared materials that have already undergone the scrutiny of selection and the polishing of rewrite and editing. A starting place among these are the commercial teaching magazines such as *Instructor, Teacher, Learning,* or *Mailbox.* Professional journals such as *Social Education, Social Studies and the Young Learner,* and *The Social Studies* will be worth a look through, too. A trip to a university library for a browse of indexes and ads may be very fruitful. The desired topic may jump out at the teacher in the first few minutes or it may take several hours, but it is time well invested if it saves days and weeks of planning. It would be a smart idea to check out the text series other than the one(s) in use in your school, too. The teachers' editions may hold some pleasant surprises. Certainly, any gems found in these outside textbooks will require some adaptation, but that will be true of most any "borrowed" material. One other resource worth a look through in a university library will be other methods texts in social studies. Some of these contain provocative unit ideas.

The second rule is, "Always be on the lookout for materials for teaching." At conventions, in the rooms of other teachers, at the teacher center (if your system is lucky enough to have one), browsing on-line or even in the dentist's office, the very thing needed may be waiting for the alert person who takes the initiative and the time to nose through the available material. One of the resources for teacher prepared units is the Association for Supervision and Curriculum Development, which publishes a list of available units and curriculum materials available for school systems.

To use prepared units effectively, the key concern is adaptation. The focus in adaptation has to be on the intended learning outcomes. If the teacher begins with concern for how a unit plan can bring significant learning, then all other kinds of needed change fall into place. A second and related focus has to be on the vitality and motivational appeal of the activities for the children. Will the children be excited, interested, and stimulated by these activities? A third related concern to the teacher has to do with whether or not the necessary resources are available to successfully bring off the activities. This may have to do as much with a realistic self-assessment of time, energy, and initiative as with material resources, but both are needed.

PLANNING FOR SHORTER INSTRUCTION SEQUENCES

The most useful and important among shorter instructional sequences is, of course, the single lesson plan. A lesson plan is in many ways a unit in miniature, and lessons contain similar key elements such as objectives, procedural descriptions of activities, and identification of resources.

Any lesson plan design which is going to be particularly useful will be one that is structured to help students better retain what they are taught. The Hunter (1990–1991) lesson sequence has been a helpful model, especially for teachers in the early stages of their development because it is structured in a series of distinctive, easily constructed steps. A lesson design developed from the elements in Hunter's sequence follows.

1. Get the learners' attention and prepare them for what they are going to learn. The teacher needs to think of ways of capturing and focusing interest on the topic of study. This part of the lesson may also review previously studied related material, making a transition and aiding understanding by relating new material to the old. The major purpose is to develop readiness for learning the new topic.

2. Explain the objective(s) or purpose(s). A key element in the Hunter approach is that the students have a good idea of the ends the teacher has in mind. This step includes a clear communication of what the teacher intends to accomplish. In a sense, though, it is something more than that; if possible, the teacher and the students need to reach a consensus so that there can be shared goals that are understood by both.

3. Do direct teaching. In this step, the teacher is communicating the new information of the lesson, teaching concepts, and so on, using a variety of techniques.

4. If it is appropriate, model what you want the learners to do. Though not all lessons require this step, in many it is essential. Basically, it involves demonstration or the completing of examples by the teacher. The teacher shows the students how each step in a process is completed (e.g., finding a location using map coordinates).

5. Check for understanding. This is sometimes referred to as the monitor and adjust stage. It is a point at which the teacher determines if the students understand what the lesson is all about. It requires some activity in which students give and receive feedback. This may involve a signaling device in which all students participate, a questioning technique using selected students, or individual responses from every student.

6. Provide guided practice. The teacher gives students a chance to use new skills or concepts. Again the emphasis is on monitored practice with feedback from the teacher.

7. Provide opportunity for independent practice.

Though this lesson planning model will not and should not be suited to every lesson, it can provide a useful pattern for many. As a model the seven steps in the lesson plan show very clearly the importance of developing detail, specificity, and sequence in the procedure of a lesson plan. Following is an example of a plan developed along the lines of the Hunter model.

Lesson Plan Title: African Nations

Level: Fourth grade

Objective: Students will learn the relative locations of the African nations.

1. Get the learners' attention and prepare them for what they are about to learn. Show a large wall map of Africa. Ask a series of questions about the countries, such as: How many countries are there? What is the largest? The smallest? Where are some of the countries that have been in the news? What nations are in the North? The South? The East? The West? At appropriate times, point to the appropriate countries or have children locate them. At this point, remove the labeled map, replacing it with a large, laminated unlabeled map. Ask how many could label some of the countries. If there are any hands, allow a few trials. End this portion of the lesson by saying that it might be useful to get a better idea of where the nations are located.

2. Explain the objective or purpose. At this point, tell the children that the purpose of what they are going to be doing is to become more familiar with the names and the locations of African nations.

3. Do direct teaching. Explain the materials and the activities. In advance, prepare a series of transparencies all of the same scale, which together form a complete map of Africa. Assign each child a nation or a set of contiguous nations so that all the nations are divided among the children. Either by scheduling or some other design, have the children in pairs use the transparencies to draw enlargements of their nation(s) on sheets of butcher paper. A taped mark on the floor will, with a little reminding, keep the maps the same scale.

4. If appropriate, demonstrate or model what you want the learners to do. Explain the materials and the activities. In advance, prepare a series of transparencies, all of the same scale, which together form a complete map of Africa. Assign each child a nation or set of contiguous nations so that all nations are divided among the children. Either through scheduling or some other device, have the children in pairs use the transparencies to draw enlargements of their nations on large pieces of butcher paper. Keep reminding them to keep all the map parts to the same scale.

5. Check for comprehension. When all maps are drawn, have the children take their own. Go to a gym or any large open area. (Outside is fine if the

wind is not blowing.) Use a line or some other marking. Go through a series of question and response discussion-adjustment exercises based on the following kinds of tasks:

- Every nation south of the Sahara desert stand to the left of the line; all others to the right!

- Name a nation and ask all children holding nations that touch it on the map to stand to the left of the line.

- All nations on the west coast of Africa stand to the front of the rest.

6. Provide guided practice. Return to the classroom. Have each child in turn use a pointer to show his or her own nation(s) on a large unlabeled wall map. Play the "Name 5" game. Divide the class into two teams. In turn, each team's members get to name and label up to five countries (using a felt-tip marker). The team gets a point for every nation that is right, but it loses two points for wrong guesses.

7. Provide for independent practice. Give each child an unlabeled map of Africa. Using one another as resources, have the children label their own maps, then check them against a labeled map. Cut out and laminate the children's maps. Have children continue to practice as a free-time activity using these maps as part of a large jigsaw puzzle.

TWO ALTERNATIVE TYPES OF PLANS

Teachers may find it useful to have alternatives to unit and lesson plans. Schedule pressures may seem to prohibit use of extensive units, while single lessons offer seemingly isolated learnings that are not easily envisioned as part of some larger learning sequence.

1. Modules

One alternative is a type of planning package that is referred to as a *module*. Modules provide for one to a series of lessons, sometimes consisting of several activities centered around one or a series of closely related ideas, usually concept statements or generalizations. Modules may be used in isolation, as part of or in conjunction with a unit, or in clusters. Built into modular teaching is the notion of *mastery*. Mastery, in this case, means that the module teaches the idea to a point where some specified or at least defined level of understanding is reached. Evaluation and reteaching, then, are necessary for module construction.

As the following examples of topics for modules might indicate, modules may aim at developing definitional understanding of concepts, at helping students reach evaluational judgments, or at providing experiences that cause students to arrive at a commonly shared generalization as a way of thinking. The following are examples of definitional topics:

- A *map* is a model representing some part of the surface of the earth or some other area and it is subject to various inaccuracies.

- A *president* is the head of a nation, organization, or business, having specific executive functions and powers for a defined length of time and under restricted conditions.

- *Laws* are rules recognized by a governing body as binding upon the members of the group.

Evaluation Judgments

- A good country

- Responsibility

- Playing fair is more important than winning

The following are examples of generalizations:

- Urban communities tend to change more rapidly than rural communities.

- Though all members of a community are consumers, only some are producers.

- A single event may have several causes and produce more than one outcome.

Once the topic is identified, the module itself consists of an array of activities including examples and identified nonexamples along with identifying experiences. The activities have the express purpose of bringing an understanding or mastery of the topic.

2. Case Studies

Case studies provide another alternative to units. Case study approaches have become increasingly more viable with the development of computers and databases. The term *case study* implies a kind of intense examination of a particular event, person, or thing, or a grouping of these. The one case is looked at as an example or model that can be studied in depth and even intently over time. In medicine a doctor might study the medical history of a few patients. From these selected cases, it is hoped that insights about others who have similar medical history may be derived. In law, a case study may be chosen because it represents a landmark decision or provides a precedent in court procedure. Sociologists, historians, and psychologists may construct fictional cases to demonstrate typical behavior. In fact, the case study approach is used by almost all professions looking at human behavior simply because of the complexity of human thought and action.

A case study is an intensive use of example(s). The example(s) provides a database for inquiry and concrete illustration(s) of principles, concepts, and ideas.

Case studies used in the social studies can be a way of helping the students see the personal and human aspects of a culture or of a time. Students look at one person, one family, one village rather than reading generalizations about a country, culture, or period of time. Human qualities seem less abstract. The short unit on Lewis and Clark presented earlier in this chapter differs from a case study only in the approach used. Essentially, it was the teacher not the student who used the database. So, instead of being a student-directed study of the details of the expedition related to a single problem or a set of problems, the unit is a series of teacher-controlled activities in which students only use the Lewis and Clark material as content.

Procedure in Preparing a Case Study

1. Identify the problem to be studied and the purpose to be accomplished.

2. Tentatively identify a research procedure for students to follow.

3. Select the appropriate example (or case).

4. Develop detailed procedural plans.

5. Collect resources related to the case. Examples of resources include

   - Maps of varying sorts

   - Background information sheets

   - Interviews on related topics

   - Letters

   - Descriptions of objects

   - Diaries and journals

   - Records and public documents

   - Newspaper clippings

6. Organize the data bank of materials and data related to the case. For example, one usable pattern of organization consists of

   - A single narrative or a series of narratives describing the facts of the case. These may include first-hand accounts, scholarly summations, and even slanted or biased descriptions.

   - First person (witness) interviews with principals in or witnesses to the case (transcripts or tapes of these)

- Pictures (photographs, drawings, etc.), films, and other media visualizations (including actual film coverage of an event) of the setting, the people, and the chain of events in the case across the time period involved

- Exhibits (artifacts, realia)

- Maps, graphs, charts

- Background information (including anecdotes)

7. Plan activities and materials structured to help or guide students as they examine the case or inquire into the evidence.

A Few Types of Activities to Use with Case Study Material

- Research-based discussions and individual reports of controversies

- Problem-solving situations calling upon data in the case

- Role plays involving the principals of the case

- Developing reports or answering questions in which they draw from data

- Debates involving controversies or points of view regarding the same or related cases

- Creative writing to or about the principle characters in the case (e.g., letters, hypothetical diaries, fictional stories, etc.)

- Question-generating sessions

- Data-generating sessions to build additional cases or to extend data bank

- Reenactments of events

- Artistic endeavors (e.g., murals, models)

- Projective analysis (What are outcomes to be anticipated beyond the data?)

- Analysis sheets and questions to be answered by studying the data

LOOKING BACK

The quality of planning makes a difference in the quality of teaching. Teachers fail to give adequate time to planning for a variety of reasons, but by determined systematic effort, planning can add to teaching effectiveness and satisfaction.

The term *unit* is most often used to describe the long-term planning a teacher does to teach a topic to a group of students. The teachers' editions of textbooks also use the term to describe the activities provided for teaching particular content, usually chapters. Whether a textbook unit or a teacher-made unit, considerable planning is involved. Teacher-made units may be of several types, including collaborative or team units, which are usually resource units; teaching units, which are prepared with a specific case and sequence of activities; and sketch units, which are less thorough and usually require much more additional planning later. Each of these types of plans has its uses.

Short-term planning most often takes the form of lesson plans. Hunter (1991) has designed one format of such plans, which has enjoyed wide use. It particularly is suited for learning retention.

Alternative types of planning are also sometimes useful to social studies teachers. Among these are modules, based on mastery learning principles, and case studies, which reflect inductive learning. The questions and activities which follow may be used to help you think about what you have read in this chapter.

- Brainstorm a set of unit titles and topics related to technology or some other area where science and the social studies are better integrated.

- Review some textbook units. Identify their strengths and shortcomings.

- Profile your own planning abilities. What are your assets and what are the areas where you need improvement?

- Design a single activity to teach the concepts of city, state, and nation.

- Design a survey to discover how often teachers prepare their own instruction units. Discuss the findings.

- Identify several types of quality lessons that could not be fitted to the model presented in the chapter. Determine the reasons that this model does not work for every type of lesson.

- Practice webbing a unit topic.

- Make up a "People Scavenge" for the unit included in this chapter.

SELF-TEST

1. What are some reasons that teachers cannot always plan as effectively as they should?

2. What are some of the characteristics of a classroom where good planning is going on?

3. How do the varying types of units discussed in this chapter differ?

4. What is a collaborative unit?

5. What are the elements necessary in a unit plan?

6. What is a case study?

REFERENCES

Brophy, J., and Good, T. (1978). *Looking in classrooms*. New York: Harper and Row.

Hunter, M. (1991). Hunter lesson design helps achieve the goals of science instruction. *Educational Leadership*, 48 (December/January), 79–81.

National Council for the Social Studies. (1994). *Expectations for Excellence: Curriculum Standards for the Social Studies*. Washington, DC: NCSS.

Turner, T. N. (2000). What to do when you burn out. *Tennessee Association of Middle Schools Journal*, 26, 1–2.

Woodward, A., Elliott, D. L., and Nagel, K. (1986). Beyond textbooks in elementary social studies. *Social Education*, 50 (January), 50–53.

SUGGESTED READING

Chaney, S. (2000). Changing roles of teachers. *The Delta Kappa Gamma Bulletin*, 66(2) (Winter), 25–9.

Chapin, J. R., and Messick, R. G. (2002). Planning for social studies instruction. Chapter 2 in *Elementary Social Studies: A Practical Guide*. Boston: Allyn and Bacon.

Kindsvatter, R., Wilen, W., and Ishler, M. (1988). *Dynamics of effective teaching*. New York: Longman.

Hostetler, K. D. (1997). *Ethical judgment in teaching*. Boston: Allyn and Bacon.

MacDonald, R. E. (1991). *A handbook of basic skills and strategies for beginning teachers*. New York: Longman.

Meyen, E. (1981). *Developing instructional units*. Dubuque, IA.

Mioduser, D., and Margalit, M. (1997). TTIPSS—a computer-based system for training, problem solving, and educational planning. *Journal of Special Education Technology*, 13 (Summer), 1–13.

Van Der Linde, C. H. (2001). Strategic quality planning for teachers in the new millennium. *Education*, 121(3) (Spring), 535–538.

Winitzky, N. E. (1992). Classroom organization for social studies. In Shaver, James P. (Ed.), *Handbook of research on social studies teaching and learning*. New York: Macmillan (pp. 530–539).

3 The Social Studies Program

LOOKING AHEAD

What topics and themes are to be taught? What is to be taught about these topics and themes? Questions such as these are constant and troubling for those involved in social studies education. Though there is little disagreement that the selection ought to be related to carefully selected goals and that the teaching itself should be done in a purposeful way, what is taught and what materials are used are ongoing problems in the social studies. In this chapter, we will look at some of the forces influencing the social studies program and at how those forces have changed the social studies. You need to be aware of how these developments will affect you, how you will teach, and what you will teach. This awareness will help you understand that the social studies curriculum is evolving.

Recognizing that the social studies has a strong knowledge base, we will also want to look at the social science disciplines. These disciplines all examine the world from a different perspective, with different emphases and foci and, often, using different scholarly tools. The social scientists working in these disciplines provide the scholarship, methods, concepts, and information that are the basis for the social studies curriculum in the elementary schools. The better we understand them and their relationship to one another, the better we can utilize and select from what they have to offer.

CAN YOU? DO YOU?

Can You

- Identify reasons why there is controversy in the social studies?

- Describe the Expanding Environments curriculum?

- Identify the social sciences and tell how they relate to what children learn in the social studies?

- Name the social sciences and tell what each one is all about?

Do You

- Have an understanding of the learning program?

- Know how the social studies curriculum is organized?

- Know what an instructional theme is?

WHY IS THERE CONTROVERSY OVER SOCIAL STUDIES PROGRAMS?

Social studies has been, and will continue to be, constantly under attack by critics. The content taught in social studies is constantly being examined. The root reason for this is that learning social studies is a lot more complex than developing an ability or skill such as reading and mathematics. It is almost without boundary or borders.

There are, arguably, five overlapping social studies curricula existing in most elementary and middle schools. First, there is the formal curriculum that is the basis of social studies classes. It usually is prescribed for, or determined by, the teachers and has clearly defined goals and parameters and is embodied in a course of study or sometimes by the textbook used. Second, there is a curriculum that is very pronounced in the primary grades and much less so but still existing later on that has to do with events and with the calendar itself. Holidays, birthdays, seasons, weather, and current events all conspire to form this curriculum which is, by its very nature, more fluid and flexible than the formal curriculum. This second curriculum may be reasoned out by the teacher to relate to the formal curriculum and have corresponding goals. The third curriculum is really embedded in the materials used to teach other subjects, especially reading and language arts. The stories in readers and the literature program deal with people, places, and events, and readers have traditionally paralleled social studies content. Through fictional and nonfictional literature, children are made aware of how people live, think, and get along with others. Science and arithmetic similarly present social studies content, particularly with reference to the stories behind discoveries, inventions, and theories. The fourth curriculum has to do with the organizational functions of the school and the classroom and is embodied in what is taught about the ways to work together and alone, the development and following of class and school rules, and the way that students are taught to act throughout the school day. This curriculum is very closely tied to the fifth curriculum which is becoming increasingly more manifest in schools, the program specifically to develop values and/or character.

With this richly varied array of curricula, which may, at times, be contradictory, there are at least five factors that contribute to the controversial nature of the social studies.

1. Anything that human effort produces is, by definition, imperfect. Before we even get a curriculum together, we and others begin to see the flaws and problems. When we put something into use, those flaws become glaringly apparent to us.

2. Cultural change is constant. We live in an era of immense societal complexity and rapid change. As rapidly as we develop a program, changes occur that require adjustments. Social studies curricula are responsive to changes in the social climate. Changes in emphasis are likely to reflect the times. Wars, depressions, periods of prosperity, international relationships, and a host of other things that influence the public climate impact the social studies.

3. People have differing values, priorities, and viewpoints. The social studies is not just a skill subject. In a democratic society, there is little likelihood of long-term consensus and none at all of universal agreement on what ought to be taught and from what viewpoint.

4. Special-interest groups influence curriculum. In our society, there are pressure groups with their own agendas and expectations. They want to influence or even control what is being taught in the schools.

5. Social studies represents an enormous changing body of knowledge. The social studies simply defy coverage or even adequate sampling. We can never have enough depth or breadth.

The term *social studies* is, to a great extent, a product of the twentieth century. It was officially adopted as the name for the curricular area in 1916 by the Committee on Social Studies, a subgroup of the Commission to Reorganize Secondary Education, which had been set up by the National Education Association (Jarolimek, 1981, 5). That committee also recommended the following curricula for grades five through eight, which were traditionally considered part of elementary or grammar school.

Fifth grade	American History
Sixth grade	World History (Western Civilization)
Seventh grade	Geography
Eighth grade	American History

In the late 1930s, Paul Hanna proposed a sequence of instructional topics that was to revolutionize elementary school social studies. This framework, known as the Expanding Communities Model or Expanding Environments curriculum, was based on a theory that children's ability to understand their world progresses through a series of developmental stages and that social studies programs should be structured to coincide with those stages (Hanna, 1957, 1963). The progression was from a study of the children themselves and their homes and families through increasingly larger communities which were more remote and abstract to children's thinking.

In spite of all the pressure for change, the Expanding Environments concept has been the major influence on social studies curriculum for over 50 years. The first eight grades of the twelve-grade Hanna model are shown in the following list.* Alongside it the dominant pattern of curriculum organization currently used in textbook and school curricula is shown.

Grade	Expanding Environments Model	Contemporary Curricula
Kindergarten	(Kindergartens were not mandatory at this time.)	Self, school, home, families, community
First	The child, the home, the family, the school	Families, community
Second	The neighborhood, neighborhood helpers	Neighborhoods
Third	The larger community, cities	Communities
Fourth	The state, the region	State history, geographic regions
Fifth	The United States and its neighbors	American history
Sixth	The world (Western civilization)	World cultures, the Western hemisphere
Seventh	World geography	World geography
Eighth	History of the United States	American history

The beauty of the Expanding Environments model was its logic. It made sense to a lot of people both from the standpoint of its reflection of a reasonable pattern of child development and as a logical way to organize the social studies. Hanna's model was developed at a fortunate time in many ways. The social climate of the nation was ideal with America coming through a depression and a world war from which it emerged as the leading power in the free world. Technology and communication as well as the economic conditions were also right. Hanna's model was soon adopted by many school systems and by textbook publishers. It is, to this day, the most common model used in elementary schools in the United States.

From the 1960s to the 1970s a spirit of reform gripped the social studies. It manifested itself in a series of well-warranted criticisms of the expanding environment curriculum as it was by then represented in textbook series

---

*Information for the list above was adapted from Hanna (1957, 1963), Superka et al. (1980), and from a survey of contemporary social studies textbooks.

and school curricula across the country and in the development of new curricula, many of which were closely tied to the various social science disciplines. Critics pointed out that social studies teachers relied too heavily on textbooks and that there was too much memorization of facts. But there was major curricular criticism as well. Critics charged that the social studies lacked sufficient substantive content; that African Americans, Hispanic Americans, women, and other groups were insufficiently represented, stereotypically represented, or misrepresented, and that significant issues and content topics of controversy were avoided. Theories of reform efforts and projects that resulted from this criticism are sometimes referred to as "The New Social Studies." Spurred in part by federal funding and in part by the social consciousness and concern of the period, the lasting changes injected into the social studies by these reform efforts during this era included:

- A greater sensitivity to the representation of various ethnic groups and women in social studies material

- Focus on inquiry and values

- Greater global consciousness

- Focus on social sciences other than history and geography as sources of insight and methods of inquiry about the world

- Greater awareness of and ability to deal with controversy in the social studies classroom

- An emphasis on learning concepts and generalizations rather than isolated facts

More recent efforts to set direction for the social studies have reaffirmed the importance of history and geography while at the same time accepting a less structured and more incidental social studies content for the primary grades. Perhaps the most prestigious of the recent groups to examine the future of the social studies have been two curriculum task forces. The first of these was the Curriculum Task Force of the National Commission on the Social Studies in the Schools, which published a report, *Charting a Course: Social Studies for the 21st Century.* In it the task force advocated a curriculum of stories about people accompanied by holiday study and following up time and place location information in reading stories, mathematics, and other materials. The Task Force suggested that such a program was sufficient to ensure elementary understanding of world geography, the civic and political traditions of the United States, and human life in different continents and at different times in the past (Task Force of the National Commission on the Social Studies in the Schools, 1989, 9). The Task Force envisioned three courses being taught in grades four, five, and six, which would include (in no specified order) (1) United States History, (2) World History, and (3) Geography.

The second group, set up by the National Council for the Social Studies, was called the Task Force on Standards for the Social Studies. It worked over a period of three years before coming out with its report, *Expectations of Excellence: Curriculum Standards for Social Studies* (1994). The standards approved were intended to influence and guide curriculum design and overall student expectations for grades K–12. The standards established 10 basic themes for the social studies:

1. Culture

2. Time, continuity, and change

3. People, places, and environment

4. Individual development and identity

5. Individuals, groups, and institutions

6. Power, authority, and governance

7. Production, distribution, and consumption

8. Science, technology, and society

9. Global connections

10. Civic ideals and practices

INCORPORATING THEMES FROM THE STANDARDS IN SOCIAL STUDIES EDUCATION

The focus themes identified by the standards task force, to some extent, are taken from the social science disciplines and represent their essential lines of inquiry. Following a kind of candlewick principle, these themes can run through topics of study and across grade levels, drawing essential content and skill development to themselves.

Thematic units represent one approach to implementing the standards. Such units are integrally related to literature-based whole-language programs and unify the content of the social studies with other curricular areas. In nongraded settings, thematic units can be part of an internal structure.

Following is a series of both typical and less usual examples of thematic unit topics at each grade level. The list is not presented as a sequential model curriculum and certainly will not precisely reflect any particular school or textbook curricular program. These unit topics are presented here simply to give an idea of topics that might be taught, suggest their connections both to the standards and to the specific discipine, and to illustrate the notion of thematic threads.

Unit Topic	Possible Theme(s)	Themes from the Standards	Core Social Science Discipline(s)
Kindergarten: School social studies typically begins with topics related to home, family, and school. Emphasis is on the immediate environment, but there needs to be plenty of opportunity to look at the world beyond.			
Who am I?	Identity/personality	4	Psychology
Our families	Interdependence	5	Sociology
Friends away from home	Socialization	4	Sociology
Rules we need	Responsibility/authority	6	Political science/ psychology
Who makes the school work?	Authority/careers	4/6	Sociology
Being careful, going shopping	Authority, society	5/7	Economics
The world, the continents, the oceans	Location	3/10	Geography
First Grade: Units on this level begin with the local area and associate it with the larger world. Often comparisons are made. Emphasis is on individuals.			
The shopping mall	Consumption/exchange	7	Economics
People we need	Interdependence	3/4/7	Economics
What happens in the factory	Production	7	Economics
Great men and women	Leadership/individual differences	2/3	History
Families in India	Cultural diversity	1/9	Anthropology
Second Grade: Contact, travel, and relationships among neighborhoods are often emphasized.			
Moving around and telling others	Transportation/ communication	3	Geography/ history
Neighborhoods changing	Cause and effect/ local pride	3/2	History/ geography
Farms and cities	Resources/culture	1/2/3	Culture/ geography
Fast foods	Exchange	7	Economics
Suburbs	Adaptation/location	2/3	Geography
Money and banks	Exchange	7	Economics

Unit Topic	Possible Theme(s)	Themes from the Standards	Core Social Science Discipline(s)
Third Grade: The larger community is generally the focus with the intent of developing an understanding of the conceptual characteristics of a community, community differences, and community changes.			
How the city changes	Adaptation/change	1/2/3	Political science/ geography/ history
Special cities	Physical differences	3/8	Geography
Towns and cities in early America	Historical change	3/6/10	History
Feeding the people	Production/transportation/ exchange	7/8	Economics/ geography
People who made change	Historical judgment	2/5/9/10	History
Fourth Grade: Environmental features of the earth are emphasized and regions of the United States are studied. How to go about adopting and adapting to the environment and the home state are sometimes part of the focus.			
Living in the deserts of the world	Region/adaptation	1/3/9	Geography
History all around us	Change	2	History
Rain forests	Location/physical features	1/3/8/9	Geography
The Midwest	Regions	1/3	Geography
Regions of the United States	Regions	3/7/9	Geography
Fifth Grade: The history of America is studied at this level with emphasis on the United States, the United States and Canada, or the United States and South America.			
New lands, new promises	Cause and effect/ location	2/3/10	History/ geography
Forging the nation	Historical judgment/ authority and responsibility	2/6/3/10	History/ political science
African Americans	Identification/change/ equality/tolerance	1/2/3/4/5/10	History
Trappers, miners, and settlers—the American west	Historical progression/ location	2/3/4	History/ geography

Unit Topic	Possible Theme(s)	Themes from the Standards	Core Social Science Discipline(s)
The end of compromise—the American Civil War	Change/causation/ historical judgment	2/6/10	History/ political science
The rise of American labor and industry	Change/adaptation causation/ historical judgment	2/3/6/8/10	History/ economics/ political science

Sixth Grade: The program at this level may include a study of Latin America and Canada or may emphasize Western civilization or the history of Europe and Asia.

Models of government: ancient Greece and Rome	Citizenship/authority/ changes	2/9/6/9	History/ political science/ geography
Castles, moats, and drawbridges	Adaptation and adoption/ cause and effect	2/5/6/9	History
New visions and dreams: renaissance and reformation	Change/cause and effect/ individual impact	2/3/6/8/9/10	History/ geography

Seventh Grade: The home state is often studied at this level. Another common topic of study is world geography.

Our state and how it came to be	Physical features/historical judgment/location	2/5/6/10	Geography/ history
Africa: a continent of nations	Location and physical features	1/3/9	Geography
Land with the most people—China	Historical causation/culture	1/2/3/6/9	History/ geography
The nations of the third world	Scarcity/distribution of resources	1/3/7/9	Geography/ economics
World resources and their distribution	Distributing resources	7/8/9	Geography/ economics
Looking to the future	Predictions/problem solving	All	All

Eighth Grade: The return to a focus on the United States and its heritage is common at this level, with a chronological approach.

A virgin land	Adaptation/cooperation	2/3/6	History/ geography
Building a new nation	Cause and effect/ conformity and authority	2/6/9	History/ political science

Unit Topic	Possible Theme(s)	Themes from the Standards	Core Social Science Discipline(s)
Those who made the new nation	Historical judgment	2/5/10	History/ political science
New lands for the new nation	Change	1/2/5	History/ geography
The irreparable rift: Civil War and Reconstruction	Cause and effect/conflict	2/3/5/9	History/ political science
Industry and power	Production/science	3/6/7/8	History/ economics
A world power	Interdependence/ science/change	2/7/8/9	History
Into the age of technology	Change/technology	8/9	History/ economics/ sociology

MULTICULTURAL DIRECTIONS IN THE SOCIAL STUDIES

Multicultural education has been a transforming force in social studies since the 1960s, yet even its strongest advocates differ widely about what, exactly, multicultural education should be. Beginning in the 1980s, a body of scholarship has emerged related to multicultural education. From this, agreement has emerged, at least about certain ideals. Gorski (2000) has asserted that these include:

- All students should have equal chances of achieving their full potential.

- Students must be prepared to live and work in an increasingly intercultural society.

- Teachers should be enabled to effectively facilitate learning for every individual student, no matter how culturally similar or different from her- or himself.

- Schools have to be active in ending oppression and prejudice, first within their own walls, then by developing all students to be socially and critically active and aware.

- The role of schools is essential to laying the foundation to change society and eliminate oppression and injustice.

- The goal of multicultural education is to effect social change.

Multicultural education goes beyond teaching tolerance. It means reaching comfort levels with curricular issues that give us discomfort, raising and addressing issues that are difficult, and asking questions that challenge thinking and beliefs. To bring about the changes advocated for multicultural education, these ideals must be embodied in all social studies curricula. Teachers themselves need to become more sensitive and aware of both obvious and subtle incidents of prejudice and bias or intolerance.

How Children Learn

Social studies is a content subject, and, therefore, social studies experts have given a good deal of attention to theories and research about how children learn. And well they should, since it is logical that a teacher's concept of the way in which children acquire and retain knowledge should instruct teaching methodology. The last generation of teachers has largely rejected the notion that they could simply present information and it would, somehow, be absorbed and learned. They have also pretty much cast aside behaviorism, with its view that learning occurs through systematic stimulus and response, punishment and reward. These explanations of learning have simply been inadequate descriptions of how knowledge is acquired and understood.

The learning theory which most social studies experts do subscribe to is called constructivism. Von Glasersfeld (1987) has suggested that constructivism has two major principles which I paraphrase here:

1. Knowledge is actively constructed by the learner, not passively received from the environment.

2. *What the learner knows* is constantly adapting and being modified by experience.

To put it another way, we make sense of the world by fitting new information and new ideas with what we already know. We construct meaning or explain what we encounter. An oversimplified example is found in our love of the use of analogy in explanation and definition. We are always trying to find some basis of comparison that our audience already does understand.

The basic ideas of constructivism were expressed by John Dewey and later by psychologists Jean Piaget and Jerome Bruner. The basic idea is that learners have to construct meaning for themselves. They do this individually and socially. Learning is an active process in which sensory input is used.

WHAT IS THE PLACE OF THE SOCIAL SCIENCE DISCIPLINES?

Social studies is the name given to a broad curricular area taught in elementary schools and middle schools. The focus of the social studies is on the child learning to understand, interpret, and live in his or her world and we have looked, in Chapter 1, at the basic goals of that broad area. Social studies is also an inclusive term for that broad field of study which includes courses in middle and secondary schools that focus specifically on history, geography, sociology, economics, psychology, government, and related subjects. Some people use the phrase "the seamless web" to describe the relationships among all these subjects. They like to see the social studies as an interdisciplinary curricular area that draws its content from what scholars in a variety of disciplines know about the social world.

The disciplines themselves would more correctly be called social sciences, and each of them offers different content emphases and different methods of inquiry than the others. The study of scholars in each of the social sciences has produced a vast number of concepts, generalizations, and facts. When social scientists start counting off the social sciences, different numbers are likely to be given. That is partly because there are some disciplines such as philosophy and religion, that some people accept as social sciences and that other people see as humanities or even natural sciences. An additional factor is that each social science keeps dividing as specializations develop. As a specialization gathers more scholars and knowledge, its perspective and methods of scholarship change too. Over time, it becomes as different from its parent discipline as that discipline is from every other one. Some see archeology as a part of anthropology, and others as a branch of sociology.

For our purpose, let us admit to eight social sciences, while recognizing that someone else might have a longer or shorter list. The eight we will look at are, in alphabetic order: anthropology, economics, geography, history, political science, psychology, religious studies, and sociology. We will look at each of them in turn, basically to refresh our memories and clarify our thinking about the chief concerns of these disciplines and the essential roles each plays in elementary social studies. Though we introduced them initially alphabetically, we will begin our descriptions with history and geography, often seen as the root or core disciplines of elementary social studies. Then we will move to the other six. While we need to keep in mind that each of the social sciences utilizes concepts from all of the other disciplines, we also need to recognize that each discipline has unique contributions.

History

History is the study of the past, or at least the surviving record of the past. Generally, we limit our study to the human past, but that in itself is very broad. There is a history of scholarship, of military events, and of economic, cultural, and social phenomena. History examines, in fact, the whole spectrum of humans in interaction with one another and with the earth.

The problem of history is that the record of the past is always incomplete, full of bias, and very distorted. This problem has produced two schools of thought regarding historical inquiry. On the one hand, narrative historians, sometimes called humanist historians, suggest that the inadequacies of the record and the complexity of the past defy any attempt to make generalizations. They conceive the historian's job as one of basically describing the past more accurately, insightfully, and fully. Scientific historians, on the other hand, attempt to use scientific methods, often with quantitative data.

The historian studies documents and records of all sorts from personal letters and diaries to business and legal papers such as inventories, wills, and bills of sale, to public records such as newspapers and government papers. Historians also study and compare the physical remains of the past from buildings, roads, and walls to the smallest of objects either preserved through time in someone's safekeeping or found in such places as ruins and tombs. Historians also look at such things as paintings, recordings, photographs, and, for most recent times, video recordings. Finally, historians use people as a resource through approaches such as interviews and observations.

Elementary social studies programs usually include the learning of historical facts as one of their purposes. Some critics of the social studies feel that this should be an even stronger emphasis. Involving children in the narrative or the story and drama of history and in the quest for historical knowledge is essential if history is to be learned effectively. Historical fascination is the key to historical learning.

History deals with questions through which a picture is reconstructed of how events actually occurred, why they occurred, and how they impacted on subsequent events. Teachers can stimulate a genuine interest in what life was like in the past. When children are led to examining history as a series of mysteries and problems, they can be naturally led to look at some of the primary resources that historians use. It is really exciting to watch what happens when children have experienced a few "Aha!" moments when they discover history for themselves. Once they begin expecting and seeking this, concepts like historical change, cultural bias, civilization, colonization, and cause and effect begin to be perfectly logical to them and to come with the learning.

Geography

Though maps and globes are among the major tools of geographers, and a particular branch of geography, cartography, is devoted to the science of mapping, the field of geography is far broader, encompassing the study of the earth's surface and how that relates to human beings. Geographers are interested in how humans adapt to various living conditions and how humans alter the geography. Physical geographers tend to focus on the earth's natural features (topography, landforms, climate, bodies of water, vegetation, animal life, etc.). Cultural geographers are concerned with people and with the factors that influence their location as well as how humans use and impact resources.

Basic to geographic understanding is some knowledge of where places are located in the world. Many educators feel that children and their teachers as well lack very basic information about their world. This seems very sad when you consider what fascination maps can have for children. With the great variety of colorful, interesting, and attractive maps available to use with children today, there is little excuse for not drawing children into hours of map study. In a world where people have become much more mobile and where people are drawn closer by communication and transportation revolutions, it seems fairly clear that children need more place location knowledge than ever before.

Geographic knowledge is basic to understanding and knowing about the world and its people, and geographically related problems are among the most important ones facing the world today. Children in elementary school are aware of many of these problems and need to be informed and knowledgeable about their impact on their world. Children often have only heard enough to frighten them about geographically related problems, ranging from overpopulation to pollution, from the depletion of the ozone to the destruction of the rain forests, from the rapid consumption of fossil fuels to world famines and droughts.

As defined by the Joint Committee on Geographic Education of the National Council for Geographic Education and the Association of American Geographers, geographic education is focused on five themes.

1. Location: Position on the earth's surface

2. Place: The characteristics that distinguish and define each place

3. Relationships within places: Advantages and disadvantages for human settlement

4. Movement: Interacting of humans

5. Regions: Areas that display unity in terms of selected criteria

The questions that geographers ask deal with where people live and why. They are interested in the factors that make the earth habitable. They are also concerned with how variations in geographic factors influence economic development, culture, and sociopolitical organization.

Children can easily be drawn into a study of other settings and other people. The variety and quantity of visual materials of all types is almost unbelievable. The fact that everything has geographic setting and the realization that we understand events and people's actions better when we know more about that geographic setting make the study of geography important for every subject children study throughout life. Flora and fauna or minerals and rocks they study in the sciences, stories and poems they read in literature, and the people and events they study in the past all relate to numerous geographic factors.

Anthropology

Anthropology is the study of culture, especially human culture. *Culture* may be defined as a system of beliefs and values, behavior patterns, and customs that is shared by a society of people. A sense of sharing and of oneness with others in this society is often part of what defines and distinguishes particular cultures. Scholars in the field generally like to think of their approach as holistic because they are interested in everything there is to know about a culture. Anthropologists study everything from ancient ruins and human remains to existing cultures. There are numerous and varied specializations within the field, including archeology and ethnography. Because cultural change is a major concern of anthropologists, technological development within a culture has immense importance in many of these specializations.

Anthropologists look for cultural generalizations. They want to know what defines a culture and what makes it fit together. Anthropologists look carefully at a process they called *enculturation,* which has to do with how young people learn about their own culture, and the influences that cultures have on one another, especially those that result in acculturation or the cultural exchange that occurs when there is long-term contact. Like geographers, they are concerned with the natural environment. However, anthropologists have a different perspective, their concerns being mostly with how culture is influenced by environment and what part culture plays in how humans adapt.

Anthropologists attempt to immerse themselves thoroughly within a culture, often becoming very personally involved. From this experience, they expect to gather immense amounts of data about that culture for further study. There is continual concern about how much anthropologists will be influencing a less technologically advanced culture even as they study it.

The concept of culture is an essential one for elementary school social studies. Children need to become less ethnocentric and learn more about other cultures. Anthropological focus can be an important part of interdisciplinary programs, but the focus of many primary units is on comparing cultures. The social studies have also found that some of the investigative techniques of anthropologists, chiefly archeological site excavation and interviewing and observation, are highly adaptable for use with elementary and middle school children.

Economics

Economics deals with resources and with the production, exchange, and consumption of goods and services. Economics is perhaps the most problem centered of the social sciences, since its basic concept is scarcity. The resources are scarce and are always likely to be exceeded by human needs and wants.

Economists try to analyze the use of and demand for various resources in order to make recommendations about the problems that relate to scarcity.

Economics is often mathematical and quantitative. Economists continually try to predict the future and to recommend courses of action that will create a more fortunate situation in the future. Therefore, they are continually trying to find ways to look at quantities produced, exchanged, and consumed. Because in societies where there is specialization, some medium of exchange (money) is going to exist, economics is also concerned with money and other forms of capital and with related areas such as banking, taxation, and investment.

The real importance of economics to elementary children is that throughout life children will be playing roles of worker (producer of goods or services), consumer (user of goods and services), and citizen (part of a society that operates under some economic system). They need to learn a number of economic consumer skills and develop economic values that can be embedded in the social studies. These have to do with such diverse areas of their lives as handling money, banking, budgeting, buying and selling goods and services, and choosing a way of making a living. They also will need to learn to deal with how scarcity relates to and impacts on their own lives. There is also some important economic content for children both as future citizens and as students studying other countries. In both roles, children need at least some understanding of how the economy operates and how this affects people's lives.

Political Science

Political science is the study of government and of all that is associated with the governing process. It deals with human behavior throughout the entire political system and includes the study of the legislative, the judicial, and the executive process. Political scientists study governmental organizations, political parties, pressure groups, voting and elections, and other related parts of the process. They also study different types of government and different types of performance by those involved in governing.

Political science attempts to give an accurate and complete picture of the way that the political process works both generally and at particular points in time. Certainly, the basic tools of the political scientists are analyses of documents, court cases and governmental acts, and media coverage of political events. But political scientists also attempt to predict, based on the notion that when conditions are similar, it is likely that outcomes and results will tend to repeat.

In the elementary school, children are in the process of becoming aware of the forms and functions of government. Their political awareness is often closely linked to their geographical and historical understanding. Research seems to support the notion that children are "politicalized" by the age of 12. Throughout the elementary grades, they are developing numerous political concepts, including right and wrong, justice, authority, power, security, and politics. They become aware of their own exposure to vast barrages of propaganda.

Political science is the source of a great deal of useful information and concepts in the process of learning about government. Since political science is largely based on questioning the process, in looking analytically at every event, the methods of the discipline are also useful at the elementary level.

Psychology

Psychology is the study of the behavior and thinking of individuals, especially humans. One branch of psychology, social psychology, is even devoted to behavior in groups. Psychologists study development across the entire life span. They are interested in a number of factors that relate to the social studies, including individuality and self-concept, motivation and attitudes, learning and cognition, human personalities, and behavior of individuals in groups.

Psychology provides us insights into social behavior in the classroom and into several elements related to learning. As elementary children learn about other people and other times, they need to understand why people behave as they do. They also need to understand something about the kinds of action taken by different types of leaders.

Religious Studies

Religious studies examines the systems of beliefs and the various practices associated with the various faiths of the world. It is an extremely broad field. Scholarship in religious studies reaches from large formal religions such as Buddhism, Islam, Christianity, Hinduism, and Judaism, to small, relatively obscure cults. Likewise, the spectrum goes from ancient religions that have not been practiced for centuries to modern religions with both ancient and recent origins. Religious study scholars also have great interest in political philosophies that contain substantively religious ideas and have important ramifications that impact on religious practices. Confucianism and communism are examples of such.

The importance of religious studies to elementary social studies relates to the importance of religious beliefs in people's lives. As children study other times and other places, they need some understanding of the religious context. Geography and history are at least partly attributable to religious factors.

It may also become important for children to understand that religious views may impact on some of the activities of the classroom as well. They need to understand the difference between studying religious views and advocating them. There may be families represented in the class with religious beliefs that will not allow the children to participate in some school activities. In the last half century, a related issue has been the place of religious beliefs in the schools. Several questions have been raised about traditional school practices that are related to religious beliefs. These questions have brought about a number of constitutional controversies involving infringement on freedom of religion and the concept of separation of church and state.

Sociology

Sociology is the study of how people act in groups. Sociologists are interested in different kinds of groups, both formal and informal, and in how these groups operate and interact with other groups. They are interested in individuals only with regard to the roles they have within groups. They are very much aware of the influence that societal values and norms have on an individual. An essential assumption of sociology is that individuals need groups in order to survive.

Sociologists study many groups that are very important to elementary age children. They examine the family, the classroom, the school, the community, and numerous types of organizations within the community. Sociology's important contributions to elementary social studies have to do with what the discipline tells us about group behavior. Sociologists offer perspectives about how people act in different institutional and community settings. Sociologists also examine how changes in the institutions occur. They look at social order and influence and authority within groups. They examine the different roles people play and social relationships. They study the impact of technological change on social institutions.

LOOKING BACK

The social studies program is constantly changing because of the variety of influences and pressures for change. The elementary curriculum for over a half century, though, has in some way related to the concept of expanding the world of the child. The most significant changes over the past two decades have been an increasing emphasis on multiculturalism, a move toward thematic topics, and a concern for the importance of children's literature in social studies instruction.

Social science disciplines have had a continued and important role as the source of content of the social sciences. Each of the social sciences, history, geography, anthropology, sociology, economics, political science, psychology, and religious studies, offers a body of knowledge, a unique perspective about the world, and a method of inquiry from which students can learn.

SELF-TEST

1. What factors contribute to controversy over what is taught in the social studies?

2. How does the Expanding Environments curriculum relate to the curriculum of contemporary social studies programs?

3. What is the difference between the terms *the social sciences* and *the social studies?*

4. How would you define constructivism?

5. Why have social studies programs tended to focus on history and geography?

6. How has geography in elementary school gone beyond the image of studying maps and globes?

7. How does anthropology relate to and differ from geography?

8. Why is economics important to elementary children?

9. Why do children need to be politically aware?

10. Does the study of religions conflict with the American constitutional concept of separation of church and state?

REFERENCES

Gorski, P. (2000). *Multicultural education.* McGraw Hill Supersite www.mhne.com/socscience/education/multi/define.html.

Hanna, P. R. (1957). Generalizations and universal values: Their implications for the social studies program. In *Social studies in the elementary school: Fifty-sixth yearbook of the national society for the study of education.* Chicago: University of Chicago Press (pp. 27–47).

Hanna, P. R. (1963). The social studies program in the elementary school in the twentieth century. In Sowards, G. W. (Ed.), *The social studies.* Glenview, IL: Scott Foresman.

Jarolimek, J. J. (1981). The social studies: An overview. In Mehlinger, H. D. and Davis, O. L. (Eds.), *The social studies: Eightieth yearbook of the national society for the study of education.* Chicago: University of Chicago Press (pp. 3–18).

Superka, D. P., Hawke, S., and Morrisett, I. (1980). The current and future status of social studies. *Social Education,* 44 (October), 362–369.

Task Force of the National Commission on the Social Studies in the Schools. (1989). *Charting a course: Social studies for the 21st century.* Washington, DC: The National Commission on the Social Studies in the Schools.

Task Force on Standards for the Social Studies. (1994). *Expectations of excellence: Curriculum standards for social studies.* Washington, DC: The National Council for the Social Studies.

Von Glasersfeld, E. (1987). "Learning as a constructive activity." In C. Janvier (Ed.), *Problems of representation in the teaching and learning of mathematics.* Hillsdale, NJ: Lawrence Erlbaum.

SUGGESTED READING

Fritzer, P. (2002). *Social Studies Content for Elementary and Middle School Teachers.* Boston: Allyn and Bacon.

Massialis, B. (1992). The new social studies—retrospect and prospect. *The Social Studies,* 83 (May/June), 125–128.

NCSS. (1991). Position statement: Social studies in the middle school. *Social Education,* 55 (September), 287–293.

Wilhelm, R. W. (1996). Learning the practical power of the social studies frameworks. *Social Studies and the Young Learner,* 9 (November/December), 8–11.

4 Making Textbooks Work for You

LOOKING AHEAD

Whenever educators and researchers have examined the teaching of the social studies, they have inevitably come to two conclusions: (1) that social studies curriculum is generally textbook driven; and (2) that the teachers, responsible for teaching the social studies, depend on textbooks.

The latter may be an even more common practice among beginning teachers who need the security, structure, and help that a textbook can give. This dependence is a cause of concern and the focus of a great deal of criticism. Concerned social studies educators are critics because they fear that textbook-driven teaching means that teachers do not really know what they are teaching or why. Without mastery of the material, a teacher cannot concentrate on teaching in creative ways that stimulate students to be involved and interested. The research seems to support the notion that teachers without knowledge will simply follow lockstep patterns that are textbook centered and teacher centered. Such social studies programs will not be creative, exciting, or in any way motivating, and will not focus on thinking skills and inquiry. These critics are not unsympathetic to the teacher; they just feel that textbook-centered instruction gives up too much.

The good news is, of course, that these criticized practices do not have to be realized. There are strategies that can allow the teacher to fall back on the obvious advantages offered by textbooks as resources and still have an exciting, problem-solving classroom at the same time. In this chapter, we will focus on using the textbook as a tool rather than letting the textbook be both the curriculum and the teaching approach. This focus actually helps the teacher and the students go far beyond the textbook. The approach described here can be applied to any resource, including material found on the Internet, that the student is going to need to read. Because the social studies is an information-centered curriculum area, notions about how to enhance students' abilities to use print materials can be extremely useful.

CAN YOU? DO YOU?

Can You

- Identify the specific reading abilities students need in the social studies?
- Tell how we can use textbooks with students who cannot read?

Do You

- Know several ways to teach new concepts and new vocabulary?
- Know some ways to actually shorten what students have to read?
- Know why it is important for students to understand the organization of reading material?

TEXTBOOK UNITS

Textbook programs dominate elementary and middle school classrooms (Educational Market Research, 2001; Ball & Feiman-Nemser, 1988). You may remember the discussion in Chapter 2 which pointed out that using textbooks does not eliminate the need for preparation but does reduce the amount of preparation and does, to some extent, take the responsibility for making decisions about what children ought to learn out of the teacher's hands.

Textbook units offer some important instructional advantages. For teachers who use such units, there is a common reading material containing the same information for all students. This is of tremendous advantage, for it makes it possible to give single assignments and to unify instruction. Another important positive about this type of teaching is the security of knowing that those who have prepared the material have knowledge and expertise in the field, have done a good deal of research into content, and have given thorough professional attention to the preparation of the text. There is added teacher peace of mind in knowing that modern technology has made it possible to keep the reading level of textual material more precisely at the intended grade level than at any point in educational history.

Textbook-centered units emphasize, usually above all else, getting information from print, most specifically from the textbook. Assignments involving reading pages, portions of chapters, and entire chapters in order to answer sets of questions or do other types of written exercises are most common.

MAXIMIZING EFFECTIVE TEXTBOOK LEARNING

Reading is an interactive process. Real reading is not taking place unless the reader is finding meaning. For that to occur, the reader has to be making a conscious, purposeful effort to be mentally engaged and involved and is showing at least a small amount of interest. Although even the best of scholars in the field of learning do not totally understand the reading process, educators like to think that effective reading involves coupling decoding and comprehension skills with background knowledge and an awareness of the interrelationships of elements in the text (Vacca & Vacca, 1993, 15–20). The questions that a teacher needs to ask before using textbooks with students in the social studies include the following: How can we make textbook assignments have the most meaning and usefulness to the greatest number of students? How can we aid students in relating background and in seeing the interrelationships of parts of the text? How can we maximize interest in the reading?

The fundamental issue is making anything that students do with the textbook meaningful, important, and purposeful. If verbal intelligence is not the learners' strength, then the task is all that much more difficult, but it still has to be achieved. This was brought home to me very powerfully by a visit to an intermediate classroom a few years ago. I have tried to preserve faithfully the details of a short exchange between the teacher and the class.

After placing me in an advantageous spot to observe her social studies lesson, the teacher opened by saying, "Let's turn to page __ in our social studies book." (She named it, but out of respect to the publishers and authors, I will not.) At this point, an audible groan rippled through the classroom.

The high twangy voice of a girl in one of the favored seats near the front piped up at this point, "We've already read that!" Her tone was one of complaint.

The whole thing was starting to embarrass the teacher. (Remember, I was there as an invited guest, sitting in the back of the room.) Turning to the girl sternly, she replied with a forced brightness, "Not orally! I want you to read that without missing any words."

Unfortunately, the incident is not that different from what seems to go on in a lot of classrooms. In fact the major criticism of textbook teaching is not so much an attack on the textbooks as on teachers who seem to make text assignments that just do not have any real meaning or purpose. Some older research seems to indicate that though teaching in content areas such as the social studies is textbook centered, reading to learn strategies is not an important component of teaching (Smith & Feathers, 1983; Ratekin et al., 1985). Assignments are given and perhaps checked and counted. But doing the assignment really does not matter because it does not relate to evaluation or even to other class activities. However, I have been involved with some preliminary research more recently that may be indicative that social studies teachers, at least at the middle school and secondary level, have become more concerned with developing reading skill (Turner et al., 2002).

If textbook units are to be used effectively, students are going to have to view work as something more than a series of things to complete and teachers need to see curriculum as more than a number of pages to cover (McCutcheon, 1981). But this is going to be true of any social studies approach in which students are using any kind of print or computer materials to get information or ideas. Let us look, then, at what teachers need to do to use textbooks and similar reading materials effectively.

- Give specific purposeful assignments. Not only does the teacher need to have clear and important purposes for having students read material, the students need to understand what these purposes are. Talking with students about what they are reading for should be as important as telling them what to read. It also means that the teacher will need to have a fair degree of certainty that the students can actually accomplish those purposes.

- Stimulate interest in doing the reading. Fortunately, teachers have several ways available to arouse interest, most of them involve creating curiosity. The teacher can, for instance, ask questions that can be answered by the reading material, point out curious and interesting illustrations that are explained or further described in the text, start and leave incomplete stories that are finished in the assigned reading, or give thumbnail sketches of people, places, or events in the text.

- Make sure that students have the skills needed to do the assignment. Many reading skills are needed in the social studies. A partial list of these appears on pages 75–76. If the teacher does not know the mastery level of a needed skill, it is a good idea to provide at least a review demonstration and monitored practice before the students do the assignment.

- Provide supervision, monitoring, and help where needed. Monitoring is important for a number of reasons. First, it is an effective form of teaching and at least in some instances allows the teacher to keep students from deep learning of incorrect ways of doing assignments. Second, it helps teachers spot cases of "frustration" easily so that directions can be clarified or help given to students who do not understand assignments. Such help, particularly the right kind of help, is not always available to a child outside the classroom. Third, monitoring gives the teacher feedback about the effectiveness of the preteaching, the clarity of the assignment, and the ability of the students.

- Follow up on reading assignments. If students are required to read and do tasks associated with reading, it should be because this will help them learn important things. What they learn needs to be applied and used in ways that make learning from print important.

READING ABILITIES AND SKILLS NEEDED IN THE SOCIAL STUDIES

A number of identifiable reading activities and skills are important if students are going to get meaning from textbooks and other reading materials. Following is a list of those activities and the skills involved.

1. Recognize the organization of reading materials.

   - Show students how to use boldfaced headings as cues to content organization, and that they can use these to make the content more meaningful.

   - Help students learn to recognize topic sentences and show them how to use these in skimming and scanning.

   - Teach them to identify main idea(s).

   - Model and give them experiences in finding supporting ideas and facts that relate to main ideas.

2. Bring meaning to reading.

   - Help students learn vocabulary and concept meaning by recognizing and using context definitions and identifications.

   - Show them how to use glossaries and outside resources to find the meaning of vocabulary.

   - Give them experiences which help them learn to use structural analysis and context clues to obtain vocabulary meaning.

   - Help them to relate what they read to personal experiences, observations, and past learning.

   - Relate new material to previous studies.

   - Teach them to recognize and follow relationships in text (e.g., sequence, chronology).

   - Help students to relate what they read to particular problems and purposes brought to the reading act.

3. Read for a purpose.

   - Before they read, help students understand questions and problems so that they will recognize appropriate solutions when they encounter them.

   - Teach them how to skim for overall meaning.

   - Teach them to scan for specific information, answers to questions, and useful related ideas.

- Help them develop the habit of using the table of contents and index to find specific information.

- Show them how to obtain information from maps in the text and how this can contribute to overall understanding of the reading material.

- Teach them how to use and interpret charts and graphs in the text.

4. Read critically.

- Help students learn to recognize author bias.

- Teach them to recognize discrepancies, contradictions, and missing information.

- Teach them to identify relationships among elements (e.g., cause and effect).

- Help them learn to distinguish opinion from fact, description from interpretation, and so on.

READING PROBLEMS AND HOW TO DEAL WITH THEM

There are a variety of strategies and techniques for helping students who have problems reading textual and reference material. Some are simple and direct, while others are complex. What you want as a teacher is for students to be able to get maximum use of printed social studies material of all types. I would like to suggest a kind of grand, four-step strategy.

1. Preteach difficult vocabulary prior to reading.

2. Reduce the length of independent reading tasks.

3. Provide specific clear purposes for reading.

4. Help students get a sense of the "story" that the reading material is telling, developing their predictive skills so that students use features of the text (such as pictures and boldfaced headings) and features of tasks (such as key-in question words) to anticipate more accurately.

By specifying a series of steps, I am not suggesting that this is a locked-in, lockstep sequence. The precise order of the steps as well as the decision to include any one of these specific steps may change greatly according to individual teaching style, the topic of study, and other individual and classroom factors. More importantly, I do not want to give the impression that these steps can only be carried out in one way. I want to suggest general approaches not specific techniques. Some notion of the range of possibilities is indicated in the examples that are given in the following sections describing each step, but the possibilities are far greater.

Strategies for Developing Vocabulary

The single most important factor in reading comprehension is vocabulary meaning (Shanahan, 2001; Gersten & Baker, 1999; Davis, 1968). Every student develops and extends four basic vocabularies throughout his or her education: reading, listening, speaking, and writing. For most students, substantial listening and speaking vocabularies exist when they enter school. They attach a set of meanings to many words they hear and use a large number of words in speaking. Most of the materials designed specifically for early reading instruction are limited to include only those words that the child is likely to know. Because the listening vocabulary far excludes all other vocabularies throughout the elementary years, this is not a particularly limiting factor. Most of the words they encounter in reading are words they have heard and for which they have conceptualized meanings.

However, the social studies deals with world cultures, with historical times, with social and governmental processes, with an endless variety of often strange names of people and places. This makes the field vocabulary rich. Many words are introduced for which the student has few, if any, related experiences or concepts. Proper nouns, particularly names of people, places, and events, are abundant. Many complex abstract concepts are also given word labels in the social studies. In fact, the most important new words that children encounter in social studies reading materials are terms which are entirely new to them, terms that are not in their speaking or listening vocabularies. Teachers are responsible for providing enabling experiences and building necessary concepts and vocabulary. New vocabulary to be understood by the child must be fitted into perceptions and experiences that form the child's existing view of the world (Smith, 1975). New concepts then become part of the child's worldview only when they can be related to that view as it already exists.

If children are to be successful in understanding or making sense of social studies reading tasks, they must learn to think about new words before they read. Preteaching of essential new words and the concepts they represent prior to any reading task will save both teacher and student frustration. Many types of activities and techniques can be used for developing vocabulary meaning prior to reading. A few ideas are suggested and described.

Teacher Explanation of Meaning

Often the most efficient way of introducing vocabulary words is for the teacher simply to explain the meanings of crucial terms prior to reading. If several terms are involved, writing the words and definitions on the chalkboard or providing a duplicated list may help. A list may even be provided in the text, but unless the teacher pays attention to it the students will most likely ignore it. For computer work, the teacher may want to provide a vocabulary that can be accessed and run off before material is read. However the words themselves are provided, the teacher needs to help students see them in context, relating the importance of the terms for the particular reading assignment. The words need to be seen and heard by the students, so they do need to be in written form.

At its simplest, the teacher explanation involves pointing out to the students where the text uses and defines particular terms. Teacher definitions might point out pictures, maps, and charts in the text that illustrate the concepts involved in particular terms. For some words, actual objects can be used from which students might get term-related multisensory experiences.

Though it is the *quickest* way to introduce vocabulary, direct teaching may also sometimes be an ineffective method. Students will not always feel a need to listen or look, particularly if the routine of the explanations becomes too tedious and regular. When the teacher uses this approach, how she or he presents words and their definitions needs to be varied, exciting, and with reinforced student involvement. This way of teaching vocabulary should be interspersed with other approaches to vocabulary development.

Classifying Experiences

Using classifying charts helps students see how terms fit into various systems of concepts. Charting is an effective way to help children categorize and see relationships among words and terms. Though such charts are more often used in reviewing after reading, they can also be ways of helping children build a conceptual framework for new words. For example, the terms *bayou* and *canal* might be understood better if shown on one or both of the following charts.

CHART 1

Term	Features	Natural or Constructed	Examples	Related Geographic Features
bayou	Shallow; sometimes navigable	Natural	Bayous in Louisiana delta	Low-lying marshlands; May drain into an ocean/river
canal	Shallow; navigable; may have locks to change elevations; often connects two bodies of water	Constructed	Erie Canal Suez Canal Panama Canal	Major transportation route links

CHART 2

Waterways	Landform	Types of Vegetation
bayou	isthmus	deciduous trees
canal	delta	savannah
lake	cape	Taiga
river	island	desert

Other classifying experiences may simply involve the students in sorting and prioritizing terms and words or a series of questions that bring out previous associations in pupil's minds which will enable them to classify the terms.

Extended Teacher Definitions

If one or two words or terms are central to understanding total reading selections, then the teacher may need to give a more extended definition including illustrations. For example, the terms *pioneer* and *frontier* are both abstractions. Both would be crucial to understanding entire units and entire chapters of text in the study of American history. Since the terms have several meanings and describe very complex and involved ideas, the teacher may want to go to elaborate lengths to develop the depth of understanding needed. She or he might want to read aloud descriptions of features of pioneer life, show audiovisual materials, use websites on the computer, plus provide a wide range of real experiences prior to reading. An extended discussion to reach a group consensus about definition would be still another way to introduce terms.

This in-depth approach might need to be used with many critical abstractions. The following questions might serve as a guide for developing a consensus definition of the abstract term *democracy*.

- What are your first thoughts about the meaning of *democracy?* (This might start a round of association play.)

- What are the features or characteristics of a democracy? (Prepare a list on the board.)

- Do *all* leaders in this country (depending on pupil knowledge, you might ask about particular contemporary or historical individuals and their differences) have the same concept of democracy?

- Does democracy mean equal opportunity? Participation in government? Equal wealth? Freedom (what freedom)? Equality?

- If a country has democratic ideals, does this mean it will have democratic practices?

Teacher-Provided Experiences

Some terms may be better understood if the teacher can provide real or vicarious experiences to illustrate the concepts involved. Names of articles of clothing or utensils from a culture, for example, may be better understood if the children see the objects and try to use or wear them. Foods that can be tasted may leave a more lasting impression.

Where real experiences are impossible, vicarious experiences may also be useful in developing concepts. These experiences may include hearing or reading fictional stories, seeing and hearing audiovisual presentations, and other activities where the child can identify with the people involved.

**Student Research to Find Definitions and Meanings
of Words, Names, and Terms**

Finding meanings for new words can be an exciting new adventure for the children themselves if it is well planned. On the other hand, it can also be routine, unpopular "busywork." The number of words that the students research is the first consideration. This number must be limited with special thought to age and ability so that the task does not become drudgery. Student involvement and participation in the discovery of new definitions will slow the instructional process, but will ensure a greater understanding. The techniques are numerous and only a few can be described here.

- The word experts: Each student is responsible for just one word, or, at most, two that appear in a unit to be studied. The job of the *expert* is to become so knowledgeable about that word that if any question about its meaning is raised, he or she will feel comfortable in attempting to answer.

- Picture definitions: The students are responsible for the meaning of a term or word in visual form. Posters, collages, and rebuses are among the many possible forms these defining visuals may take. Collages may be especially useful in depicting abstract concepts such as democracy, as well as in developing a concept of a particular person, their character traits and accomplishments.

- Sound pictures: A few particular social studies terms lend themselves to sound pictures as a way of vocabulary introduction. In some cases, a student may have to take a tape recorder to the best place to collect the sound picture. For example, the call of a muezzin or the singing of a cantor might be ways of gaining concepts of what these individuals do in a study of religion. A foreign language or dialect, a musical instrument, a type of song or dance melody, and other similar concept words can be defined through experiencing the sound.

- Word look-outs: Each student is responsible for one or two words and their meanings. Over a period of several days' class activities, every word will come into discussion. When an individual's word comes up that person is responsible for noticing, defining, and writing the word on the chalkboard or on a classification chart.

- Contextual locating: Many terms are defined either directly or indirectly by the reading context. As a skimming exercise, have students look for and read definitions of words and terms as the text defines them.

- Creating context: Often the best way to learn what a word means is to use it. In this technique, students are demonstrating that they know the meaning of a word by inventing a context where the word can be used properly. The particular context required of the student may vary greatly—a story, a descriptive paragraph, a single sentence, a poem, a poster or cartoon caption, a bumper sticker, a picture title, a type of poem. These and many others can be creative applications of words through written contexts. Following are examples of a "Diamonte" (a diamond-shaped poem) which defines the word *scimitar* and a descriptive paragraph for the word *senator*.

Scimitar

Keen

Curved blade

Defense of Islam

Saracen

Sword

Senators

No matter how big your state is or how many people it has, there are always two *Senators*. *Senators* are elected every six years. There are fewer *Senators* than there are Representatives.

Ways of Reducing the Amount of Reading in the Social Studies

Reading is the means not the end of dealing with social studies materials. Understanding and being able to understand the idea content of materials is the goal. Therefore, more comprehension can be achieved by cutting the number of actual pages of reading. For some children, a reading assignment of two pages of print versus one of twenty pages of reading may mean the difference between their being willing to read the material or unwilling to read it.

One of the most creative ways a teacher can help a child with reading difficulty in the social studies is to control the amount of material that the student has to read. The trick is to find ways of focusing the individual student's reading effort on the particular information that he or she absolutely needs to know. Because social studies materials are most often written at or above grade level reading ability, reducing reading may be helpful for many students. Following are several ways of reducing the reading load:

- Use student-written summaries instead of the text.

- Use teacher-written summaries instead of the text.

- Use textbook cut-ups.

- Try textbook highlighting.

- Experiment with question write-ins.

- Cooperate with class divide-ups.

Using Student-Written Summaries
One way to reduce reading is to collect, over a period of several years, student-written summaries of chapters or sections of printed material. These can be put in binders or folders with illustrations and then used as

reading material for students unable to read the text or the resources. The time needed to collect good summaries puts the beginning teacher at a disadvantage. A teacher may have to have several classes before a sufficient number of good summaries can be assembled. Cooperation from a teacher and class in a high grade may be one way of overcoming this difficulty temporarily. Good student-written summaries have several advantages.

- They are usually closer to the language that students speak and hear daily both in sentence structure and vocabulary than are printed materials.

- They reflect digested rather than raw content. That is, they include the message that one child has received from print.

- They are usually brief and to the point, leaving out many things a teacher would include.

Before student summaries are used as a substitute for textual materials, the teacher must do some careful editing. This can be very time consuming. The following example was done by a sixth-grade student. The teacher read and corrected the paper, and, after a conference, the student rewrote it. A few minor corrections were still needed and these could be made on the copy that was to be used. In fact, there may be some advantage psychologically to the student experiencing reading difficulty to see that the material he or she reads has errors. This may help the child's self-confidence and willingness to try to write themselves. This summary is a child's view of an entire chapter of a social studies textbook.

Example of a Student Summary*

The first industry to grow in the United States was the textile industry. This happened after Samuel Slater brought the idea of cotton spinning machines to the United States and Francis Lowell built machines for making cotton cloth. Eli Whitney came up with the idea of mass production and interchangeable parts.

After the Civil War, more money went into industries and many industries grew. Andrew Carnegie built the steel industry into an empire. When he was 66, he sold all his companies and retired. Other industries that grew were the banking industry and the oil industry. Industries got so big that they became monopolies.

There were also new farm machines and scientific developments during the industrial revolution. One famous scientist was George Washington Carver. People moved off the farms and into the cities. Many people also immigrated from other countries to the United States. In the cities, people began having problems because of houses with poor safety and sanitation.

---

*Summary of Chapter 13, "An Industrial Nation," *The United States Yesterday and Today* (1990). Morristown, NJ: Silver Burdette, pp. 280–297.

Using Teacher-Written Summaries

Well-prepared teacher summaries of printed materials also take a great deal of time to produce. However, they may be written when the teachers *have* more time available than they do in the classroom. I have written them in the summer, on airplanes, in hospital waiting rooms, and in other locations when I just *needed* something to occupy my mind. Such summaries are especially useful because they may be written to include all specific facts and ideas that the teacher especially wants children to know. They can be written to fit the test or evaluation if necessary. Vocabulary can be specifically controlled and limited. The teacher should have a clearer and more complete understanding of the conceptual content of the material than do children and be able to give the purposes and themes more emphasis. Teachers are also less likely to make spelling and grammatical errors than are children. Clear references to pictures, diagrams, and other features of the text can be inserted.

Because of the time that summaries require, the teacher usually should not try to write summaries for all readings the first year. In a few years, though, a substantial number can be collected. Such summaries may be duplicated and used with an entire class, with groups of students, or with individual children with special reading problems.

Following is a teacher's summary of the same selection covered by the student write-up. Similarities and differences in style and completeness can be noted, but the one crucial quality of shortening the material read is the same. Thus, both make good substitute reading materials.

Example of a Teacher Summary*

The Industrial Revolution brought changes to life in the United States. This "revolution" began in the first half of the 18th century with the textile industry in New England. Two men made this happen—Samuel Slater and Francis Lowell. Slater was an Englishman who built the first cotton spinning machines. Lowell built factories with weaving machines that made cotton cloth. The Industrial Revolution was also aided by Eli Whitney, the inventor of the cotton gin, who introduced the ideas of mass production and machines with interchangeable parts.

After the Civil War, the development of a national market due to transportation developments made more money available for industry. Among the great industrialists were Andrew Carnegie who built a huge steel making industry and J. P. Morgan, who built a large banking industry and later bought Carnegie's steel empire. Another leader was John D. Rockefeller who founded Standard Oil. This was one of the businesses that grew so large that it could put competition out of business. The government became so

---

*Summary of Chapter 13, "An Industrial Nation," *The United States Yesterday and Today* (1990). Morristown, NJ: Silver Burdette. pp. 280–297.

concerned about such businesses that it tried to regulate them through a law called the Sherman Antitrust Act (1890).

New farm machines and scientific developments revolution-ized farming and caused many people to move to the cities where jobs were available in factories. Large numbers of immigrants also came from Europe and Asia to the cities. Cities grew so quickly that they developed problems due to crowded areas and poorly built buildings. Sanitation and safety in tenement (apartment) buildings was very bad.

Attempts to deal with the problems were called reforms. Lim-its were set on immigration. Laws were passed to improve hous-ing and sanitation. Settlement houses were founded to provide services. One of the reformers was Jane Addams who founded a settlement called Hull House in Chicago.

Textbook Cut-Ups

Textbook cut-ups require that the teacher have a free rein with the printed materials. It also demands extra copies of materials and a ruthlessness in destroying books and similar materials that repels many teachers automat-ically. It may be an especially good way of salvaging texts no longer in use.

Two copies of each page to be used may be needed for every cut-up version unless the material is printed on only one side or careful editing is done. The teacher cuts out only the most important sentences, pictures, and other things appearing on the pages and glues or pastes them in order on a clean sheet. A textbook chapter can usually be reduced to a few pages. The print authority is preserved as assurance to the child that he or she is reading a real book. But the overpowering and discouraging number of pages that may keep many children from ever attempting to really *do* an assignment is not present.

Textbook Highlighting

A felt-tip highlighter or underliner is needed for the old college student trick. Go through the chapter before the student does and highlight the parts which he or she really needs to pay attention to. Warn the student about what is important and what is not, instead of letting the child figure it out. Make sure the child knows what has been done and why before he or she reads the material.

Write-Ins

Writing in the text is something that students have done and which teach-ers have discouraged. This technique causes a breaking of the taboo. It is a technique that is easier if only a few problem readers are involved where the teacher aids them by marking up their texts.

The teacher draws attention to major points and to questions an-swered by writing notes in the text. If textbook questions are used, they may even be cut out and taped directly next to the answer. Arrows can be drawn to maps, pictures, and charts from the descriptive references to these in context.

Class Divide-Ups

Instead of having every child read every part of the text, assign only portions of the text to each child for reading. All can still have the benefit of the information in the entire reading. Each child might be assigned half the chapter and have a partner assigned the other half. The partners then have to prepare one another with the important and useful information in the other half. Another way to work this is to have various groups each assigned sections. After reading the section, the group meets to decide what they need to teach the class from their section and *how* this can be done most effectively. Until the children become good at this, it will be necessary and helpful for the teacher to sit in on the meeting of every group to provide guidance.

Helping Students Develop a Sense of the "Story" by Aiding Predictions

Every piece of reading material, textual or otherwise, has a message or story. Knowing what the story is about, a sense of its purpose, organization, and direction before we read helps us understand it better when we read. Effective previewing or surveying of reading material helps in the following ways:

- It provides purposes for reading in the form of expectations.

- It heightens anticipation and interest.

- It helps determine in what way materials relate to particular interests, questions, hypotheses, and so on.

- It provides advance organizers for thinking about what is read.

- It aids in predicting.

According to Smith (1975), greater accuracy in prediction is highly important to reading comprehension. That is, if the individual has a better idea about the nature of the reading content *before* reading, he or she will understand it better. Studies of skills development key in on such predictive skills. Herber (1978), for example, has described a technique called SQ3R, a five-step procedure consisting of steps labeled:

Survey

Question

Read

Recite

Review

Of these steps, surveying or previewing the material seems to be most important because effective surveying helps all other phases. If the student can predict, he or she can follow the direction of the writer and anticipate his or her thoughts. A number of teaching techniques, including the following, can help students predict more accurately the content of reading materials.

- Point out the headings and boldface type so the students recognize them as organizers.

- Have students discuss speculations from titles and headings about what content is logical.

- Point out pictures before reading and discuss them. From the pictures and the captions, intelligent guesses are possible about the accompanying written material.

- Point out specific references in the text to maps and illustrations so the students will know to look for these during reading. For example, the text might refer to stone ruins which an illustration will show.

- Provide an outline or introduction overview and discuss it. A simple outline for the selection involved in the student and teacher summaries used previously might be

    I. The textile industry grows in the United States

    II. Transportation aids the growth of industry after the Civil War.

    III. Machinery revolutionizes farming.

Purposeful Reading

If asked, "Why are you reading this?" most students in social studies classes respond with a shrug of the shoulders or, at best, answer, "Because the teacher told me to." The most effective readers are very aware of their purposes for reading and areas to find very specific types of information. This alertness to purposes allows students to cover printed material more rapidly, use context and format clues in locating information, access and use such features as an index or table of contents, and even determine appropriateness or inappropriateness of the material. Reading to achieve specific purposes aids in developing predictive skills described earlier.

To help poorer readers use their social studies textbooks and other reading materials with a better sense of purpose, social studies teachers need to set purposes for such students that are specific and clear, guide them so that they read to understand those purposes, and follow through to emphasize the importance of the purposes.

The major learning students need for some purposeful reading is that the objective of reading in social studies is not simply to read the material.

In fact, reading is incidental and only a tool by which the student gains the necessary information. Some very common procedures of social studies textbooks focus on providing purpose for reading regardless of whether the teacher is aware of this purpose. These procedures include:

- Providing guide questions before reading which identify specific types of information and understandings the student is to gain.

- Providing study questions that ask the student to identify the ways an author thinks and to go beyond the author's thoughts. For example, after reading material on historical periods, questions might be asked to get the student to explain how people in those eras might think about the way we live in the present.

- Alerting students prior to reading to follow-up tasks that will employ particular knowledge and concepts. For example, in the chapter on the industrial change in America, students might be asked to build a model of a farm before the change and another to show how farming was revolutionized.

When tasks related to *reading* are given to students, the purposes need to be made clear. It should not be assumed that students understand why they are reading or know what to look for.

Practice exercises such as skimming and summarizing for particular facts, details, or headings can help students become more aware of the importance of purposes in guiding how and what they read.

Teaching Students How to Read Questions and Task Statements

Many students have difficulty in reading social studies materials simply because they do not make effective use of question clues that could help them be more purposeful in their reading and more accurate and correct in the way they respond. Teachers can incorporate direct teaching about question clues into social studies or reading study skills instruction. One of the most fundamental skills in dealing with questions has to do with getting an immediate idea of what a question is asking and being able to relate that to the reading material. One of the ways that effective readers do this is by being sensitive to the nature of question words and to the nature of the answers these words demand.

Question words such as *who, what, where,* and *when* call for particular kinds of answers. One does not have to have any knowledge at all of the reading material itself to know that the answer to "Who was the English king who was a leader in the Third Crusade?" will *not* be, "The Long Bow," "The Battle of Agencourt," or "The Holy Roman Empire." The question word *Who* dictates a particular kind of answer, including the name or description of a person or group of persons. Any question, in fact, offers clues to the length and nature of acceptable answers by the question words that appear in it.

Many students intuitively learn this as they develop their skills in reading and the social studies. For some, though, it is crucial that the teachers develop their sensitivity to the influence of key words on question meaning.

Even alerting students to organizational features of textbooks related to questions may be useful to them. For example, students should realize that answers to lists of questions in the text are usually found in the same sequence that they are asked. As simple and logical as this may seem, there are many students with reading difficulty who may need to be reminded often.

Another feature that students should recognize is to question reversal and parallel structure. These both refer to questions that are written in exactly the same language as the text but with a change in sentence order. A question such as, "What was the ruler of Ancient Egypt called?" will probably be answered in the text with a statement such as, "The ruler of Ancient Egypt was called the Pharaoh."

Teachers of the social studies constantly grapple with problems students have in grasping and retaining content through reading. The teacher needs to remember that the social studies objective is not to have children read so much as it is to have them learn to use reading as one way to master concepts, learn facts, and obtain information relative to problem solutions. If this is kept in mind, a more purposeful and effective strategy can be developed.

LOOKING BACK

The social studies textbook is often the major teaching tool in the social studies. In order to teach effectively from a textbook or any reading material, the material has to be meaningful and purposeful to students. Teachers need to give purposeful assignments, stimulate interest, make sure that students have the skills needed to do the required reading, provide proper and sufficient supervision and monitoring for reading tasks, and follow up effectively.

When students have problems reading content material, there are several strategies that teachers can use. Among the most important of these is preteaching vocabulary, reducing the actual length of reading assignments, providing sufficient and clear purposes for reading, and developing predictive skills.

SELF-TEST

1. Why is making anything students do with the textbook meaningful, important, and purposeful the fundamental issue of this chapter?

2. Name several things that teachers can do to make the use of textbooks more effective.

3. Describe several ways of teaching concepts and vocabulary to children.

4. What is SQ3R?

5. What is meant by the term *purposeful reading* and why is the concept important?

REFERENCES

Ball, D. L., and Feiman-Nemser, S. (1988). Using textbooks and teachers' guides: A dilemma for beginning teachers and teacher educators. *Curriculum Inquiry,* 18 (Winter), 401–423.

Educational Market Research. (2001). Social studies market: Core textbooks currently adopted December, 2001. Educational market archives. Article ID 36. On the web at http://ed-market.com/d_c_archives/display-article.php?article_id =36.

Gersten, R., and Baker, S. (1999). Reading comprehension instruction for students with learning disabilities: A research synthesis. Executive Summary. National Center for Learning Disabilities. Available on the web at www.ncld.Org/research.ncld_reading_comp.cfm.

Herber, H. L. (1978). *Teaching Reading in Content Areas* (2nd ed.). Englewood Cliffs, NJ: Prentice Hall.

McCutcheon, G. (1981). Elementary social studies teachers' planning for social studies and other subjects. *Theory and Research in Social Education,* 9 (Winter), 45–66.

Ratekin, N. et al. (1985). Why teachers resist content reading instruction. *Journal of Reading* (Fall), 348–354.

Shanahan, T. (2001). Chapter 4. The National Reading Panel: Teaching children to read. International Reading Association. Available on the web at www.reading.org.advocacy//nrp/chapter4.html.

Smith, F. A. (1975). *Comprehension and Learning: A Conceptual Framework for Teachers.* New York: Holt, Rinehart, and Winston.

Smith, F. R., and Feathers, K. M. (1983). Teacher and student perception of content area reading. *Journal of Reading* (Fall), 348–354.

Turner, T. N., Coffee, D., Sharp, K., and Wilson, P. (2002). A survey of middle school and secondary social studies teachers and their teaching of reading skills in the social studies. Unpublished pilot study.

Vacca, R. T., and Vacca, J. L. (1993). *Content Area Reading* (4th ed.). New York: HarperCollins.

SUGGESTED READING

Alleman, J., and Brophy, J. (1996). Considering textbook limitations and strategies for compensation. *Social Studies and the Young Learner*, 9 (November/December), 4–7.

Fordham, N. H., Wellman, D., and Sandmann, A. (2002). Taming the text: Engaging and supporting students in social studies readings. *The Social Studies*, 93(4) (August), 149–158.

Smith, B. A., and Larkin, A. G. (1990). Should place vocabulary be central to primary social studies. *The Social Studies*, 81 (September/October), 221–226.

Vocke, D. E., and Hahn, A. (1989). What does reading research say to social studies teachers? *Social Education*, 53 (September), 323–326.

5 Purposeful and Authentic Assessment and Evaluation in the Social Studies

LOOKING AHEAD

Assessment is essential to good social studies teaching, not because politicians say so or because there is so much stress on grades and test scores, but because it informs teachers and learners. Good assessment tells what we are doing right, and what we need to do to improve. Assessment, at its best, should reflect what teachers and schools are trying to accomplish.

This chapter focuses on the tools that teachers use in assessing students. We want to stress that all assessment in social studies should be firmly based on the goals and objectives of the social studies program. We also want to stress that the students themselves need to be importantly involved in the assessment process.

There has been a lot written about authentic assessment over the last decade. Authentic assessment means that the focus is on what students do and produce rather than on scores on objective tests. The notion of authentic assessment is consistent with the problems approach that we are advocating here. Solid authentic assessment involves the learner in the evaluation process. They become more aware of what they need to solve the problem of their own learning.

CAN YOU? DO YOU?

Can You

- Tell why grades and test scores are so emphasized in schools?

- Tell how teachers go about determining grades?
- Explain what authentic assessment is?

Do You

- Know why evaluation is always comparative?
- Know how evaluation should be different in the problems approach?
- Know the weaknesses and strengths of objective and subjective tests?

THE ROLE OF ASSESSMENT IN THE SOCIAL STUDIES

Teachers and students have a tendency to equate terms such as assessment or evaluation with grades. This is like thinking that art is a paint brush or that music is a voice or a piano. Grades and standardized tests are tools by which assessments are done. They are indicators of student progress and learning, of the degree of teaching success, and of areas of strength and weakness. Teacher-made tests, teacher observations, and the various kinds of work that students produce provide teachers with still other indicators. It is extremely important that teachers do not lose sight of the fact that the true purpose of evaluation in the social studies, as in any other area of instruction, should be to help children learn better.

Assessment and especially achievement test scores as well as summary grade evaluations on grade cards take on special importance to administrators, teachers, students, and parents. What makes grades and tests so important is that they are the major feedback to the students, parents, and others; they are concrete and a matter of permanent record; and they seem to be based on solid performance data.

Everyone involved can easily lose sight of the fact that feedback is only part of the reason for student assessment. Student assessment is also related to finding out how well we have taught, how well the student has learned and can perform, and what still needs attention. At its best, evaluation guides and improves teaching and learning.

All types of student assessment involve comparison of student performance. One of the reasons that many people like grades and test scores is that these provide some of the easiest comparisons and have many bases of comparison. The student's performance may be compared in a quantitative way to some particular criteria of success built into school or teacher objectives, to a performance standard, to classmates, to the whole school, to a national average, or to his or her own past performance or perceived potential. Modern computer programs make it possible to make many of these comparisons in a really short period of time. Normative performance, for example, is the basis on which most standardized test scores are analyzed. Norms or averages can be computed and used to compare the performance of one person or group to average performance in either an age or grade group or even among all people who have taken that particular test.

Another basis of comparison is criterion-based assessment. In criterion based evaluation, the concern is about the extent to which an individual is able to meet indicators of success that relate to particular characteristics. Levels of performance are set in advance on the basis of some preconceived notions of what constitutes *mastery*, for example.

When a teacher plans instruction, criterion-based assessment is often useful. The preselected criteria of success that the teacher identifies for a lesson or a unit are called *objectives*. Objectives describe the specific knowledge or skills that are expected to result from the teaching/learning activities. Objectives identify the desired learning outcomes. Many educators think that objectives can be more clearly defined and evaluated if they name some behavior that might be an indicator that the objective has been achieved.

Most educators agree that assessment and teaching will be more effective if they are based on objectives or desired learning outcomes that we can then use as indicators of the degree of success we have had in teaching. When the learning outcomes provide direction, both teaching and evaluation can be more focused and purposeful learning is more likely to occur. One approach to teaching, often referred to as mastery learning, is based entirely on the notion that instruction about any basic learning needs to continue until that standard has been achieved.

In the social studies, we have been struggling for a long time with some particular dilemmas that educators in other curricular areas may be just now starting to see. One of these dilemmas has to do with the overall evaluation of students, but most especially with that part that has to do with giving grades. Social studies learning outcomes involve the acquisition of knowledge, the development of skills, the variables of interpersonal relationships, very complex and often subtle changes in personal values, philosophies, and beliefs, and other criteria that relate to performance and to development of products that are often intricate and elaborate. For some of these outcomes, it is very easy to design ways of assessing that can be easily measured. For what may be considered the most important learning outcomes, though, measurement and assessment are much more difficult and subjective.

PRINCIPLES OF ASSESSMENT

Assessment is important to teaching and learning only when it helps both the people doing the evaluation and when everyone who is affected by its outcome thinks about and better understands how they are doing and how they can do better. Teachers, students, parents, school administrators, and even school board members and legislators can all ultimately improve what they do if the total assessment program is doing its job. Well-constructed assessment gives students and even their parents, as much as teachers, ownership in the learning process. This can only be accomplished if all are involved in deciding what the assessment will be and how it will be used.

Alleman and Brophy (1999) discuss the changing nature of assessment in the social studies. They point out that assessment should be focused on curricular goals and objectives and be used as a means of improving both the curriculum and the instructional program. They go on to assert that "evaluation of student achievement should be used solely to improve teaching and learning."

The standards movement in social studies has had a profound influence on how social studies teachers look at assessment. Success in the traditional classroom was based on the ability to remember specified information and the mastery of particular technical skills. The job of assessment has become much more complex. Information and skills are looked at differently with emphasis on students learning how to obtain information and how to learn skills. Learning to learn and becoming an independent learner are stressed. The foci of evaluation are expanded to include such factors as the ability to identify and define problems, flexibility to handle new situations, ability to apply knowledge in different settings, and openness to many ideas and solutions. The real concern is the ability of students to handle problems.

An illustration of how the tools of evaluation and grading have changed is shown in the following table of some of the evaluation tools. The table is purely hypothetical but reflects observed differences in general.

Social studies educators argue that assessment can be important to teaching and learning when it helps everyone involved think about and better understand how they are doing and how they can do better in relation to the goals of the social studies (Alleman & Brophy, 1998; NCSS, 1990). Authentic assessment gives students as well as teachers ownership in the learning process (Avery, 1999). Both goal-centered assessment and authentic assessment can only be accomplished if we consider at least five major principles.

1. The aim or purpose of all assessment in education is to improve learning by:
   A. Making sure the curricular goals are understood by all;
   B. Identifying specific areas of student strengths and weaknesses;
   C. Identifying effective and ineffective teaching practices;
   D. Being sure that assessment tasks themselves involve organization of information and decision making;
   E. Identifying the need for additional and/or different instruction; and
   F. Bringing about self-assessment and independent learning.

2. To be authentic, assessment must be an ongoing process, and a variety of tools must be used with understanding.

3. Everyone must realize that all assessment is imperfect and that flaws are inescapable. Types of error include:

   A. Sampling error—What we choose for assessment does not allow us to effectively identify what the student knows and does not know, what they can do and what they cannot do. (This could be a bad test item or an unrepresentative sample of the student's work.)

   B. Assessor error—The person doing the assessment makes the wrong assumptions and/or inappropriate interpretations, and/or incorrect judgments.

   C. Communication error—The assessment message sent to and/or received by the student is incorrect, misunderstood, or otherwise constructed so that it does not result in learning improvement.

4. Students need to develop ownership of the goals of assessment.

5. All assessment should relate to the goals of the curriculum and classroom assessment should be directly connected to soundly conceived and well-stated objectives.

6. Classroom evaluation should be based on what you intend to teach, what you actually teach, and what you intend for students to learn from that teaching.

GUIDELINES FOR ASSESSMENT

Assessment may require many different types of instruments and forms in the social studies, including quizzes, tests, examinations, observations, oral examinations, interviews and conferences, checklists, holistic evaluation of projects and papers, self-evaluations, portfolios, and a host of others. Even if we limit our concern to just grading and the other formal ways of giving students and parents feedback, the complexity of the assessment process is sometimes overwhelming. That complexity might be illustrated by taking a look at a typical six-week grading period. An intermediate level (fourth- to sixth-grade) social studies teacher, even a fairly traditional one, might have the following variety of information on which he or she would like to base grades:

- Scores/grades on one or two unit tests plus quiz grades

- Records of homework and/or seat work completed

- Evaluations of student map work of different types

- Recorded grades from several pieces of evaluated written work (stories, poems, essays, reports, outlines, questions answered)

- A holistic evaluation of a group project involving working together to produce a group report and some display (diorama, mural, table scene)

- Grades for an individual research project given both in writing and orally with artifacts made by the student
- Observations of participation in class activities and discussion
- Notations on volunteer projects including some very elaborate ones showing a great deal of energy and interest
- Student self-evaluation and peer evaluation of projects

Average Extent to Which the Tool Is Used in Student Assessment

0 Not Used at All

1 Used Sparingly/Occasionally

2 Used Frequently

3 Of Critical Importance in Evaluation

EVALUATION TOOLS	TRADITIONAL TEACHING	STANDARDS BASED TEACHING
Daily assignments	2–3	1
Short quizzes, review	2–3	1
Short quizzes, problems	1	2–3
Objective tests, recall	2–3	1
Objective tests, application	2–3	2
Essay tests, informational	2	1
Essay tests, problems	1	2–3
Individual Projects	1–2	3–4
Reports, written	1–2	3–4
Reports, oral	1	3–4
Group/collaborative		
Projects	1–2	2–3
Reports, written	1–2	2–3
Reports, oral	1	2–3
Teacher observation	1	2–3
Self-assessment	0–1	1–3
Journals	0–1	1–3
Stories and other writing	0–1	1–3
Games and active discussion	0–1	1–3

Problem-solving activities	0–1	1–3
Dramatic activities	0–1	1–3
Participation in community service projects	0	1–3
Personal portfolios	0	2–3

The first obvious problem is that, if some numerical averaging traditional evaluation is to be used to determine a grade, this teacher has more than one option for determining each of the various numbers to plug into the grade mix. The second problem has to do with coming up with an overall formula that accounts for or weighs differences in importance and effort for each activity. Subjective decisions have to be made about the relative value or percentage of a grade to be allotted for different tasks and performances. A third and even more important difficulty, though, is that only some of the activities on the list may be evaluated in such a way as to yield definitive and objective grades. Some of the most important student work simply has to be evaluated in very subjective ways. Even checklists, which can produce only some very questionable quantitative information, just will not provide any true evaluation of this work.

The point is that assessment, even the small part of it that we call grading, is never easy and never without flaws. Teachers have to make difficult arbitrary decisions. These decisions can be, and probably will be, questioned and debated. To provide at least a small help in the decision making, I want to offer 10 broad principles or guidelines for assessment:

1. Both the form and the substance of assessment tools can best be defended if they are based on teaching objectives. Only if we think through in advance what we want learners to accomplish and what an effective way of evaluating these accomplishments is can we establish an acceptable approach to assessment.

2. We need to assess what we teach, not what we should teach; both teaching and assessment should reflect what we want as learning outcomes.

3. We need to focus assessment on what is important rather than on what is easy to measure.

4. Ongoing assessment is preferrable to endpoint; we need to incorporate evaluation into regular activities.

5. Assessment of teaching should be based on what students learn rather than on what they already know and can do; therefore, we need to find out what they already know before we teach.

6. If we give students a clear understanding of the purposes of any assessment and the reasons for the assessment, they will perform better.

7. Students need to perceive the assessment as fair and honest, not tricky or directed at "catching" them.

8. Assessment procedures should be built around the notion of finding ways of improving instruction.

9. Effective assessment gets the student involved in self-evaluation, thinking about how he or she can do better, and taking responsibility for his or her own learning.

10. A teacher should always remember that assessment is, at its very best, a subjective and risky affair.
    A. Anyone *can* be wrong about a grade or any kind of assessment and everyone *is* sometimes wrong.
    B. Anyone can make mistakes about the information upon which evaluation is based.
    C. Anyone can misjudge a student or a student product.
    D. Anyone can be wrong about what they should be evaluating and teaching.
    E. Everyone will be guilty of "A" through "D" on a regular basis.

Many of the approaches, techniques, and tools of assessment are well known because we have experienced them as students ourselves. Even so, an overview of the various tools of evaluation can help teachers find a more purposeful and fair personal approach to grading and evaluation.

AUTHENTIC ASSESSMENT AND PORTFOLIOS

Educators have become more concerned in the last decade about how well the various means of assessment that we have been using are working. One issue is a growing belief that tests alone are inadequate as measures of ability and learning. Educators can easily identify students who do poorly on tests and produce and do wonderful things in class or show great knowledge and skill in conversation. They see the same kind of discrepancies with students who have high test scores and do poorly outside the tests. There are many questions about the validity of the tests themselves, since scores seem to be influenced by reading ability and cultural background. Then of course, there is real concern that the quality of learning simply does not lend itself to being quantified.

Going beyond issues relating to testing to the broader one of giving grades, many educators feel that students need to take an active part in the evaluation, instead of having the traditional receptive and even passive roles. In even the best situations in the past, students have taken part in only a limited number of in-class experiences where they have graded their own work or that of other students. Students have been given few, if any, experiences where they have had the opportunity or the need to examine their own thinking and work reflectively and diagnostically.

The term *authentic assessment* was coined to describe a broader approach to student evaluation that tries to bring teachers, parents, and students together to look at the whole body of work that reflects student ability and potential. The term *authentic* is used because the basic premise of the approach is that we need to look at all types of real work that students do in order to see their accomplishments and potential. Types of assessment that we have used in the past, especially tests, simply do not have any relation to the ways that skills and knowledge are used in the real world and in jobs later on in life. Educators involved in this effort are looking more to methods of evaluation, which involve all kinds of performance and products of performance that show what children can do, particularly what they can do over more extensive periods of time.

One of the major changes advocated in authentic assessment is a new reliance on individual portfolios or collections of student work assembled over time. The student takes an active and important role in the development and organization of the portfolio. He or she usually helps decide what goes into it. The student may also be responsible for organizing and record keeping with regard to the contents of the portfolio. Some emphasis may be given to student initiative in conferences with the teacher. The individual items in the portfolio become the basis for student-teacher conferences and the base of comparison for future work. The student who learns to gather and organize his or her own material for a portfolio, and to help select the best material for it, is not only more active in his or her own evaluation but is learning skills that will be of benefit in the world of work.

One way that a teacher can control the size of a portfolio and insure that students actually do some selective decision making, is to limit each portfolio to a certain number of pieces. Another way is to require that the portfolio include examples of particular types of work (e.g., book reports, essays, answers to comprehension questions, poems, stories, maps, pictures, problem-solving activities, and group reports). The form that portfolios take can also help the teacher manage their size in order to make them meaningful, evaluated work instead of unorganized collections. In some cases, the portfolios may be physical, organized scrapbooks, but they can also be computer folders, in the form of videotapes, or take a number of other shapes.

Ideally, portfolios bring teachers and students together in ways that help the student improve his or her work. Even so, there are obvious problems when it comes down to how they are used in evaluation. The success of portfolios depends upon several factors: (1) Students, and others as well, including the teacher, have to see them as important and purposeful; (2) Time has to be spent in interaction between the teacher and the student, both in the development of the portfolio and in its evaluation; (3) Acceptable procedures for organizing and evaluating the portfolio have to be developed; and (4) There have to be clear-cut ties between the portfolio assessment and traditional grades. Portfolios can be evaluated in a number of ways, including group and individual conferences, written descriptive feedback, and diagnostic and evaluative checklists, to name a few. The evaluation, whatever form or forms it takes, should be the one that makes the best sense to the teacher and the students.

ASSESSMENT THROUGH TESTS AND QUIZZES

In a world of high stakes testing the very first thing many people think of when the subject of assessment is mentioned is tests and quizzes. Tests always involve performance, and we use them because they are the quickest way available of finding out what people (or animals or even inanimate things, for that matter) know or can do. Nationally normed standardized tests, though not as well known in social studies as in reading and mathematics, are given systemwide and statewide because they have been viewed as a way of comparing and evaluating students as to their mastery of information and skills. Though many responsible educators are dissatisfied with these tests and the way the data from them are used, there has been a movement toward national testing programs.

In the social studies, the most widely used forms of tests are written ones that involve answering questions or performing specified tasks. Generally, we label those tests that involve little or no judgment in grading as *objective measures*. Included in this group are true-false tests, multiple-choice tests, labeling of diagrams and maps, matching, and some short-answer and fill-in-the-blank tests. Most of these tests can also be called "high-cue" tests because they contain a lot of clues and may even supply the correct answer (e.g., matching). The kind of thinking that is required may involve recognizing rather than remembering information.

The advantages of objective type measures mostly relate to the unchanging quality of the test items. The correct answers are thought to be verifiable and absolute. Except when the teacher makes a detectable and documentable error, there is little or no danger of misinterpreting or wrongly grading an answer. In addition, such questions can cover the material to be tested by sampling what is important in a very equitable way based on pre-established criteria, and performance data can be gathered to establish the value of individual items. Once such tests are established, the teacher or anyone else can correct them fairly quickly.

However, there are many dangers in objective tests. Some of the criticisms help us realize that such tests are really not objective at all. Many such criticisms have to do with test-item construction. Here are some of the typical criticisms.

• Insufficient information is given to call for one specific answer (multiple-choice stems and completion or fill-in-the-blank: e.g., All of the _____ were _____ .)

• Items are written deliberately to be tricky or misleading (e.g., True-False: Cortez conquered the Incas in Mexico.)

- Test items tend to concentrate on the less important and even trivial aspects of a topic of study (e.g., Short answer: How many Pilgrims survived the first winter in Plymouth?).

- Test items require the students to share an opinion (e.g., True-False: The greatest woman of the nineteenth century was Florence Nightingale.) .

- Questions are often long, wordy, and confusing.

- More than one alternative is plausible as an answer.

- It is difficult to write objective items that involve creativity, evaluation, and application, and few objective tests include such items.

- Objective tests often work to the advantage of lucky guessers, and chance plays too large a role.

Teachers in social studies are still going to find objective tests useful. First, there is no doubt that objective tests are efficient. They can be taken and graded quickly. Students easily learn the skills they need to answer objective test questions. What is more, those skills that they develop taking these tests are useful in standardized tests.

Social studies teachers who want to use objective tests, but want to use them in the best way, can improve the quality and usefulness of their tests over time. First, they need to make sure that every question relates to some important objective or learning outcome. They also need to realize that high success on the test is their goal, because if most students do poorly it is an indicator that they have not taught effectively. If almost all students miss a particular question, something is wrong. It probably means that the question was either worded in a way that was vague or difficult to understand, that the material was not covered, or that what was taught was either not understood or had no impact.

Those tests which require value judgments in evaluation are described as *subjective measures.* Subjective measures include nearly all types of essay and problem-solving work where the process is as important as the answer and where thought and creativity are often part of the judgment. These can be called "low-cue" test items because they depend almost wholly on the ability of students to remember information relative to the question and use it. Little or no information is actually supplied.

Subjective tests are supported by some people because they are believed to require students to think and to structure their thinking, recalling the appropriate information. They also allow different students to use different arguments and information. There are as many common criticisms of essay tests as of objective measures. Critics claim the following:

- There is no fair and consistent way of grading an essay test.

- Students who do not write well do not do well on essays.

- Many students are able to be too creative in their answers.

- The kind of thinking required in essay tests is beyond the ability of most students, so the measures are unfair indicators of what they know.

- Essay tests can only sample a smaller amount of the material covered, not all of the objectives.

- Essay tests take much more time to grade and must be graded by someone who both knows the material and, at least according to some, knows how it has been taught.

One of the answers to many of these criticisms seems to be an approach to grading essay work called *holistic evaluation.* In this approach, the preparation procedure includes supplying students with thorough descriptions of various performance levels for essays. These descriptions range from descriptions of characteristics of poor answers on up to the attributes of superior essays. These criterion-based descriptions become the basis for the grading, which, in essence, is the process of categorizing essays into particular levels. They are generally referred to as rubrics.

Holistic evaluation has been a way of responding to legitimate recognition of a testing problem. It is a good way to show that simply by knowing the pitfalls of any form of test or test question, it is possible to avoid or at least reduce the dangers. The form of test or quiz and the kind of test questions that a teacher uses should be a matter of sense and judgment. Some tests provide information specifically to help planning and teaching (formative evaluation); some are merely diagnostic; and others are intended to be final, exit evaluations (summative). Any good test for the social studies, whether it includes subjective or objective questions or both, and regardless of its intended use, is going to do the following:

- Measure what it is supposed to measure (prerequisite knowledge, what is important, what has been taught and learned, etc.)

- Require the thinking skills that the teacher wants the students to use

- Allow the teacher to evaluate how well the objectives have been achieved

- Be an additional learning experience for children

- Be constructed and evaluated with fairness

- Be carefully and clearly worded and understandable to the students

- Not be a test on which children fail because of the lack of reading ability

- Be constructed so that the students can be expected to complete it in the time allowed

- Relate to all objectives in an equitable way

- Be of a length and type that is appropriate to the students, the material covered, and the way the material was covered

Developing a test or quiz and even deciding to use one that has been prepared to go with a text or other educational material should be a thoughtful and purposeful procedure. The first consideration should be the purpose that the test or quiz is going to serve. A number of additional thought-steps are needed, which might include the following:

1. Think about your specific purposes in the evaluation, what you are trying to find out about what the students have learned or what they can do with that knowledge.

2. Consider how much time you want the test or quiz to take, accounting for attention span, ability level, the breadth and depth you want in the evaluation, and the importance attached to the particular evaluation.

3. Decide what kind(s) of activities or behaviors you want the test or quiz to include.

4. Develop a plan for dividing the test or quiz into its component parts. (This may take such forms as outlines, sets of objective statements, and organizational plans allocating percentages.)

5. Prepare the individual items.

6. Carefully check the items for content, wording, clarity, readability, and so on.

7. Have someone else read the items to see if they understand them as you intended them and if they see any ambiguity, possibility of multiple interpretations, trickiness, and so on.

8. If possible, have someone do the test to see how that person interprets it and answers the questions and how long it takes to complete. (As a rule of thumb, multiply adult time by three to get an estimate of child completion time.)

9. Observe students as they take the test to note ease or frustration, commonly experienced difficulties and individual problems, and differences in rate of completion.

10. When grading tests, become aware of instances where student answers consistently vary from what you believe is the correct answer.

PROBLEMS IN ASSESSING PROJECTS AND REPORTS

Projects are extremely difficult to assess fairly. They often involve art ability or other abilities outside of those which are directly related to social studies learning and thinking; sometimes reflect parent help and/or differences in financial and other resources; and, even for a similar assignment, vary immensely in type, complexity, and learning value. When projects are done by groups, various members may make vastly different contributions. All of this is almost an essential part of the nature of this type of activity. Project work, at its best, involves a tremendous amount of thought and effort in conceptualization which may not be reflected to the evaluator in the finished product. One of the problems of project work is that students may turn it into copy work, reflecting almost no thought or originality. The teacher may or may not detect this when it happens, depending of course on how carefully the material is read, how familiar the teacher is with the resources and/or the style of the language used in them, and what the teacher expects from a style. It is a simple reality that a poor student is more likely to get "caught out" than a good one. Flashy and impressive projects may, in the final analysis, reflect little learning or teaching; unimpressive projects, on the other hand, may be the result of much more time and thought.

Even so, it is within the very qualities that make projects difficult to evaluate that the true value of project work is found. Projects involve students; they make them think and apply what they learn; they require conceptualizing, problem solving, and solution finding; they provoke research and questioning; they necessitate planning and organization; and, in the case of group projects, they involve group interaction skills and teach some valuable lessons about how other people operate and think.

Reports, whether oral or written, present all the same evaluation difficulties. They involve language abilities of different types, and the student's self-confidence and ability to communicate to and/or in front of people may influence how good the report seems as much or more than the actual thought and work involved. Availability of resources may also be a factor, as may the nature and form of the assignment. A well-structured report assignment, for example, should produce better results.

Projects and reports may be evaluated in a number of ways. The most common of these are any number of types of subjective evaluation with or without comment, checklist evaluation, analytical evaluation, peer evaluation, and self-evaluation.

SUBJECTIVE ASSESSMENT

The teacher's overall subjective judgment has always played a role in assessment. It is authoritarian in style and relies almost entirely on the teacher's professional judgment. The reasoning is that the teacher observes a project or report through its development, has an intimate knowledge of individual children, and has had a great number of past experiences with student projects and reports. Subjective assessment assumes the authority of the teacher and his or her right to be the judge. Students are discouraged from questioning any grade or judgment from the very beginning. At least an unconscious reason for this discouragement is that the criteria for judgments is not easily verbalized and is not very consistent. In fact, a teacher or a child could bring almost any factor into a justification argument. It is very difficult to give instructive and useful diagnostic feedback in this approach. When instructional suggestions and comments are made, they tend to be interpreted by the student as the teacher's rationale for the grade given. This may not actually be true.

Flaws in writing mechanics (or the absence of such flaws) and the appearance of projects sometimes influence teachers' judgment of substance and ideas. Often ideal models are used to show students in advance what a good report or project looks like. This may or may not have positive effects. On the other hand, seeing the models may reduce creativity in some cases or even cause student frustration at not feeling able to complete equivalent work. On the other hand, models may provide students with clarification about expectations.

PEER ASSESSMENT AND SELF-ASSESSMENT

Peer assessment and self-assessment by the students themselves represent the aim of all evaluation. Social studies teachers need to be constantly working toward the point where they can develop constructive ideas about what constitutes good work and make adjustments to achieve it. The basic process, whether involving peer assessment or self-assessment, begins with educating students to think of first efforts as preliminary stages. The process also means that students develop high standards, a desire to produce quality work, and an acceptance that such work can be achieved through revision. Students become involved in actively seeking to understand what it takes to produce good work. This is always a goal, and the process of moving students in the direction of the goal is at the center of standards-based teaching in the social studies and of what we have called a problems approach. The students perceive their own success in terms of work that they can take pride in; intrinsic goals replace extrinsic ones.

The process is one in which students learn to judge their own reports and projects, to know what they ought to contain, and to have a refined concept of the features that distinguish outstanding efforts. Obviously, this is an ideal and, as such, is something that teachers need to work toward, not expect at the outset. Teachers need to carefully structure instruction so that students learn how to make judgments. Follow through is needed, and a developmental approach is an absolute requisite to achieve more than superficial assessment.

CHECKLIST ASSESSMENT

Using checklists to assess produces an assessment that, at least in appearances, is more criterion based. The checklists may identify the features that the project or report is to include and the characteristics that the teacher expects in a report or project. When checklists are given to students in advance, they help the student in clarifying teacher expectations and give them some sense of security about how they can be successful in meeting these expectations and getting a good grade. Such thinking may produce some very regimented work, though, and cause students to work too much on meeting the criteria and too little on creative problem solving.

Following is one example of a checklist that might be used with an upper-grade reporting activity. The items on the checklist might be treated with a simple check mark indicating acceptability or might be rated in some way showing how well each criterion has been met. The report

- _____   Has a clear, creative, descriptive title.

- _____   Attempts to solve a problem or answer a question.

- _____   Deals with an important topic.

- _____   Is well organized with at least three subtopics.

- _____   Has a list of references (in correct form).

- _____   Shows that the references have been used.

- _____   Covers the topic completely.

- _____   Is presented in an interesting way.

- _____   Shows that the writer or presenter is knowledgeable about the topic.

- _____   Uses visual material (pictures, charts, maps, etc.).

- _____   Shows concern for mechanics (grammar, punctuation, and spelling).

- _____   Has a good summary and conclusion.

ANALYTICAL ASSESSMENT

Analytical assessment is based on careful examination of student behaviors or products in the light of clearly identified criteria. This approach may take several forms. When projects or reports are evaluated analytically, the teacher usually examines them very carefully and gives a detailed reaction. Sometimes this is a preliminary evaluation after which the students have the opportunity to revise, change, and improve. This view treats the work that has been done as a phase in the process of learning how to do this type of project. It is a draft. Whether the analysis is merely a step in the process or comes as a final feedback session, it can take one of two basic forms. One approach is for the teacher to begin with no criteria, basically letting the work itself dictate how it is analyzed. The idea is to give feedback of strengths and weaknesses that will allow students to improve. Another analytical approach involves the examination of a report or project to see how well it meets a number of standards. Comments would then be made relative to each of these standards. For example, the following categories might be the basis for evaluation of a project:

- Topic (What thought is evidenced in the selection of the basic idea?)

- Approach (How unique and interesting was the approach used?)

- Effort (Does the project show industry and care?)

- Purpose (Is the project purposeful and instructive?)

- Visual quality (Does the project attract attention and interest?)

- Mechanics and content (How well does the project reflect research and knowledge and is it done with a care for correctness?)

TEACHER OBSERVATIONS AND ANECDOTAL RECORDS

Teachers have very little time to take notes on children. What is more, descriptions of such observations do not easily translate into a form that can be considered in grading. In spite of these arguments, teacher observation is an invaluable tool in evaluation. One of the reasons is that the development of the child is full of subtleties and nuance. Teachers need to be reminded that the essence of an individual is not really something that can be quantified.

The best teachers of the social studies are those who are most reflective. The records of day-to-day actions of children often give such teachers the very best substance on which to reflect. In addition to the paper trail of children, these records are of two broad types: criterion based quantitative observations which usually take such forms as checklists; and qualitative observations that take the form of narrative descriptions. If either type is used, it needs to be done in a systematic regular way, and it needs to be kept up over a longer period of time. Because this record keeping cannot be done when teachers are presenting to the class, the logical times for such record keeping are when children are engaged in activities that require little teacher supervision and at times during and at the end of the school day when children are not present.

What becomes obvious with only a little knowledge of the techniques of teacher observation is that they incorporate checklist techniques in a particular way. In observation, checklists are shortcuts to developing systematic records of how children are behaving and progressing. They give the teacher a record that helps him or her make sense of the class, and they do so with very little time spent outside class, beyond determining and setting up what qualities the teacher is going to look for. Checklist assessment also relates well to determining the actual accomplishment of at least certain kinds of objectives.

Checklists may take a number of forms. One of the most common is a list of very specific competencies or knowledge (e.g., knows the cardinal directions). When a child masters an item on the list, his or her name is checked. A checklist might be set up to keep systematic track of group activity as well. The following list might be one that the teacher might carry about the room during independent group work activity.

Date _____

Name	Works without conflict	Gets on task	Problem solves	Shows leadership	Behavior is appropriate
Group 1					
Billy					
Maria					
Heather					
Eric					

Name	Works without conflict	Gets on task	Problem solves	Shows leadership	Behavior is appropriate
Group 2					
Jason					
Freddy					
Michael					
Starla					

While checklists save time, anecdotal teacher observation records demand a lot of time. Anecdotal material may reflect specific observations during the day. It is narrative in form and describes actual behavior. Such comments may not need to be lengthy or provide a lot of detail, but they do need to be complete. The teacher may or may not want to create categories for such notes prior to observation. Some may be behavioral, for example, "When John lost his place in line at lunch he shoved several children and made threatening remarks." Others may reflect participation, for example, "Caroline raised her hand for several questions in discussion. On two occasions that I called on her she answered completely."

Such notations of observations mean little unless they show a pattern. The patterns emerge when dated observation notes are kept for longer periods of time. Until recently teachers could not verify conclusions from such observations unless an outsider observed the classroom over a period of time. Technology is quickly giving us another tool for observation, one through which teachers can verify or disprove their impressions of students. More and more teachers are doing at least some videotaping of regular classes, not just special lessons. With the focus of such taping away from the teacher and on the students we have an additional tool for looking at patterns of behavior.

The time required by anecdotal-observation approaches to evaluation almost demands that such observation be focused on particular problems or particular children. The data can be very helpful in instances where faculty are going to meet and discuss a particular child or where reference material is being gathered to recommend special attention for a child. This type of information may also help a teacher deal with a particular classroom management problem. However, the approach takes a great deal of time, which may be beyond that available in many classrooms.

LOOKING BACK

Assessment is an important and complex part of the social studies. Assessment tools allow teachers to examine their own effectiveness as well as the learning of their students. Sound evaluation begins by comparing what has been learned to what the teacher intended to teach. In other words, achievement is measured against objectives.

Teachers assess this learning through student behaviors and student products. They need to be constantly aware of the need to focus on what is important, not just on what is easy to measure. There has been a push in the last decade toward what has been called authentic assessment. The argument is that tests and other traditional measures do not measure in a "real" way what a child is capable of doing. One approach to authentic assessment is through student portfolios, collections of different types of work that the student assembles over a long period of time. The most traditional assessment tools are tests, quizzes, and papers, but evaluation based on these tools alone does not give a true or authentic picture of student capability. Other student activities, some much more difficult to assess, are as important or more important than tests and written papers. Teachers may attempt more complete assessment by using observational tools including checklists and by recording students in action.

SELF-TEST

1. What does the term "basis of comparison" mean in assessment?

2. Explain why both the method and the content of assessment should be based on the teaching objectives.

3. What is meant by the term *authentic assessment*?

4. Identify the criticisms of both objective and subjective tests.

5. What are the traits of a good test?

6. What are the steps in building a test?

REFERENCES

Alleman, J., and Brophy, J. (1998). Assessment in a social constructivist classroom. *Social Education,* 62 (January), 32–34.

Alleman, J., and Brophy, J. (1999). The changing nature and purpose of assessment in the social studies classroom. *Social Education,* 63 (October), 334–337.

Avery, P. G. (1999). Authentic assessment and instruction. *Social Education,* 63 (October), 368–373.

NCSS. (1990). *Social Studies Curriculum Planning Resources.* Dubuque, Iowa: Kendall/Hunt.

SUGGESTED READING

Adams, D. M., and Hamm, M. E. (1992). Portfolio assessment and social studies: Collecting, selecting, and reflecting on what is significant. *Social Education,* 56 (February), 103–105.

Burroughs, S. (2002). Testy times for the social studies. *Social Education,* 66 (September), 318.

Darling-Hammond, L., and Falk, B. (1997). Using standards and assessment to support student learning. *Phi Delta Kappan,* 79 (November), 190–201.

NCSS. (1991). Position statement: testing and evaluation of social studies students. *Social Education,* 55 (September), 284–285.

Wood, J., Miederhoff, J. W., and Ulschmid, B. (1989). Adapting test construction for mainstreamed students. *Social Education,* 53 (January), 46–49.

Worthen, B. R. (1993). Critical issues will determine the future of alternative assessment. *Phi Delta Kappan,* 74 (February), 444–456.

6 Reading, Writing, and Technology: Tools for Social Studies Learning

LOOKING AHEAD

If we were to imagine the social studies as a huge monument, the very base on which the weight rested would be an area we call information and communication skills. The social studies cannot stand without these skills. We simply have to be able to find, process, and use information in order to do problem solving or to make decisions. When we have questions to answer, our success depends on either knowing or being able to find the specific information that those questions require. In addition to all of these information skills, social studies requires us to interpret information and create from it. What this all means is that children's ability to deal with information is a critical one.

This chapter deals with the development of those information skills most essential in the social studies. It focuses on some of the types of materials and assignments that teachers traditionally have found to be useful as well as on types of materials that have become available in this age of technology. The chapter also speaks to the pitfalls and problems that teachers and students encounter in using these tools.

CAN YOU? DO YOU?

Can You

- Name the four basic purposes for reading and writing assignments in the social studies?

- Think of ways to use fiction books in the social studies?

- Describe different ways of using computers in the social studies?

- Help children use the Internet for research.

Do You

- Know what children dislike most about using references?

- Know how to break children out of the "copy from an encyclopedia" or "cut and paste" on the computer reporting mode?

- Know how to make social studies book reports interesting?

- Know how to help children learn to organize their writing?

- Know how to help students use computers in research?

EFFECTIVE READING, WRITING, AND COMPUTER-USE ASSIGNMENTS IN THE SOCIAL STUDIES

Reading and writing have long been important and related tool skills for the social studies. Technology has only added to the complexity of the skills needed. Obviously, students need to learn to get information. On the other side of the coin many kinds of social studies activities require writing. Students must write to show that learning has occurred or that they understand that learning. Skills are most often needed for independent seat work or homework assignments. Assignments which involve students using the computer, while usually completed in class, are almost always completed independently. Lee and Pruett (1979) have suggested that such assignments are used for one or more of four basic purposes:

1. Practice or follow-up work

2. Preparation or readiness work

3. Extension or application where students transfer a skill or a concept to some new situation

4. Creativity where students produce a new response

Both teachers and students need to first understand the purpose that a particular reading, writing, or computer assignment serves in order for it to be completed in an effective, meaningful way. Effective assignments will also exhibit several other traits.

1. They will seem interesting or provoke the curiosity of at least some of the students.

2. They will have a minimum amount of teacher supervision and an optimum frustration level. (Though students need to overcome difficulties

and solve their own problems, the difficulties and problems cannot be so great as to cause the student not to do the assignment. The trick is to make work challenging without making it seem impossible.)

3. They will be devised to be accomplished in an amount of time that is appropriate to the age and the ability of the students. The students need to think that they can accomplish the tasks. (Sometimes we have to break large assignments into segments in order to accomplish this.)

4. Students will have a clear and complete understanding of what they need to do and how to do it. (Studies have shown that lack of clarity is the most common problem of teacher assignments.)

5. Students will know the answers to procedural questions such as the kind of heading they are supposed to use, the acceptable length, the kind and size of paper, the types of resources they should use, etc.—before they even begin. (In fact, they will have a clear understanding.)

USE OF REFERENCE READING PROVIDING FOR INDIVIDUAL DIFFERENCES

In order to find information, children need to know how to use reference materials. We also want children to learn to take delight, and have their curiosity stimulated, in a good browse through a variety of reference materials. If we do our job right, they will become more excited when they find better materials, not easier ones. They will be drawn to the Internet, not because it is easier to cut and paste a copied report together, but because the Internet offers more and better maps, data, and other types of information and because that information is more up to date than what they can find in their local library.

DICTIONARIES, GLOSSARIES, AND INDEXES

While adults often consider sources such as dictionaries, glossaries, and indexes as shortcuts to understanding and finding information, this is not the feeling that most children have. Many simply hate having to look things up. Nothing could be greater drudgery, no task more tedious.

The trick, then, is to make looking up stuff easy and fun. I like to tempt children by showing them what they *do not* have to do to look things up. For example, they *do not* have to be able to spell words accurately. They *do not* have to read every word or even most of the words. Beyond just knowing alphabetic order, three skills do have to be mastered, to use these kinds of resources: (1) When searching for a topic, students have to be able to think of alternative words to look up if their first guesses don't pan out; (2) they have to be able to think of likely spellings for words; and (3) they have to be able to scan or go down a page quickly to find one word.

The "shortcut" feeling can be enhanced in the social studies by making dictionary, glossary, and index work collaborative. The teacher can help younger children build a class dictionary for any unit of work. The children can also build their own card files of personally owned words. (*Owned words* are those that they can consistently recognize and are therefore among their own personal sight words.) Older children can keep either a personal or a group notebook dictionary with each topic studied. Dictionary and index work can also be turned into competitive, speed and accuracy games too. The skills and shortcuts apply to computer sources as well as print ones.

ENCYCLOPEDIAS, ATLASES, AND ALMANACS

Children need to learn to choose special reference materials. The first problem is always in identifying in which source, whether print or technological, to look. To choose, children need to know the amount and kind of information they need and how quickly they need it. Structured exercises with encyclopedias, atlases, and almanacs will help children learn the contents, organization, and style of different types of references. Following is an example of an encyclopedia scavenge. I have the children work in pairs, each pair with a different volume of the encyclopedia. Each pair is in a race to complete all the items and to do so first.

1. Find an entry of at least two pages.

2. Find a country and tell its population, area, and one other fact.

3. Discover a biographical entry and tell two types of information it includes.

4. What is the shortest entry you can find?

5. What is the longest entry you can find?

6. Find a reference that sends you from one entry to others.

7. Make an educated guess about how many entries there are in your volume. (Tell what reasoning your guess is based on.)

8. Find an entry that is not a proper noun.

9. Identify three entries that deal with the same broad topic. (You do not have to limit your suggestions to your volume.)

10. Name the first and last entries.

BIOGRAPHIES AND OTHER NONFICTION

For more depth and information, students need to learn how to identify, use, and appreciate biographies and other nonfiction literature material. Increasing numbers of such nonfiction books that are boldly exciting and informative are being written for children. Biographies are written at many levels. Some nonfiction books have real depth and feeling as well as interest-arousing information. Such books can be used in a lot of ways in addition to standard classroom browsing "interest" tables and reporting activities.

Through the grades, well-written, carefully researched, colorfully illustrated nonfiction picture books of high quality are becoming more abundant. These can be used for highly effective read-aloud experiences in social studies through the grades. Some of these describe other cultures or life in other places. Others richly describe events and the details of life in different times. The accurate illustrations add to the delight that children experience and to the learning value.

Biographies at the primary level have to be full of anecdotes and stories. Some of the best ones have eye-catching illustrations and many have humor that this age group can understand. S. N. Monjo's *The One Bad Thing about Father* or Doug Quackenbush's biographies are examples of the kind of book that works well at this level. The teacher can read or tell the story wearing the costume of a character or a friend of a character. This can make the story characters more real and believable for children through the middle grades. Children will also benefit from drawing a picture of the character they have read about and then telling about their picture.

Photographs and illustrations in a number of books make them ideal for thumbing through with a "what's that?" attitude with small groups. The Silver Burdett series, *The Human Story,* is typical of large, heavily illustrated books developed especially for upper-grade children, which are ideally suited for this purpose. The same kind of curiosity browse can be done with younger children using books such as Peter Spier's *People* or Virginia McLean's *Chasing the Moon over China.*

Some books like the *Turning Points of History* series from Silver Burdett or Aliki's *A Medieval Feast* or *Mummies, Made in Egypt,* are almost ideally suited as manuals for laying out historic events geographically and walking through them in a step-by-step pantomime. These books, or others such as Macaulay's *Castle* or *Cathedral,* can inspire the young "architectural artists" in a class to draw and build models.

In the upper grades, it is important to choose biographies which show the real and human side of their subjects. Books such as Jean Fritz' *Where Do You Think You're Going, Columbus?* present historical figures in an interesting way with their human problems and weaknesses. An idea worth trying with biographies is based on the concept of the meeting of minds. Instead of giving a book report, the students take the role of the title character. Then in small groups they talk about issues and questions in role. The biogra-phied characters need not be contemporaries. In fact, it adds an element of interest if they are not. What would Alexander the Great say to Napoleon or to Susan B. Anthony? Other biography book-report alternatives for the upper grades are the quiz show and the news magazine show. Both are based on television models and involve children in taking on character roles. Examples of quiz-show models include a "Who is the mystery guest?" panel show or "Who is the best _____?" (based on two or more people who have read about the same figure, each playing that per-son). News-show formats can vary from interviews to "You are there" spots with the character being his or her own reporter.

FICTION AND POETRY

Another way that social studies learning can occur is through fiction that children encounter in the reading and language arts curriculum and as recreation. Fiction is about people, events, and places, often about real ones. Even animal characters in stories often personify human qualities. Fiction deals with solving problems and often centers on values and emo-tions. Fiction is often culturally routed, and story forms such as myths, tall tales, and folk tales tell much about the culture of their origin.

Poetry also offers social studies learning opportunities. We can learn and remember a lot about the beginning of the American Revolution, for example, by doing a readers' theater based on Longfellow's *Paul Revere's Ride*. Poetry is the most economically worded, intense, and focused form of verbal communication. The basic job of poetry is to express personal feel-ings and thoughts either in song or story form. What this means, in effect, is that the content of all fiction and poetry can be called social studies.

One reason for using fictional material in the social studies is that fiction is most often more appealing to children than nonfiction. Good stories just read better than textbooks, where the task of covering specific content con-trols the writing. Fictional characters and plots are imaginative, exciting, and appealing to the emotions, while bare fact material of any sort is not always so interesting. Many children who will give only minimum effort to textbooks and other nonfiction are avid fiction readers. They can often be led to discover history, geography, and other social studies content through fiction. In fact, many grow to love the social studies after first hav-ing their interest stimulated by fiction.

What kind of fiction do you want to guide children to? To my way of thinking, a book is going to be good social studies material if it meets some, but not necessarily all, of the following conditions:

- It tells a good story well.

- It develops strong, real characters who are confronted with important and believable problems.

- It contributes something to the child's knowledge and understanding of the world (other people, other places, other times, the self).

- It provokes the reader to think and feel about some human problem or situation.

- It helps the child deal with his or her own problems.

There are many types of fictional and poetry books that relate to the social studies. Though far from complete, the list given here provides a fair sampling of the varieties of story types that can be used as part of the social studies program.

Fiction

Folk tales and myths

Legends and hero stories (Robin Hood, King Arthur, William Tell)

Tall tales

Historical novels that focus on particular events, or times

Biographical novels with real and important individuals as their subjects

Biographical novels written about real, but relatively unknown historical figures

Novels in different geographic settings

Books dealing with personal survival

Books dealing with the problems of family living

Books that deal with contemporary social problems

Books that present characters who have admirable and desirable qualities

Poetry

Poems that tell the story of real or legendary events

Poems that deal with historically significant individuals

Poetry that is a folk art form of a particular culture

Problem poetry

Lullabies

Work songs

Holiday and calendar-related poetry

Geography and weather poems

Some excellent teachers make it a daily practice to find time to read aloud to classes, exposing the children to at least a portion of some really powerful and interesting books with solid social content. One reason for doing this is that the children really enjoy it. In addition to the motivational value, reading aloud to children is good modeling; children see the teacher who they admire and look up to reading. Research and common sense tell us that children can often listen with understanding, memory, and appreciation to books and stories that are too difficult for them to read themselves.

Fictional books and stories as well as poems are usually rich in drama and can be turned into skits, role plays, pantomimes, and other acting-out experiences. Some poetry lends itself to choral reading and independent read-aloud activity.

Fictional books also may be a really superior alternative to topical assignments for children to practice reporting skills. Oral reporting in the social studies often turns into futile and meaningless drudgery as children read aloud, and with great difficulty, papers copied verbatim from encyclopedias. We will talk more about reporting skills later in this chapter. But here are ten ideas that, with a little thought and planning, a teacher might use to get children to do some different and interesting fiction book reports.

TEN DIFFERENT TYPES OF BOOK REPORTS THAT WILL MAKE REPORTING A MEANINGFUL ACTIVITY

Fiction and nonfiction reading can add meaningfully to social studies learning. Sharing the reading is important, yet book reports are notorious as meaningless assignments in which students do copy work. Oral reports have an even worse reputation as meaningless, boring activities. Here are 10 different ways to have students do book reports which can be more fun and have much more impact both on the reporter and on the audience.

1. Economic book reports: For a story or book, draw two circle graphs. On one, show the expenditures of the main character. On the other, show that character's income. The circles should be segmented estimating the percentage of the total budget the character would have had to pay on today's market for the goods and services received in the story and the sources of income.

2. Archaeology book reports: Create a shoe box dig for a book or story. Having read the story, try to imagine that archaeologists are digging into the site of the main story events hundreds of years after the story happened. In the shoe box, create in miniature the artifacts they might find at the site.

3. Story museum reports: Create a miniature museum exhibit commemorating the events depicted in the story. This can be done as a diorama or through a series of drawings.

4. Comic book reports: Create a comic book for the book or story using cartoon drawings to show the story events.

5. Shoe box story parade: Read a fictional book about a historic event or a biography of a historical character. Create a float out of a shoe box showing the most significant or memorable scene from a book or story. When everyone in the class has done a different float, they can be formed into a parade with each person serving as commentator as his or her float passes by.

6. Book trials: After a significant number have read the same book or story, stage a mock trial of one of the story characters or a trial of the author(s) for "corrupting the youth." Assign the roles of attorneys, defendants, witnesses, and jurors.

7. Historical creation book reports: Create documentary evidence that traces the history of a book.

8. Story geography: Map a book or story showing the location of the episodes and events described. Then give a map talk taking the major character(s) through these events step by step.

9. Sociometrics of books: Develop diagrams showing the relationships of people in a book. Small circles represent individuals, dotted lines show kinship ties, and solid lines with arrows stand for positive feelings of like or love. The oral report consists of explaining the diagram.

10. Publicity and review reports: Do a promotion for a book as it might be sold in a television commercial or develop a review that might be given on a television review program if the book were a movie.

ORGANIZING TO WRITE: NOTE TAKING, QUESTION ANSWERING, AND OUTLINING

Reading and writing activities or assignments in the social studies may take several forms. Follow-up of a class or group reading assignment might include having students do any of the following activities:

- Answer questions.

- Write a summary.

- Write a solution to a problem using information from the reading material.

- Make up a story involving the time or place described.

- Write a description.

- Write book reports on single books read independently (e.g., biographies, books about events, "You are there" type books, viewpoint books, etc.).

- Write summaries of articles in magazines and newspapers.

- Make written plans for a project or activity.

- Write letters requesting information or materials.

- Write letters of appreciation.

- Imitate literature types from other cultures or times (e.g., Japanese Haiku poetry, tall tales, ballad type songs, etc.).

- Do in-role writing activities in which the student pretends to be in another culture, place, time, or position.

- Write dramas and skits related to unit topics being studied.

- Write narrative reports of library research on a topic using one or multiple resources—an experiment conducted, a series of observations, an interview or conversation.

- Make up rules, generalizations, hypotheses, cause and effect statements, etc.

Students experience two major kinds of difficulties with writing assignments in the social studies. The first of these has to do with the clarity of the assignment. The teacher simply needs to be sure to explain an assignment clearly and completely. To be assured that she or he has done this, the teacher needs to cross check, asking children to repeat and even paraphrase and explain in their own words. Providing a written down version of the assignment also helps. The second difficulty has to do with how well prepared the students are for an assignment. Avoiding this difficulty involves being assured that the students have the ability or readiness to do the assignment. It also means that they have been taught in such a way that they know how to do the assignment.

The base or prerequisite skills needed for many if not all writing jobs include note taking, writing answers to questions, and outlining. All of these skills involve having the ability to see what is most important and the ability to discern what is relevant for particular purposes. For children to develop these abilities, they have to, first, be able to see the essential purpose of the writing job itself. Secondly, as they read, listen, or observe, they must be able to pick out central messages. Thirdly, they need to be able to scan for messages related to particular criteria.

You are making a big mistake if you assume that students have already developed skills to the level that you want them to have. The first thing to do—always—is to determine where they are. It has been my experience, and that of most teachers with whom I have talked, that the best way to do this is through monitoring and observing what the students do. Once you have determined what skills they do and do not have, you can set about to gradually develop the needed abilities. This saves frustration and anguish for both you and the students.

The trick is to keep the possibility of excitement and interest alive. Note taking, question asking and answering, and outlining can be boring, especially if the students do not understand the assignment or if the content you work with is dry material. I think that part of the mastery of this trick is to work with fun stuff to learn the skill. Outline the sports section of the newspaper or a Shel Silverstein poem, for example, or take notes on a comic book or a travel brochure. The other part is to be *absolutely sure* that students do understand what it is they are supposed to do. One procedure to try is the following:

1. Define the skill that you want the children to have and analyze the steps they will have to go through in performing that skill.

2. Find out what the children can do by giving them a very simple and short supervised task involving the skill.

3. Model the skill, using a question-and-answer format to get the children to look at what you are doing analytically.

4. Repeat the model, going step by step with new content, allowing the children to do the work as a class. Monitor to make sure that they are all with you.

5. Supply exercises in which part, but not all, of the structure is in place.

6. Gradually withdraw the structure until the children can perform without it.

Such a systematic procedure sounds simple and logical, but the majority of teachers seldom follow this kind of procedure. Research indicates that teachers rarely make certain that students understand the questions in textbook assignments (Anderson, 1984) and that there are often major comprehension problems inherent in the questions themselves (Cooper, 1986). The questions may be unclear in their wording. Students may lack the background knowledge needed to understand them or may be unable to see just what it is that the questions are seeking.

In spite of these problems, research supports post-reading questions as contributing to learning (Walberg, 1986). This would seem to indicate that if teachers would be more careful about assignments and about preparing students for them, such assignments could be beneficial.

Sometimes you really have to plan to keep an assignment within reach of a particular group of students. By "within reach" I mean that the assignment is one that these students can do in what is *for them* a reasonable amount of time. One approach that has been very successful is cooperative learning, which involves students in a helping relationship with one another. Other approaches that seem to be successful suggest that reducing assignment length (the number of questions to be answered) while providing more guidance and feedback, is beneficial (Barron et al., 1998; Slavin, 1987). Mechanisms for doing this include dividing work among students, segmenting assignments, and identifying assignment mentors (Turner, 1989).

Following are a few guidelines (adapted from Turner, 1989) which may make textbook question assignments more meaningful:

- Assign questions only after reading them carefully.

- Give clear, complete directions both in writing and orally, taking time to explain and answer questions.

- Call attention to special problems and trouble spots students are likely to encounter.

- Point out where questions call for the student to evaluate, be creative, or give interpretation.

- Teach the students about question words and that questions in texts are answered in the order that they are asked.

- Follow up completed assignments by going over them in a meaningful way.

- Wherever possible, use visual graphic organizers.

DEVELOPING RESEARCH AND REPORTING SKILLS

Students are often asked to make reports in the social studies. Such activity may serve one or more of several purposes

- Writing both necessitates and helps thinking. By asking students to do reports we are giving them valuable practice in thinking skills (Turner, 1989).

- Writing is developed by practice. By involving students in writing activities, we help them develop their writing skills.

- Reporting activities allow students to pursue individual interests and work at their own levels.

- Giving a report gives a student a sense of authority. He or she becomes an expert and gains ownership of a unique and special knowledge.

- Reporting can help a student develop and improve self-expression.

- Presenting a report can be an application of the entire spectrum of language skills.

- Reports can give oral and visual display of writing and/or speaking.

- Reporting can be structured to foster social interaction.

- Reports provide checkpoints where student learning is observable and in a form where such learning can be evaluated.

Reports can be written, oral, or both. The first reporting activities are informal but prepared kindergarten and first-grade experiences such as show and tell. Writing an experience story as a class in early school experiences is also a preparation for reporting, especially if one child reads the entire story back after the class has composed it. Reading, writing, and oral language skills are combined in reporting. Among the most common problems associated with reporting assignments are wholesale copying from reference books, students' lack of comprehension of their own reports, stumbling and stiff presentation of oral reports lacking in meaningfulness or purpose, and inattention of students to one another's reports. It is easy to see that all of these problems are somewhat related. Fortunately, they are also avoidable.

None of the problems associated with student reports is attributable to the nature of reporting itself. They seem to be more related to the lack of thought by teachers relating to the clarity of reporting assignments and the readiness of students for particular types of reporting assignments. Problems also come due to the failure of teachers to teach children how to write reports and to lead them through the steps of preparing the report.

Let us first look at the assignment stage. Reporting assignments may be set in several contexts: (1) as assignments everyone does (everyone reports on the same thing), (2) as parts of sets of assignments from which everyone chooses (students may choose among two or more projects), (3) as a form of recognition or distinction to better students (reporting activity is done only by students that the teacher sees as capable and likely to put forth the effort), (4) as volunteer activities that are encouraged and rewarded (extra credit and praise). None of these forms is inherently better or worse than any of the others. What is important is that the students know and understand which set(s) of rules is operating. A logical rule of thumb seems to be to keep the system simple, especially with younger students.

There are a number of types of reporting assignments. Earliest reporting activity in elementary school begins with sharing or show-and-tell activities and with language-experience approaches. Sharing activities are important because they develop children's ability to talk in front of an audience and can help them learn to distinguish important and appropriate things from those that have less significance and relevance. Language-experience approaches, which are a form of teacher-led corporate reporting, have similar value and teach children sequencing and ordering skills as well.

One type of individual reporting that can begin very early is experiential reporting. "What I Did/Learned/etc. on My Summer Vacation," the most trite example of this kind of report, gives this type of assignment a bad name. At its best, an experience report is a positive learning experience. It involves having students give true accounts of events that have reality to them. There is a natural narrative and sequence and an opportunity to learn the importance of supporting detail, noting cause and effect relationships, and drawing conclusions.

The same can be said for observational reports which are accounts of events witnessed and sometimes staged and orchestrated by the student.

Observational reports can be made about movies, television programs, dramas, field trips, and other events witnessed by the students both as individuals and as groups. They may even be done collaboratively (see Chapter 4).

Both direct and phone interviews can be the basis of interesting reports. Children need to be given a structure of questions to ask in the interview. This can be provided by the teacher or developed in a guided class discussion. Audio or video recordings of the interview can be useful both in report write-ups and in segments as part of oral reports.

Reports may also take the form of demonstrations. Children can show either directly or by simulation how something was or is done in a culture. They may also use drama as the vehicle for the report. (More ideas related to this will be presented in Chapter 10.)

A real danger in reporting is that of mindless, copied reports. This danger can be averted by clear directions that specify how the report is to be organized.

Whatever form of reporting or writing students may be asked to do, success rather than failure can be expected if the teacher follows certain principles.

1. Assignments should be stimulating, interesting, and challenging to students.

2. Writing assignments ought to be clear. Teachers need to provide both a written description and an oral explanation of the assignment and then see feedback about how well students understand it. Teacher failure to determine student understanding of assignments is rated in research as a major problem.

3. Assignment length and complexity need to be within the capabilities of the students. This can be achieved by
   A. Limiting the length of the assignment.
   B. Segmenting the assignment into logical steps or components.

4. Provide a structure for the report. Among the many structuring devices that might be used are outlines, sets of questions, dramatic devices (e.g., job applications for biographical reports on historic characters), a list of key points, or chronologies.

5. Successful and satisfactory writing assignments result from embedding the teaching of necessary directions and skills development into the writing assignment process.
   A. Such assignments specify and direct length by specifically defining length (number of words or sentences or pages) or space provided.
   B. Such assignments embed the teaching of such skills as summarizing, paraphrasing, skimming, and scanning into the development of the assignment.

     C. Such assignments provide a structure of steps to follow in doing the assignment.

     D. Such assignments specify and provide the resources to be used and direct students on how to use them. (School librarians are often very helpful. Use them, but be sure resources are available.)

WRITING CREATIVELY

Writing can actually make the social studies more fun. The variety of creative-writing tasks that can relate to any social studies topic is really limited only by the teacher's imagination. Any idea used ought to be mentally tested with three questions before it is tried. (1) Is doing this task really going to serve some purpose related to understanding what is being studied? (2) Can the students do this task and do it in a reasonable amount of time? (3) How is this task going to affect or relate to the other activities that we are doing?

A number of beneficial writing activities can be described as in-role writing. In-role writing means that the writer is pretending to be someone else as he or she writes. One kind of in-role writing involves trying to go through some authentic writing exercise from a particular time period, such as writing letters, wills, and epitaphs for famous and nonfamous historical characters. Another type of in-role activity involves imagining how a historical character might deal with some of the paper work we deal with today. For example, how would that character fill out a job application or some questionnaire. Students can also write in-role autobiographies and poems.

One unique type of creative writing assessment which has several twists involves imitating a writing form of a particular culture. Children studying Japan can, of course, write Haiku poems. The study of Germany and France invites fairy tales, the American West suggests tall tales, ancient Greece and Rome might produce myths and fables, and the New England colonies bring sampler messages and Horn Book type sayings and stories. Reading stories or poems that come from any culture can provide models for meaningful creative writing.

A third type of writing that holds exciting promise is problem-solving stories. Usually the teacher provides a story starter which is a problem scenario. The children then have to write a story in which the central characters try to solve the problem. For example, I gave a fifth-grade class a scenario about two children from the North who found themselves deep in the heart of the Confederacy at the outbreak of the Civil War. They had to write a story in which the children figured out how to find their way back. The teacher may have a little trouble thinking of such problem scenarios. If so, plots of books and movies offer rich sources of problems.

One activity that I find particularly satisfying, though, utilizes simple stories that children make up about fictional children that they imagine in the cultural setting they are studying. With older children, I sometimes set this up as a long-term project. I try to get them involved to the extent that they feel that they are actually doing research in order to write the story. It gives them what amounts to a real scholar's purpose for studying. This might be in the form of a diary that they make entries in every day. These could involve such calendar events as travelling with Columbus, Marco Polo, or any explorer, going on a cattle drive with cowboys, taking a wagon train or a railroad train west, going on a modern trip to a preselected set of selected sights, or any one of a host of other journeys.

Another activity that I like is collaborative writing. In one form of it I have the students write a story in groups. Their story is structured by a handout which gives the skeleton story in a series of topic sentences. Each student or pair of students independently writes a paragraph beginning with one topic sentence. When all have finished, the group works together to smooth out the inconsistencies and write in transitions. Here is an example of a set of topic sentences that might be used for students to collaboratively write a "Robin Hood" story.

Sample Topic Sentence Set

Because of the greed and the cruelty of the Norman nobles, many a good and honest man had turned outlaw. These outlaws roamed the king's forests foraging what they could. The most famous of all the outlaws was Robin of Locksley, better known as Robin Hood. Robin was himself of noble blood, but had been dispossessed of his land and titles by trickery. Along the roads that led through Sherwood Forest, no rich Norman traveller was safe from Robin's merry band of outlaws. According to legend, Robin Hood robbed from the rich and gave to the poor. You can help to build yet another story to add to the Robin Hood legend.

1. The Sheriff of Nottinghamshire, unable to catch the outlaw known as Robin Hood, at last had hit upon what he thought would be a foolproof plan.

2. Disguised as peasants, the Sheriff and three of his archers slipped into Sherwood Forest quietly.

3. As they passed through a glade in the forest, an arrow whistled through the air, missing the Sheriff's ear by little more than an inch.

4. The Sheriff did not realize that Robin Hood had seen through his disguise immediately and told a story of how he and the others had been forced off of their land in the north.

5. Blindfolded, the four strangers were led through a twisting, turning way to a secret glen.

6. Secretly, the Sheriff left a trail of white pebbles for his soldiers to follow.

7. When the blindfolds were removed, the Sheriff's men were amazed at the great group of busy and happy people they saw.

8. The outlaws treated their visitors royally, feasting and toasting them through the late afternoon.

9. With a mischievous grin, a small man came strolling through the boisterous crowded tables to pour out a bag of white pebbles in front of the Sheriff.

10. As Robin and a half dozen or so men surrounded them, Sir Guy and the archers looked at each other fearfully.

11. The Sheriff and his men, relieved of the weight of their purses, their weapons, and their shoes, wandered in the forest for days before they were found, and the Sheriff was not a happy man.

MATHEMATICS AND THE SOCIAL STUDIES: CHARTS, GRAPHS, AND MAPS

Mathematics goes to work in the social studies. There are many ways in which measurement and calculation skills can be of help to children in their world. Mathematics is also a tool for learning about that world and about how social scientists work. It is important to help children learn to use mathematical tools. The place to begin is with everyday things that can be part of children's lives. The experience can begin as a class activity and then slowly move to group and individual practice. Charts and graphs can be used to show such information as:

- Each child's attendance

- Completed work

- Teacher conferences

- Children's independent reading

- Class opinions

- How related ideas are alike and different

- Days remaining until some special event

- Competition among groups

- Numbers of different kinds of objects

- Work completed

Use of measurement as well as charts and graphs can provide important, conceptually related experiences as children study other cultures and other times. They can measure areas equivalent to the sizes of the ships of explorers and colonists, or of the log cabins of famous historical characters such as Abraham Lincoln. They can look to the content and weight of packloads of soldiers of various eras. In fact, measuring is one of the most important ways of making verbal descriptions visual and tactile. Mathematics enables students to look comparatively at such things as personal income, shipping, manufacturing, mining, and farming in very concrete ways.

Mathematics is also an important tool for making and reading maps. Practice in measuring distances on maps is a critical part of learning about scale and about place relationship. With intermediate grades, you can have children create their own ruler from a piece of string and then make a game out of measuring distances. Making grids to draw smaller and larger maps can also help children with measurement skills. Younger children can begin with a map divided into four, numbered quadrants, where they locate places by quadrant.

USING COMPUTERS FOR SOCIAL STUDIES LEARNING AND RESEARCH

You may consider yourself the furthest thing from a "techie" type. In fact you may think that many of your students are likely to be far more computer savvy than you are. Nonetheless, technology is increasingly important as a tool for research and learning in school. We are only beginning to realize the enormous potential of technology in the social studies. The following are only a few of the possible ways in which technology may be utilized.

- Drill and Practice/Testing Activities: These are among the oldest forms of computer-assisted instructional activities. With user-friendly software, teachers can use and even create their own work materials and tests. One advantage of computer drill materials is that they can give instant feedback for correct and incorrect answers. Another is that students quickly learn to do the activities without teacher help.

- Word Processing: Students can use the computer to write, spell check, edit and rewrite, and store on discs and in folders. Desktop publishing programs enable them to clip and paste in pieces of art, quotes, and information, and even video and audio segments, thus enabling them to research and produce sophisticated reports and presentations.

Classes can write class books, do "foxfire" or cultural journalism projects in which they combine their reporting and do investigative reporting using community resources, produce class and school newspapers and magazines, produce personal journals, write fiction, and create fiction anthologies related to unit topics.

- CD and Video Disc Reference Materials: Encyclopedias, atlases, and an abundance of specialized reference materials are now available on CDs. These are set up so that students can use them with great flexibility, even copying print, audio, and action video segments from them. Finding information is even easier and certainly quicker than with print reference materials. With the right equipment, anything that appears on a computer screen can also be projected, allowing for use of these materials in teacher presentations and student reports.

- Interactive Book CDs: A number of very good children's books useful in the social studies are now on CD. The added advantage is that these are now interactive. If a child has trouble with a word, the computer will pronounce it and even define it. Added visual and sound activities, including animation, make these books an adventure for younger children (and even their teachers).

- Games and Simulations: A constantly growing list of game and simulation materials, appropriate for a variety of ages and content topics, is becoming available for purchase or through the Internet. Field (1997) has identified a number of recent content-focused software packages that can involve children in decision making and provide information in story scenario formats. The role-play aspects of these activities are inviting to children, and they learn unconsciously.

- The Internet: The resource with the most varied potential is the Internet. Not only is it possible for children to find information and resources related to almost any topic, but through the Internet they can be in communication with others interested in their topics as well. The Internet offers the possibility to identify and exchange electronic mail or be in instant communication with pen pals, even international ones. It also makes it possible for a class or school to be adopted by and to communicate with seagoing ships, long distance truck drivers, and communities and schools in other countries. Students can receive files, including a tremendous amount of different government materials, on the Internet (Wilson, 2000; Watson & Marsh, 1995), gain access to any number of games and activities, and even receive and read magazines and books.

- Databases: Computers are best at storing and manipulating data. When large amounts of information are stored in an organized way so that particular summaries and analyses of that data can be called for, it is called a *database*. Teachers and children can learn a great deal from using existing databases, creating their own databases, and manipulating the data to help solve problems and answer questions. A database in a classroom may store information learned in a unit study, or be a collection or file of some kind. A number of geographic and historical databases are available on the Internet (Watson & Marsh, 1995; Budin, Kendall, & Lengel, 1986). There are also databases that can be purchased for particular studies.

- Record Keeping: Teachers and students can use the computer to store and compute many different kinds of information, including research data for the student, and grades, financial ledgers, attendance, and behavior for the teachers.

- Graphics: There are a number of relatively user-friendly programs available now through which graphic organizers and diagrams can be created to help explain ideas and organize information.

Computers offer growing opportunities for a variety of individual, group, and whole class activities. To get the best use of computers, though, social studies teachers first need to choose software carefully. According to Braun, Fernlund, and White (1997), a technology product should promote meaningful social studies learning, help provide challenging instruction, and actively engage learners. But before they buy software, teachers need to know something about their computers and their children. Both the machines and the students have limitations. Choose a piece of software that requires too much computer memory, and it will be useless because the machine and the user will both be frustrated. Choose one that is beyond the ability of students, and it will be useless because the children will be incapable of using it. To use computers in the social studies classroom with the best possible results, teachers need to follow some guidelines.

1. Be sure that students have the knowledge and skill that they need before turning them lose on a particular computer activity.

2. Recognize that your students will sometimes have more computer expertise than you do and learn from them and utilize that skill.

3. Develop monitoring and control mechanisms to keep students on task. Though one of the good things about computers is that they can lead users in directions that they never imagined, with children, the teacher is the one who has to be sure that they stay focused. Teachers have to set limits, too, on the time that students spend on particular computer activities.

4. Do not allow a few students to monopolize the available computers.

5. Provide time and opportunity for explorations, allowing students to discover new and exciting things, but be aware that there are things on the Internet that are not appropriate for children.

6. Recognize and help students deal with the frustrations related to working with technology.

7. Take into account the differences in skill level, experience, ability, and aptitude among your students

8. Be aware of and teach students about ethical and moral issues related to computers and the information obtainable from them.

9. Be open to new and ever changing technology.

LOOKING BACK

The social studies is knowledge based, and that knowledge has been most readily communicated through print. Students need reading and writing skills to succeed in social studies. This need has only been intensified and compounded with the growth of the use of technology. Computers themselves as well as computer software have the capability of storing and organizing vast amounts of information. They also make unlimited resources available through the Internet. Teachers give reading, writing, and computer-based assignments for the purpose of reviewing information, preparing for new studies, extending what goes on in the classroom, and developing creativity. Children need to learn to use a variety of resources, including children's literature, print reference materials, and those available through technology.

There is a growing unity of purpose between social studies and the language arts as the literature connection becomes more apparent in social studies and as the whole language movement continues to influence the language arts curriculum. Writing skill is emphasized in both areas and social studies teachers are seeing imaginative writing as a way of motivating interest and research. Computer software and word processing offer effective, imaginative tools for such writing activity.

Research skills and the writing skills needed to communicate research are critical concerns. Educators know that writing ability grows through practice and that writing is linked to thinking. They also know that mathematics is an important research and problem-solving tool. It is especially important that teachers move beyond those reporting assignments that require little thought other than that needed to copy or to do rote, word-calling types of reading. This becomes even more important as the Internet offers information sources so far reaching as to be completely beyond teacher control or management.

SELF-TEST

1. What are the four basic purposes for which reading and writing assignments are used in independent seat work?

2. What are the qualities that you need to look for in a nonfiction book?

3. What are some different kinds of fictional material that can be used in the social studies?

4. How does the social studies relate to whole language?

5. What are the purposes of learning research and reporting skills?

6. How are guidelines useful in making textbook questions more meaningful?

7. Why do teachers have students write reports and give them orally?

8. What place does mathematics have in the social studies?

9. Identify some of the different ways that computers can enrich the social studies.

REFERENCES: PROFESSIONAL MATERIALS

Anderson, L. W. (1984). What teachers don't do and why. *Education Report 27, no. 3.* December.

Barron, B., Schwartz, D., Vye, N., Moore, A., Petrosino, A., Zech, L., Bransford, J., and The Cognition and Technology Group at Vanderbilt. (1998). Doing with understanding: Lessons from research on problem and project-based learning. *The Journal of the Learning Sciences, 7,* 271–311.

Braun, J. A., Jr., Fernlund, P., and White, C. S. (1997). *Technology Tools in the Social Studies Curriculum.* Wilsonville, OR: Franklin, Beedle and Associates.

Budin, H., Kendall, D. S., and Lengel, J. (1986). *Using Computers in the Social Studies.* New York: Teachers College Press.

Cooper, D. (1986). *Improving Reading Comprehension.* Boston: Houghton Mifflin.

Field, S. L. (1997). Content-focused software for the social studies. *Social Studies and the Young Learner,* 10 (November/December), 29–30.

Lee, J. F., and Pruett, K. W. (1979). Homework assignments: Classroom games or teaching tools, *Clearing House,* 53 (September), 31–35.

Slavin, R. E. (1987). *Cooperative Learning: Student Teams.* Washington, DC: National Education Association.

Turner, T. N. (1989). Using textbook questions intelligently. *Social Education,* 53 (January), 58–60.

Walberg, H. (1986). Synthesis of research in teaching. In Wittrock, M. (Ed.), *Handbook of educational research: A project of the American Educational Research Association* (3rd ed.). New York: Macmillan, 1986.

Watson, E. K., and Marsh, G. E. (1995). Social studies and the internet revolution. *Social Education,* 59 (April/May), 198–201.

Wilson, E. (2000). Virtual field trips and newsrooms: Integrating technology into the classroom. *Social Education,* 64(3) (April), 152–155.

REFERENCES: CHILDREN'S LITERATURE

Aliki. (1983). *A medieval feast.* New York: Crowell.

Aliki. (1979). *Mummies, made in Egypt.* New York: Crowell.

Forbes, Esther. (1943). *Johnny Tremain.* Boston: Houghton Mifflin.

Fritz, J. (1980). *Where do you think you're going, Columbus?* New York: Putnam.

Human story, The. (1987). Morristown, NJ: Silver Burdette.

Macaulay, D. (1977). *Castle—The story of its construction.* Boston: Houghton Mifflin.

Macaulay, D. (1973). *Cathedral.* Boston: Houghton Mifflin.

McLean, V. (1987). *Chasing the moon over China.* New York: Redbird.

Monjo, S. N. (1970). *The one bad thing about father.* New York: Harper and Row.

Spier, P. (1979). *People.* New York: Doubleday.

SUGGESTED READING

Helms, R. G. (1997). Exemplary World Wide Web resources. *Social Studies and the Young Learner,* 9 (January/February), pull-out section, p. 7.

James, M., and Zarillo, J. (1989). Teaching history with children's literature. *The Social Studies,* 80 (July/August), 153–158.

Jonassen, D. H., Carr, C., and Yueh, Hsiu-Ping. (1998). Computers as mindtools for engaging learners in critical thinking. *Tech Trends* (March), 24–33.

Kelly, R. (2000). Working with webquests: Making the web accessible to students with disabilities. *Teaching Exceptional Children* (July/August), 4–13.

McGowan, T., Guzzetti, B., and Kowalinski, B. (1992). Using literature studies to promote elementary social studies learning. *Social Studies and the Young Learner,* 5 (September/October), 10–13.

Means, B. (2000–2001). Technology use in tomorrow's schools. *Educational Leadership* (December/January), 57–61.

NCSS & Children's Book Council. (1997). Notable children's trade books in the field of social studies. *Social Education,* 61 (April/May), 1–15.

Risinger, F. (1999). Teaching social studies with the internet. ERIC Clearing House for Social Studies/Social Science Education. Available on the web at http://www.indiana.education/-ssdc/assintdig.htm.

Schneider, D. O., and Brown, M. M. (1980). Helping students study and understand their social studies textbooks. In Patten, W. E. (Ed.), *Improving the use of social studies textbooks.* Bulletin 63. Washington DC: The National Council for the Social Studies.

Slavin, R. (1987). Cooperative learning: Where behavioral and humanistic approaches to classroom motivation meet. *The Elementary School Journal,* 88 (September), 29–36.

7 Study, Map, Time, and Economic Skills: The Urge Is the Edge

LOOKING AHEAD

Information is only important if it can be put to use. Children often feel that they are asked to learn information for which they have no use at all. As a result of this and other factors, students do not always learn in school the skills they need to use information.

If the teacher's goal is for the students to become independent learners, and if the ability to solve problems is a major factor in that independence, then finding and analyzing information have to be viewed as critical tool skills. The focus of this chapter is on those skills that are needed to make the best use possible of information in every problems context. The chapter begins with general information skills and then moves on to two specific areas that have special importance to the social studies, map skills, and time skills.

CAN YOU? DO YOU?

Can You

- Identify several ways that you can stimulate curiosity in your students?
- Explain why map and globe skills are so difficult for children?

Do You

- Ever get the "Columbus urge" or have "Aha!" moments?
- Know that there are several kinds of memory?

- Know what a mnemonic device is?

- Know how children develop time and space concepts?

BUILDING THE DESIRE TO MASTER STUDY SKILLS

In elementary and middle school, children have to master some very complex and difficult information-processing skills. It is a tough task and a huge one. What makes the learning even more difficult is that children have to gain this skill mastery during a period when they are going through tremendous physical and emotional changes and facing stressful social changes. The majority of children in the world today are in stressful home situations and that complicates the mix. A growing number are "latchkey kids" on their own for hours after school. Many are from single parent homes. Many face physically or mentally abusive situations. Unemployment of parents, insufficient family income, or other major economic problems add to the insecurity.

There is an expression, "the urge gives you an edge." What it means is that the strong desire or wanting to do something well gives an individual a distinct advantage; it helps them to actually do well. Children often wonder about how they will ever use the learning that educators and parents are forcing upon them. It makes sense that the best opportunities that teachers have to help children acquire the kind of edge that the strong urge to learn will give them is when there are opportunities to put information to use. Learning to use knowledge is, after all, the heart of a problems approach. Once students learn that knowing information and how to get it is useful in solving real problems, it gives knowledge purpose.

Where teachers make a difference is in providing opportunities for the urge to grow. Teachers have to convince children that knowledge really does empower, because it can enable them to solve existing problems and anticipate and head off potential problems. If they come to believe this students learn because they need to know and want to learn, not because the teacher wants them to know. That "edge" has to be acquired early on, because learning to use information is not easy.

Children have to deal with information that comes from an array of sources, an almost endless variety of print and computer accessible materials. Not the most exciting of these materials or the easiest to handle is the textbook. More exciting, but sometimes requiring more interpretation, is other information that comes from technology or print in audio or visual forms, from artifacts and other objects, and directly from other people. Reading, observation, and listening skills as well as technological competencies are needed as the basis for study.

First and foremost, children need to be able to know where and how to find the information they need. As an accompanying processing skill, they have to be able to decide if information is true and accurate, relevant, important, and useful. Finally, they have to be able to remember, use, and present the information.

FINDING INFORMATION

Locating information requires a particular kind of mindset, and teachers can help students acquire it. Yes, they do have to learn about different kinds of resources and the type of information these resources contain. Mastery of accessing skills is needed too, as are using various types of indexes and tables of contents, computer menus, and search engines. Children need to be taught skimming and scanning skills. However, all of these things can be learned over time with effort if students develop the right mindset. I like to call that mindset the "Columbus urge." It is that irresistible desire to explore, to find out. Corny as the expression may sound, the "Columbus urge," which causes students to need the thrill of discovering and the sheer satisfaction of knowing that they know, transforms them into real self-starters. If children can acquire this one quality, they will be driven to learn all of the necessary skills that it takes to gather information.

The "Columbus urge" can only be encouraged, never created, by the teacher. Key teaching elements that contribute to its growth include teacher modeling an excitement about learning and developing a classroom that is a busy, exciting, stimulating place where provocative questions are constantly being asked and where tidbits of curious information of interest are constantly being unearthed and celebrated. You do not want to get too gimmicky, but here are a few ideas to develop the "Columbus urge."

- Regularly give children things to find out that really catch their interest and stir their curiosity. (Hints: You are going to have to find out about *their* culture and what interests them. You are likely to find that things like "firsts," "longests," "shortests," and "mosts" work consistently.)

- Leave questions dangling and unanswered and challenge them to find out.

- Model the excitement of researching and finding out.

- Celebrate when students discover solutions, making a big thing out of it.

- Challenge the children to come up with questions and curiositiies for you and for their classmates.

- Obtain and have children see and use as many interesting information sources as possible.

- Give children lots of opportunities to find information and then use it.

- Remember that "knowers" love to show off, so don't just let them; encourage them and even plan opportunities for them to do it.

- As a time filler, play the "I know something" game. In it the children try to discover what it is that the teacher, or someone else, knows. The children have to be trained to know that their first job is always to find out *where* the information can be found. (Is it in the dictionary? An atlas?)

- Have constantly changing displays and bulletin boards where students encounter people, actions, and things that are different and that create curiosity.

Last, yet far from least, among the classroom elements that the teacher can and must provide in order for children to develop their own "Columbus urge" is a structure which ensures students ownership in repeated successes. It is a fact of life that the greatest payoffs that self-motivated problem solvers experience are "Aha!" moments. These are those times when they actually feel the thrill of a breakthrough; a problem that they have worked on, that has eluded them, suddenly has a solution, the pieces of the puzzle fit together, the unexplainable makes sense. When a teacher can make these times of elation for students, then both have satisfaction.

Decision Making with Information

I like to give children lots of practice in decision making. I sometimes start with questions about how they distinguish things in the popular culture. Here, they are the experts. They know the differences and I, the teacher, do not. What makes a particular brand of toy different? How do you tell the differences among cartoon characters that, to me, look about the same? Playing stupid helps here, though I usually do not have to play, so I ask them about attributes of the toys or the characters that I know are not relevant but are, nonetheless, observable traits. *All* dalmatian puppies are white and black and little. *All* cars have four wheels. These are characteristics all right, but they do not help us tell things apart. With younger children who are very ego centered, I may go to the children themselves as examples. "Let's see why I like Bryan." "Is it because he's wearing a blue shirt?" You can easily see where this questioning would go. The important thing is that through it the children are learning that what may be important and relevant to one question, has no merit or use with another.

We also do a lot of listing of traits. This can be transferred to unit study. For example, if we are studying a country, a city, a state, or a geographic area, I like to make a list of the characteristics of the area with the children. I often do this as part of a "Would you like to live there?" activity. That way, we can have two columns, one of traits that make a difference and one of traits that do not. We can do a similar listing with historical people or current candidates for political office. We are just deciding different things, whether they did their jobs well, whether they are suited for office, and so on.

Once they have the idea, I move to some type of game activity. A favorite across grade levels is one I call "mysteries." These are multi-clue riddle activities and they can even be done in groups cooperatively. The number of clues and the difficulty I fit to the class. The idea is to reveal a series of clues one at a time, beginning with the hard clues that could apply to any number of possible answers and going to easier, more obvious ones. In some of these games, some clues may be irrelevant or unimportant.

Sorting activities also help children learn to distinguish relevance. One that I think works very well is called a *card sort*. The activity begins with a deck of cards with facts or single words written on them. Have labeled category boxes ready and sort the cards into these. After you have done this sorting a few times as a group discussion activity, it may be assigned with multiple decks as a cooperative group activity as well. After the groups finish, they can explain their logic. It is good to include cards that do not fit any category in the deck. Using concrete materials is good for similar sorts that can be done with large amounts of information with the proper computer software.

Remembering Information

In the social studies, students are required to remember information for three reasons. They have to understand and remember some information just long enough to work through a single lesson or class. Other information they are going to have to retain for a while longer, perhaps a few days, in order to do more extended, long-term assignments. Finally, there is information that teachers want them to remember over a long period of time. These three are referred to in various ways, but for our purposes let us use the terms, *working memory, long-term memory,* and *cumulative memory.* What we expect children to put in cumulative memory is usually related to what has been called *cultural literacy.* This term has gotten a lot of attention in education in recent years and is often used to describe what an "educated person" should know.

It is important to realize that all three types of memory are important. One of the teacher's jobs in the social studies is to help children learn how to decide what is important to remember and to distinguish whether information is needed for working-memory, long-term memory, or cultural literacy.

Part of the secret of getting students to remember information and ideas is to present that information to them in memorable ways. That means it has to be interesting, even exciting if possible. If you do not think this is important, think about the fact that children can tell all about a movie they saw, but remember nothing they read in a dull textbook. But emotional impact is not the only route to remembering information. Children have to learn that learning is sometimes work and requires a determined effort.

There are several ways that teachers can help their students learn and remember information.

- Work on a can-do attitude. This requires both encouragement and task control to keep the amount of information at a level that students can handle. Students need to feel confident that they can remember. (If they feel they cannot memorize something, their own prediction of failure will be one more hurdle to overcome.)

- Understanding precedes remembering. Yes, nonsense words can be memorized, but generally anyone is more likely to remember what they understand than what they do not understand.

- Talk with students about what they already know. If students can relate or associate information to their own experiences, it will make it easier for them to remember.

- Organize the information for them in a way that makes sense. Isolated pieces of information are often more difficult to remember than information that has patterns and structures that relate individual facts.

- Provide mnemonic devices for sets of information. Memory-jogging associations that are catchy and full of images really do work.

- Make memorizing work as much fun as possible. Play memory games and quick fun practices.

When it comes to reviewing for the purpose of remembering information of all types, the approach most often used is drill. But, watch out! Drill can be meaningless, boring, and totally useless as a learning activity. If children are tuning out mentally, they are not learning. This means that *YOU HAVE TO MAKE IT ENJOYABLE*. This can happen even if drill is the method. Even the rote learning drill can be so structured that it makes the fact that the children are learning mean something. A good drill is going to help the learner put the information into logical and meaningful structures. It will put the stuff together in a way that makes sense and seems useful. Equally important, the drill has to be one that the child will participate in fully. If children find the drill uncomfortable or boring, they will start tuning out, daydreaming, or thinking of other things. So, any and all gimmicks and games are welcome.

Generally, memories with positive happy associations are more vivid and lasting than those with negative associations. A drill is fun when everybody is getting the answers quickly and correctly. The students are also more likely to learn if they experience information with as many senses as possible repeatedly. Picture flash cards, actual associated objects, actions or movements, even odors can be part of a drill.

One of the best ways to make drill enjoyable is to turn it into a game. If it's going to work, a drill game has to be one that the children will enjoy and also one that covers the necessary information repeatedly. The best drill games are those that keep the majority of the children mentally engaged most of the time. Because more senses are involved, I like games that give the information in writing as well as orally. I also prefer small-group games with the children controlling the pacing, but this is not going to work for all teachers and classes.

Many commercial board games and card games as well as television game shows and sports activities are adaptable to fact-learning activities. Games do not have to ask questions about the facts. They simply have to get the children to see, say, and hear the information repeatedly. "Monopoly" or "Candyland" types of games can be adapted so that the various board spaces and playing pieces are labeled to represent historic or geographic facts related to a topic being studied. This will enable children to encounter these words and images over and over. Similarly, many common games played with cards can be fact-learning games with specially made cards.

TEACHING ABOUT MAPS AND GLOBES

The skills needed to use maps and globes depend on an extensive knowledge base regarding types of maps and their purposes, as well as knowledge and understanding of map conventions and symbols and of the nature of different land forms. To use these tools effectively one must know something of the structure, functions, and terminology of different types of maps and globes. Maps and globes are sources of information about the geographic world. From them we can learn about the location, size, and names of particular places, about the economy, about weather and climate, and about natural features. Maps and globes, in fact, provide important information that can help students understand their world and are tools for problem solving.

Choosing Maps and Globes to Use

We want to make children feel comfortable with maps and globes and to fascinate them with the kinds of information that they can find on them. We also want children to gain an understanding that different kinds of maps and globes can be used for different purposes. By the time they have reached the intermediate grades, if not before, children should be able to use maps and globes to answer questions and solve problems.

We can define a *globe* as a three-dimensional representation of the earth's surface or the surface of another astronomical body. A *map*, on the other hand, is a two-dimensional representation of an area. Because maps are flat, maps showing a very large area, such as the earth's surface, are going to be distorted from reality in some way.

It is important to choose maps and globes for classroom use wisely and carefully. Increasing numbers of maps can be found on the Internet and in computer programs. Obviously, since many of these sources are free and reproducible, some of the qualities listed below are not concerns. However, the capability of the teacher to enlarge, print, and use these maps effectively are issues of concern. To begin with, teachers need to keep in mind that the best map or globe for a particular lesson will depend on several factors, including

- The conditions under which it is going to be used

- The number of children who will be looking at it (e.g., whole class, small group, individual)

- The ability, background, and skill levels of the students

- The purpose(s) for which it is going to be used (i.e., the type of information that the map will need to show)

- The types of tasks that children are going to have to complete

In purchasing and collecting classroom maps and globes over time, teachers need to think about a number of things, especially the following:

- Relative cost

- Accuracy

- Readability

- Durability

- "Busy-ness" (For young children especially, maps need to contain minimal information.)

- "Mark-ability" (Maps on which you can write, draw, and erase are very useful in the classroom.)

- Store-ability (Teachers have limited space.)

- Usability (Maps must be useful for a variety of teaching purposes.)

Maps and Globes in the Primary Grades

Among the key geographic concepts that young children need to learn is what a map is. They begin learning the concept by working with very simple maps showing areas they can actually see. A map of the classroom or the scene shown in a sand table, or a map showing the location of items in a desk drawer, are examples of places to map.

Along with the concept *of* map, children need to get some concepts *about* maps. They need to learn that objects on a map have a directional relation to one another and that we have to turn a map a certain way if we are to follow it. They also need to learn that maps use symbols and that maps simplify and summarize a lot of information. They can learn all of this and more by making and then following maps of the school or playground or of places they visit on field trips. These experiences early on will also help them learn that maps show very real places and will teach them the importance of accurate depiction of relative size on a map.

Following are a few ideas for consideration that might help primary children learn more effectively from and about maps:

- Try to orient maps in a horizontal rather than a vertical position with young children because that is the way they see the world. This also prevents a confusing misconception that "North is up and south is down."

- Give children a lot of experiences with maps of places they can see, places they have actually been, and places they will and can visit.

- Give young children plenty of multisensory, manipulative experiences with maps (working with jigsaw puzzle maps, map outline and route tracing, feeling high and low places in relief maps, etc.) and, when manipulatives are used, opportunity to orally affirm things like place names and names of geographic features.

- Whenever place names are mentioned in reading stories, in class discussions, and so on, it only takes a minute to show them on maps and globes.

- Acquaint children with a variety of types of simple colorful maps, including pictographic maps, to make them aware of the map legends and symbols and to teach them that different maps show different types of information.

- Teach about scale, map distances, and direction experientially and at a developmental simple-to-complex pace.

- On a regular basis, have specific attainable but challenging objectives that relate to what children should learn about place location and geographic and map concept terminology.

Maps and Globes in the Intermediate Grades

Older children should be able to work with maps and globes containing differing amounts of information with increasing independence. As they spend more time learning about different cultures and regions, more and more information is presented to children in map form. By the time they have completed the elementary grades, children should be able to read, use, and make maps and globes in a way that shows mastery of the four basic map skills: (1) reading direction, (2) reading distance, (3) understanding map legends, and (4) orienting the map to the real world. They should be able to recognize and understand the purposes of the basic types of world-map projections and different thematic maps (rainfall, vegetation, product, etc.). Students at this level need to understand a number of terms related to maps and landforms.

Teachers at the intermediate grade level need to do map work carefully and often to develop map skills. Many of the guidelines that were suggested for younger children apply as well to the older ones.

- Never assume previous knowledge and skill in using maps without verifying that children really do possess that knowledge or skill.

- Ask questions in discussion and writing that require students to get information from maps and globes.

- Have several easy-to-play map location and jigsaw-map assembly games and activities available in the classroom and encourage their use during free time of any sort.

- Have plenty of activities such as treasure hunts and scavenger hunts, and mapping of field trips that involve *using* or following maps as a means of reaching particular objectives.

MAPS ARE TO USE

One of the reasons that children have trouble learning map skills is that the majority of map work they do in school is too often just a series of questions and tasks for which the children see no purpose. They really need to be exposed to maps in ways that seem meaningful and purposeful to them.

It seems amazing that we teach map skills without having students really use maps in the ways that adults do. Adults find they *need to use* maps. They really need them, and use them for a variety of reasons: to find out where they are going or how to get there; to find alternate routes when there is some problem with the original; to help them decide about a new job; to locate a friend or relative; to find their way around some place they are visiting; to make business decisions that require a knowledge of distance and routes; to consider distance to supplies, equipment, or marketing; to determine the weather's effect on their travel; and to determine meeting places, etc. In short, adults use maps to plan, to understand, to solve problems, and to dream about their world. Unfortunately, the teaching of map skills to children contains too little of this. Map skills are taught in a way that says to students that maps are to look at; to answer questions from worksheets; and sometimes to color, draw on, or mark. Children fail to discover that maps are useful items and that they can help in real-life activities.

This appears to cause any number of problems relating to sequential development of skills and concepts. One of these problems is that students tend to see map work as lacking in purpose. A second is that they never really learn to use maps to find specific information or to follow routes.

Following are 10 map-*using* activities in which children can participate and from which they can learn how maps can be used. "Map-using Activities" is a descriptive title for this type of exercise. It includes any method by which students experience relating maps to physical space or in relating maps to problems involving that space. To be effective, such activities should be perceived by students as having sensible purposes and should involve short-term, specific tasks that are tightly structured.

1. Map-Reading Scavenger Hunt

The scavenger hunt taxes the students' abilities to follow directions given on a map or in a set of written directions accompanying a map. It is an adaptation of the gaming sport of orienteering. Groups of students are asked to find a treasure by following a precise routine in the shortest possible time.

Each group is equipped with a compass, a meter stick (think metric), and a set of directions or a map showing them their route to and location of one portion of their own team's treasure map. Each group's route is different from those of all the others. The teacher will need to prepare in advance a treasure map or set of directions for each team. The treasure maps or directions are each cut or torn into sections and each section put into a separate capped plastic bottle or a can with a tight sealing lid. This enables the teacher to place the containers in advance without worry about weather damage. Of course, they cannot be set out too far ahead of time. Chance discovery and removal can happen too easily. The cans or bottles of all teams should be indistinguishable from one another. However, the maps inside might be color coded by team so as to be recognizable when discovered. The containers are then hidden in a pattern shown on the map or described in the directions. The sets of directions are written so that the discovery of one container gives a new set of directions leading to another. A team may, by following its own map, discover all of its own map pieces or directions. The activity should be monitored and any group that opens another team's container simply because it is discovered and not by following the map should be penalized by adding time (say, 1 minute). Teams are staggered in starting, but turns are recorded. The team completing the map in the shortest time wins.

2. Site Stakeout

For site stakeouts students are divided into groups of six to ten. If possible, work with one group at a time and keep accurate record of the time it takes that group to complete the task and any errors corrected or help needed. Each group is assigned a different site. Sites may be such things as castles, forts, museums, public buildings (e.g., city hall, the school, jail or prison), typical small frontier towns, factories, or colonial farms. Groups are given sketch map drawings showing their own site in detail. Other information about activities on the site is also provided. The group's job is to "stake" its own site by outlining the perimeter and interior features as accurately as possible. Each group uses string and small wooden or plastic stakes (clothespins work well, too). Stakes are driven into the ground and string stretched between the stakes. All groups show such things as dimensions, relative size, and so on. All parts of the site are labeled corresponding to diagram labels. Upon completion, the staked-out sites are evaluated on the basis of their accuracy, the time elapsed in completing the stakeout, and the amount of adult assistance required.

3. Orienteering Scavenge

For the orienteering scavenge some advance work will need to be done. Cooperation is needed among several people in the school and community. It is also recommended that an adult volunteer be recruited to accompany each team of children. The initial task is to identify places in the community, students' homes, places of business, offices, and so on, simply on the basis of the willingness of people in these places to participate in helping the students learn. A map of the community is drawn indicating by a number each of the places where a cooperating person is to be found. No names of people or place titles are listed on the map.

Each team is given a copy of the map and an order in which they are to visit each place. The order is indicated only by the number. (The order of the places is different for all teams.) Teams are sent out at five-minute intervals. Their job is to use the map to find, in *proper order,* the places listed on their directions. At each stop, the team records the name of the person or the location and the time of arrival. The teams must get a verifying signature from the cooperating person at the site. (They may wear badges or caps if there are several people about.) The objective for each group is to finish all scheduled stops in the *correct order* on a timed schedule (or in the shortest possible time).

4. Fantasy School Map

The fantasy school map activity is designed to help children understand the concepts of miniaturization or symbolism as they apply to maps. It is a map-making activity in which students try to translate a part of the world onto a map. Imagination and policing are needed, but it can be well worth the effort in terms of practical learning. The amount of space used may vary. A large area, such as a cafeteria, gymnasium, or playground, is best. Students imagine that the area used for the map is a part of some larger, distant geographic area. For example, it might be seen as an area of the gold fields of California, a township in the Northwest Territory, an area of land being opened for homesteading, a feudal manor, a Roman military encampment, or a contemporary community in any country.

It should be pointed out that the size of the actual area being imagined would be much larger than the actual space used. The first job of the group of children is to arrange and label the features of the area. Existing furnishings should be incorporated. A chair may be used to symbolize a building, a bookcase may be a mesa, and so on. But added features may be created simply by labeling sheets of paper. The students then map the area they have laid out.

5. Best Route

Best route involves studies in using maps to determine the best way to get from one place to another. For this activity students are put into small groups. Each group has a map of the local community around the school and a list of jobs to do. The tasks may simply be finding specific purchasable items (students need not buy, only locate where items may be purchased) or finding the best prices or set of items to deliver. But jobs could also include involvement in volunteer citizenship activities at several locations, community improvement or helping elderly or disabled individuals in which students actually do the work.

Each group is to determine the most efficient route for performing the tasks and the time it will take to complete those tasks. Groups go *together* and will need to use the map. They must anticipate delaying factors (such as hills or unmarked construction sites, heavily trafficked roads where crossing may be difficult or even incur backtracking) and keep in mind such effort and time influencing such factors as distances to carry heavy loads. A route plan and estimated time for each stop have to be submitted before the trip is taken. Afterwards, students can discuss alternative, better routes and factors influencing how well their plans worked.

6. Map Labeling

Provide students with an unlabeled map of a familiar area and have them fill in the labels. The location may be one seen and traveled regularly, such as some part of a local neighborhood or one visited one or more times. If the latter is used, informing students before the actual trip can improve observation.

7. Where Does It Come From?

Divide students into groups. Each group is given a world map and a list of 10 products, 10 animals, or 10 plants. Using reference books, the group must determine locations where the items on their list may be found. They then must chart the shortest possible route for obtaining them.

8. Shortest Route to the Habitat

Give the students a list of 10 animals and ask them to pretend that they have been commissioned to return each animal to its natural environment. Have students discover the shortest distance that these animals may be taken by plane to a safe habitat which is similar to the one in which they are naturally found. The catch is that they cannot carry animals beyond a specified total weight *or* animals that are natural enemies on the same trip. The list of animals should include some relatively heavy ones, some that are prey, and some that are predators.

9. Mapping a School Activity

Have students make and use a school and school grounds map to set up plans for a school activity. These might be a school carnival (with specific locations for all attractions), a walking field trip (with specific places of interest noted), a class party, parents' night, or open house.

10. Story Maps

Have students do story maps as book reports. A *story map* charts the geographic areas used as settings for the book. Inferences and direct statements of the author about relative distances, landmarks, and features are used by students; movements of protagonists and other characteristics can also be charted. Interior as well as exterior maps may be made. Fantasy and realistic stories set in fictitious places may be mapped almost as easily as those whose settings are real places.

A caution and guideline: Depending on school policy, these activities may be designed in such a way that they take students around the neighborhood for variety and interest. Local school policies, community cooperation, and the neighborhood will be determining factors in deciding if and how to use orientating approaches. Parent or other adult volunteers are essential precautions for many. However, simple adaptations may be all that is needed to use some such activities within school grounds.

TIME CONCEPTS AND SKILLS

Children are very aware of time. Developing time concepts and skills not only helps them understand history, but it enables them to better understand the events in their own lives. Their awareness of time and time words should become more and more specific as they progress through the elementary grades.

Time understanding for children begins with a mixture of vague and precise time references in their lives and in the language around them that is most likely to be confusing. For example, when someone says "in a second" or "in a minute," they do not mean precisely 1 or 60 seconds. In fact, the reference, in a child's experience, might have meant several hours and is no more precise than the very uncertain "in a little while." Other seemingly precise time references also have had a wide range of meaning to children. Tomorrow may have meant just that, or it may be a word used for when something was not going to happen for days if at all. Part of the job of the school is to help children clarify and distinguish both the vague references and the more precise ones.

Children's Understanding of Time

The following description of each stage of children's understanding of time is based on Thornton and Vukulich (1988).

Age (in Years)	Stage Description
3–5	Capable of sequencing daily events, can rank order family members by age
6–8	Develop the ability to use "historical numbers" to represent the past; can sometimes match dates with major events (e.g., Christmas is December 25)
9–11	Become capable of matching persons and events with textbook descriptions (e.g., colonial period)
12–14	Able to use time classifications with increasing ease (e.g., decade)

As children grow in their understanding of and ability to deal with time, they begin to have increasingly more precise reference points on the clock, the calendar, in their own history, and in the histories of different elements in their world. They begin to understand that one of the ways to understand time is to visualize time passage as space distance. Visualizations through a variety of types of time lines help children to better see events in relation to one another. In the process, children begin to learn

- The meanings of time and calendar words

- The precise meaning of time words used in the measurement of time (second, minute, hour, day, week, month, year, decade, century, millennium, etc.) and that some of these words are used with indefinite meanings as well

- How time is sometimes represented by distance (time lines including calendars and some clocks)

- How to use clocks

- Ways of using calendars

- How to use different types of time lines

- That events occur in sequence and knowing this sequence can be useful

- That the relation of events to one another is sometimes a function of the times that each occurs

- What the relationships of particular events are

Children learn about time by developing meaningful reference points. The schedule for the school day is one of the major devices used to learn about clocks and acquire shorter time references. Scheduled events at school and outside of school as well as the so-called Holiday Curriculum are the major means through which children learn about the calendar. Multisensory experiences that add meaning to events and associate their occurrence with dates help children remember the time and place of the events.

A calendar is one of the earliest time lines that young children are exposed to both in and out of school. Kindergarten or early primary teachers, for example, often use the space above eye level on all four walls of the classroom to make an "in-the-round" pictorial calendar. On it they show the seasons, the months, the weeks, and the days. Particular events are given particular attention. School starting might rate a picture of the school, birthdays a child's name and picture or a crown, holidays some picture or symbol. Such a time line not only teaches time concepts including the cyclical nature of the year, but also develops self-concepts.

Learning about the relationship of events and people through time lines continues with many different possible activities. Examples include:

- Having children make a personal time line of their own lives. This can be illustrated with drawings, photos, and/or cut-out magazine pictures showing themselves, their families, their interests, and the events of their lives. This may require taking time with each child to help them recognize, remember, and reconstruct what has been important to them.

- Have children line up according to birthday.

- Let each child do a stair-step family time line tracing one strand of his or her forbearers.

  _____ GREAT-GREAT G.M.

  _____ GREAT G.M.

  _____ GRANDMOTHER

  _____ MOTHER

  _____ ME

- Help students do human time lines in which each individual represents events and historical people. Chalk marks or masking tape on the floor can show precisely measured distances to represent decades, centuries, etc. Costume creation and reporting-type activities can be added to make it even more fun.

- Human time lines can be used to represent events relating to one another during a relatively brief period of time (e.g., events surrounding the break up of the Soviet Union), the time relations of different people or events (e.g., inventions that changed our lives), or the relationship of several important events over a broad span of history.

- Make clothesline time lines. Have the children add events as they are talked about, clipping the new events to the time line using a squeeze clothes pin.

- Give children in groups of three or four a deck of cards each labeled as a different holiday. Have children experiment sorting and ordering the holidays in different ways, including chronological order.

ECONOMIC SKILLS

Economic skills that children begin to learn in elementary school have to do mostly with their roles as consumers. However, they also need to learn something about how producers and others operate. Among the economics concepts and skills that children need to learn to use are the following:

- Different types and values of money

- How to manage their own money and time

- How businesses and governments use money and time

- What are needs and wants and how do we tell the difference

- What is meant by such concept terms as value, cost, and price

- The relative costs/values of different goods and services

- How to do comparative shopping

- How and why exchange occurs

- The skills needed for using bank accounts

- What credit is and how it works (including what interest is)

Situational scenarios and hypothetical problems related to economics can be created and used at almost any level. Even in kindergarten economic thinking can be part of many types of learning centers set up in the classroom: kitchen centers, post office centers, building construction centers, and so on. Children of all ages like and learn from trading and swapping activities, which can provide an experiential basis for discussion of relative merit and relative value. Many commercial games, perhaps the best known being "Monopoly" and "Pit," involve swapping activity and can be the basis for classroom activity.

1. Teachers can make up card decks related to particular units. On each card, an item of property related to the unit can be listed. When cards are distributed, students can have a trading period. The follow-up should relate to issues such as scarcity and abundance, the costs of production and transportation at the place and time of the unit, and other factors relating to the trades.

2. At a small cost to the teacher or perhaps with items from a school sponsor, the teacher may set up a "store." Students, over a period of time,
can "work" for "store money," which they can exchange for items on a
given day.

3. Student groups can be set up as countries with sets of resources and
needs. The game involves exchanging their resources for what they need.

4. Card decks can be created with suits of cards based on items of values.
Card games can involve exchange with the purpose of getting a monopoly by collecting complete suit of one item.

Lots of commercial games deal with banking, budgeting, and with
using and conserving resources. The teacher needs to find out which of
these the students are familiar with, extend their experiences with these
games, and help them to understand what these games teach. Beyond the
commercial games, numerous valuable classroom activities are possible.
Class banks can be set up with accounts involving checks, balances, and
other factors. Income and expenses can be assigned. The whole experience
then can be used as the basis for discussion. Students can deal with pretend shopping lists for events like Thanksgiving or other holiday meals
and make a visit to a grocery store to cost out their lists. Field trips to banks
and businesses may be valuable. They can be urged to ask questions to di-
rectors of zoos, hospitals, and other enterprises about their own expenses
and budgets. Students can deal with hypothetical budgets for families in
any period of history or in any culture being studied.

Activities that can build economic skills should be carefully planned
to suit the level of ability and the interests of the students. The following is
a list of a few possible activity types:

- Planning dream vacations

- Practicing at exchanging play money representing different values or
different currencies of countries

- Price-following activities and games (e.g., stock market, home prices,
automobile prices, etc.) over time

LOOKING BACK

Well-developed study skills give students a winning advantage, an edge,
when it comes to learning tasks or success in life. The most important
study skills include knowing how to find necessary information, being able
to make decisions about information, and being able to organize and remember information. Some study skills are specifically associated with the
social studies because they relate to one or more of the social sciences. One

of these is reading and using maps and globes. Students are more likely to develop map competency if they are exposed to many experiences interacting with maps, map problems, and problems that involve using maps. The maps used in these experiences need to be simple and purposeful. The experiences themselves should teach about distance, direction, scale, and map symbols at a developmentally appropriate level. Maps should be used purposefully in the classroom with a variety of applied map-reading and map-making activities. It should be stressed that maps can be fun and there should be an abundance of map games and other activities that children enjoy doing. Time skills also require concrete hands-on activities with concrete materials which expand the child's awareness of the time relationships among events. Lots of experiences with clocks, calendars, and other forms of time lines can help students to understand the abstractions of these time relationships.

This is a society in which the development of economic skills is essential to survival. Children need experiences in dealing with money and exchange as well as a growing understanding of credit, banking, budgeting, and economic planning, at a personal level as well as for communities up to the size of nations.

SELF-TEST

1. What are some ways to create the "Columbus urge" in children?

2. Why is it sometimes said that the social studies are information based?

3. What are some things a teacher can do to help children learn essential information?

4. What is a mnemonic device?

5. What is the difference between a map and a globe?

6. What are some guidelines for using maps and globes in the primary grades?

7. Why is it important to teach maps in a way that involves maps as tools of problem solving?

8. What are some of the time concepts that children need to learn?

REFERENCES

Thornton, S. J., and Vukulich, R. (1988). Effects of children's understanding of time concepts on historical understanding. *Theory and Research in Social Education,* 16 (Winter), 69–82.

SUGGESTED READING

Baumgartner, D., Donahue, M., and Bryan, T. (1998). Homework: Planning for success. *Teaching Pre-K–8*, 29(3) (November/December), 52–54.

Cooper, H. (2001). Homework for all–in moderation. *Educational Leadership* (April), 34–38.

McClure, J. (1989). Practical map examinations for geography. *The Social Studies*, 80 (July/August), 159–162.

Muir, S. P., and Cheek, H. N. (1991). Assessing spatial development: Implications for map skill instruction. *Social Education*, 55 (September), 316–319.

Rae, C. (1990). Before the outline-the writing wheel. *The Social Studies*, 81 (July/August), 178–180.

Schulze, M. (1996). Students as map makers: Creating Coropleth Maps. *Journal of Geography*, 95 (July/August), 168–170.

Turner, T. N. (1990). *Brainstorms*. Glenview, IL: Scott Foresman.

Young, T., and Schiene, V. (1992). Writing to learn in social studies. *Social Studies and the Young Learner*, 5 (September/October), 14–16.

8 Teaching Thinking and Problem Solving

LOOKING AHEAD

In a democratic society, developing students' ability to think, to learn for themselves, and to solve problems are all critical goals. The ultimate aim is to develop students who are independent learners who do not need a teacher as motivator and guide. Embodied in this goal is the notion that effective teachers allow, encourage, and challenge students to understand what they need to know, learn how to find information they need, and know when to search, where to search, and what to search for. If the development of independent learners is truly the goal of education, then it is more important to teach children how to think than it is to teach them what to think.

Thinking skills have been an increasing concern in the social studies. The National Commission on the Social Studies (NCSS) Task Force on Scope and Sequence (1984) asserted that, "Social studies programs have a responsibility to prepare young people to identify, understand, and work to solve problems that face our increasingly diverse nation and interdependent world" (p. 251). A later NCSS Task Force on Early Childhood/Elementary Social Studies focused on cooperative problem solving, claiming that basic skills in reading, writing, and computing were necessary but not sufficient if children are to survive in today's world. Critical thinking and the development of positive attitudes toward self and others were given priority status in this report (1989).

That same year, the NCSS, funded by the Carnegie Foundation, the Rockefeller Foundation, the MacArthur Foundation, and the National Geographic Society, and sponsored by NCSS and the American Historical Association, published a report that had been two years in preparation, titled *Charting a Course: Social Studies for the 21st Century* (1989). Among the curricular goals outlined in that report was the development of a critical understanding of the history, geography, economic, political, and social institutions, traditions, and values of the United States as expressed in both their unity and diversity, and development of critical attitudes and analytical perspectives appropriate to analysis of the human condition. Later standards have voiced similar concerns.

Presentation-style social studies, where the teacher does most of the talking, is not likely to develop children's thinking skills. Such skills require that students be involved and participate in the learning process. This means that discussion, teacher questioning, and carefully constructed assignments are very important.

CAN YOU? DO YOU?

Can You

- Tell three ways that teachers teach children to think logically?

- Identify some functions of the mind that relate to critical thinking?

- Distinguish among several different kinds of problem-solving tasks?

Do You

- Know how teachers can help children to understand and remember information?

- Know what a story map is?

FOCUS ACTIVITY

Student Decision Making in Your Class

Examine the kinds of decisions listed below. Think about various examples that you have seen and experienced as a student, observer, and teacher. How much of the decision-making power do you think ought to be in the hands of the students? To what extent does the teacher need to control and/or limit the decisions? Generally speaking, put a check in the appropriate block, then draw a line connecting the checks. What does the general pattern indicated by this line tell you about your willingness to relegate decisions to your students? How does this relate to developing students as problem solvers and as independent learners? What do you think that this says about your commitment toward developing independent learners? Who would make the decisions in your classroom?

DECISION TYPE	THE TEACHER	THE TEACHER BASED ON CLASS DISCUSSION	THE CLASS OR GROUPS WITHIN IT WITH TEACHER "VETO" POWER	THE CLASS OR GROUPS WITHIN IT WITH TEACHER GUIDANCE	THE STUDENTS INDIVIDUALLY OR AS INDIVIDUALS CHOOSING FROM TEACHER-PROVIDED CHOICES	THE STUDENTS INDIVIDUALLY OR AS GROUPS FROM SELF-GENERATED CHOICES
Deciding what unit topics they should study.						
Deciding the focus of units studied.						
Following personal interest and curiosity.						
What types of projects and reports should be done in a unit.						
What should be given for homework.						
Deciding what report topics they will do.						
What they should be evaluated and tested on.						
What particular books they should read.						
What materials to use for a report or project.						
The format of group reports.						
Determining class rules.						
Determining consequences for breaking class rules.						

THE THINKING SKILLS OF OBSERVING, LISTENING, AND COMPREHENDING

When we use the term "thinking skills," we usually refer to an array of mental processes involving remembering information and ideas, processing that information, and then using it to solve problems. We sometimes forget that thinking is part of the process of gaining information through observing, listening, and reading. We use these abilities in the gathering of information. The skills of gathering information are of particular concern to us as teachers. In fact, the recent evidence that many children and adults learn more easily through one sense than through others has caused us to revise and extend our approaches to include more multisensory learning materials. Research and experience also inform us that learning to listen and to observe purposefully are trainable skills that can be acquired and improved through directed, structured practice over time.

We need to look at two different ways of learning. The first, we usually call *rote learning*. Rote learning means that information is memorized with little or no understanding of its meaning. For example, you may have learned a nonsense poem or song at some point in your life or learned to spell and pronounce words and had no idea of their meaning. Rote learning does not provide us with useful information, because if we have no idea of the meaning of what we have learned, we cannot conceive how to put it to use.

The second and more important way of learning begins with our understanding what we learn. The more "sense" we can make of something, the more it fits into patterns and stories in our minds, the more likely we are to remember it. In previous chapters we have talked about constructivism, the theory which explains that people come to understand new ideas and information by relating it to previous experiences. From a constructivist point of view, the way that new information is presented may be as important or even more important as the information itself, because it will determine how we make sense of the information or give it meaning. The quest to develop children as problem solvers in the social studies can be traced at least to the beginning of the twentieth century when a few innovative schools began to look at a life-centered problems approach as central to the curriculum. Beginning in the 1960s and 1970s, the notion of learning to learn became crucial to every social studies program as an approach called the *inquiry method* was widely advocated. The inquiry classroom differed from traditional classrooms. The student was supposed to learn to ask questions, not just answer them. The teacher's role became less that of information provider and more that of coach and guide.

The term "thinking skills" refers to all of the mental processes that individuals use to obtain, make sense of, and retain information, as well as how they process and use that information as a basis for solving problems. The process of taking in the information likewise involves thinking skills, especially those related to observing, listening, and reading. Obtaining information and ideas is a sensory process and all of the senses are used in information gathering. Bcause there is substantial evidence that for many children and adults learning is easier through one sense than the others, teachers need to utilize multisensory learning materials wherever possible. Even so, learning to listen and observe purposefully are trainable skills acquired through directed, disciplined practice. Therefore, teachers need to help children acquire these important skills in a systematic and developmental way.

A term used to describe relating new ideas to experiences is *schema.* Schemata (the plural) are the various ways that we group ideas and knowledge in our minds. Our best chance at understanding new concepts is to tie features of those concepts to one or more of these schemata. To do this, we look for similarities, make assumptions, create analogies, and generally relate information to ourselves.

Another factor in comprehension is *metacognition,* an individual's awareness of his or her own thinking processes and of the thinking processes of the people with whom he or she is communicating. The term has come to be used to describe a person's awareness and understanding of the organizational patterns of reading material and of speakers. Research seems to support the notion that individuals who are able to form clear and accurate story maps of reading material or spoken material have a clearer overall understanding of that material. This, in turn, helps them to understand the meaning of specific parts of the communication as it relates to the organization and purposes.

To maximize student understanding teachers should provide story maps for students before they listen to, read, or view material. In effect, this means that teachers need to provide both sensitive and clear overviews of oral presentations, audiovisual programs, and reading material before students are exposed to it. Then, too, pointed reflective review of material will also help students develop their metacognitive skills. This may, in part, be why the body of research and experience in teaching has already demonstrated that such reviews increase learning and retention in a clearly measurable way. Such reviews generally involve teacher questioning, so that students become intellectually involved and, therefore, active in forming clearer cognitive maps of material covered.

Generally, teachers can help children to understand and remember information by following a few simple principles.

- Associate the new information with experiences that the children have had in the past.

- Connect each piece of new information to other pieces of information using a pattern that children can follow. (Sensory or visualizable patterns are best.)

- Repeat the information and the patterns often.

- Provide a shared purpose or use for the learning.

- Give opportunities for practice with feedback.

LOGICAL THINKING AND ANALYZING SKILLS

In the social studies, teachers can help children gain logical thinking and analyzing skills in at least three ways: by modeling, through discussion, and through guided practice with feedback. Purposeful guided tasks and teacher questions are important in logical thinking skills such as the following:

Thinking Skill	Type of Activity
Interpreting or explaining	Paraphrasing, rephrasing
Relating information to self	Advanced organizers for reading assignments
Applying previous knowledge	Charting, drawing parallels
Identifying implicit assumptions	Discussion of motives
Identifying key features and characteristics	Defining, describing, giving background
Summarizing and synthesizing	Writing summaries, reviewing, giving closure to lessons
Comparing and contrasting	Identifying attributes, pattern finding
Organizing information	Outlining, sequencing
Classifying and categorizing	Charting, sorting
Inferencing and concluding	Cause and effect exercises, following clues, guessing games, problem solving
Determining truth, accuracy, completeness, reliability	Cross checking, maps of errors, peer evaluation

CRITICAL AND CREATIVE THINKING

Someone has said that the chief dilemma of teaching is to show students where to look without telling them what to see. Helping students learn to think logically should lead them to critical and creative thought processes, not show them what to think. The teacher wants the student to be able to make informed decisions based on the information available and to have the ability and the mindset needed to come up with multiple and original ideas as solutions to problems.

Critical thinking can be defined as making evaluations or judgments of experience. When evaluation is based on analysis, as it normally is, then critical thinking involves often complex logical reasoning. Critical thinking requires comparing a personal set of experiences and values to current experiences, newly encountered data, and decision- and judgment-demanding situations. We think critically whenever we try to reason out decisions or judgments.

Critical thinking relates to some very important functions of the mind.

- **The symbolic process:** We allow words, numbers, and other symbols to stand for ideas.

- **Visualization:** We make mental pictures that represent our perceptions.

- **Characterization:** We notice the qualities of things and that which we notice, in turn, builds our perceptions of likes and differences.

- **Classification:** We sort things into classes, types, families, and so on.

- **Structure analysis:** We notice how things are made and break classes into component parts.

- **Operations analysis:** We notice how things happen, successive stages, and so on.

- **Paralleling:** We see how situations are alike.

Creative thinking also requires evaluative thinking as well as other abilities. Creative thinkers come up with new ideas, new ways of looking at things, and different ways of synthesizing or combining existing ideas. They see several logics possible in solving problems and also are open to illogical methods. They are not so much looking for *the* solution to a problem or answer to a question, as they are trying to see various possibilities. Part of the creative mindset is a fluency and flexibility of thought. Creativity implies originality, the ability to come up with unique and unconventional approaches. But good creative thinkers follow through with the same openness, having the ability to develop and elaborate ideas in solving problems. Creative thinking is what we need when we try to find new and different ways of solving both new problems that we have never encountered before and older ones that have remained without satisfactory solution. Though it would be an oversimplification to say that creative thinking is the ability to solve problems, that ability is at least a focus of creative thinking. Creative thinking differs from most thought required in school chiefly because of its emphasis on alternative approaches and solutions and on multiple solutions.

PROBLEM SOLVING AND INQUIRY

Problem solving most often begins with a situation that demands a solution or a response. For a true problem to exist there can be no already defined answer or process for arriving at an answer available. A creative problem-solving experience is one where the individual has to figure out both what to do and how to do it. Creative problem solving, as it relates to the social studies, can involve any one of the following thinking difficulties:

- Dealing with a negative or difficult situation

- Overcoming an obstacle

- Bringing about some desired outcome

- Bringing about change

In order to understand and use information, we must be able to put that information into a variety of logical structures. As this skill develops, it involves curious playfulness and a willingness to experiment with different ways of ordering and different ways of looking at information. As we learn to do this, we learn to identify relationships and patterns, to put information from different sources together, to make inferences and judgments, to recognize qualities such as relative importance, relevance, and usefulness, and to differentiate among degrees of partial, convincing, decisive, and conclusive evidence.

The most critical issue in problem solving is the ability to recognize and identify what the real problems are. Once the real critical problems are clearly and specifically identified, ways to find solutions are more easily determined.

Inquiry teaching models since that time have used variations of the "scientific method." Most of us learned some version of this method in science sometime between seventh grade and high school. The scientific method is simply a sequence of the steps involved in any research. Following is one of the ways of describing the scientific method.

Sense the problem (beginning with a doubt or uncertainty)

Define the problem

Come up with some hypotheses (possible solutions to the problems)

Gather evidence

Draw conclusions

Inquiry has proven itself to be far more than an educational fad. It has changed the way we look at teaching social studies and has provided problem-solving tools which continue to be useful in teaching children to become independent thinkers and problem solvers. One contribution of the inquiry approach has been the development of a variety of teachable creative problem-solving strategies. These strategies were conceived with the problem that defies solution in mind, and they can be learned easily through experiences in which the teacher models them in discussion formats with specific problems. The following are among the most successful of these strategies for approaching difficult problems:

- Restate the problem. Simply putting a problem into different words may make it more understandable and, therefore, more solvable. It gives the problem solver a fresh perspective.

- Segment the problem. Dividing the problem in some way, whether into identifiable components or simply into smaller pieces, is a most useful strategy. Divided, the problem can be attacked as a cooperative learning task by a group or can be dealt with one piece at a time.

- Try solving tangential problems. Look at the impact of the problem and identify side effects. Work on solving these relatively minor problems and they may provide a key to the central problem.

- Look for analogies to the problem and try solving these analogous problems. For example, if we said that our polluted rivers are similar to clogged arteries and then looked at the solutions doctors suggest for clogged arteries, it may help us identify remedies for the rivers.

- Reduce the problem. If we try to say the problem in the minimum number of words and as simply as possible, then we may understand its essence more fully and be better able to solve it.

The best way to get children to become active problem solvers is to give them lots of problems to solve. These do not have to be, and probably should not be, the brain-teaser type. Real life problems are more effective. The teacher needs to treat situations in the classroom as problem-solving activities.

As a teacher, I have often given my students a set of guidelines like the following. When we encountered problems, it was often stimulating to their thinking to lead them through the list and ask students for their thoughts about the problem in relation to each of the guidelines. The fact that every guideline did not apply to every problem was an important point to make in the discussion.

1. The best way to get super ideas is to get *lots* of ideas and then throw away the ones that aren't so great.

2. Write down your ideas before you forget them (within 5 minutes).

3. Begin with the obvious and then look for more than one right answer.

4. Ask questions, even dumb questions.

5. Remember that nearly all words have several meanings.

6. Visualize the problem. See it backwards, forwards, inside out, and all mixed up.

7. Ask how nature would solve the problem.

In these discussions, I always attempted to tolerate and even encourage the offbeat and to keep the controls and the classroom atmosphere relaxed. I also tried to help children realize that the true secret of problem solving is perseverance.

Types of Problem-Solving Tasks

Once children learn to recognize and verbally describe problems, they need to learn to identify critical elements within these problems. Recognizing the presence of patterns and features in a problem may signal a possible way of solving it. A problem of a particular type can be approached in much the same way as other problems of that type. Knowing the elements of a problem, then, may be of enormous help in identifying and using the most promising approach. Once the approach is identified, following a series of steps used in similar problems will often lead to a solution. Following are a few of the approaches that can be used as models for children. Each relates to problems of a particular type. Sample activities are given with each approach.

1. *Approaching problems that require looking at all related factors and issues involved:* In these problem-solving strategies, the emphasis is on the nature of problems that have multiple possible answers. The approach is one that is effective for complex problems for which there is no perfect set of right answers. The actual number of possible answers will vary with such problems. However, the problem solvers' task includes defining criteria for examining the appropriateness of answers. The total answer set that the problem solvers identify can be judged in so far as it takes into account those criteria or factors. Examples of this approach follow.

- **Pilgrims' Progress:** If you were embarking with the early Puritans or Pilgrims who came to settle New England, what sort of supplies would you take with you? Make a list that includes necessities as well as other things you might like to have. Remember that this is the 1600s. What kinds of supplies are going to be available, and what things simply will not. Think about the kind of place that you are going to and the kind of place you are coming from.

- **Invention Brainstorm:** Suppose we put the word *invention* in the middle of the paper. Now let us think of other words that represent related ideas; we will place these words all around the page and connect the ones that are related to one another with lines.

2. *Approaching problems that focus on setting priorities:* Prioritizing is a lifelong problem. There are always too few resources, time, money, or goods for the demands. Individuals, communities, and nations continually have to decide which needs and wants to meet first. Prioritizing problems in the social studies usually involves looking at lists of equipment or provisions as

they relate to a particular problem or being faced with a series of problems in a given situation and having to decide in what order these problems need to be solved, based on immediacy, importance, or a combination of the two. Following is an example of a problem-solving task of the second type.

• **Shipwreck Rescue:** You are the commander of a sailing ship bringing new colonists and supplies to the New World in the seventeenth century. Your ship has been caught in a terrible storm as you approach the coast. You have been unable to keep the ship from going aground on the rocky shore. The storm still is raging all about and may at any moment either wash you out to sea or break the ship into pieces. The water rushing all around is only about six feet deep and you can see a solid beach perhaps a hundred yards away. Here are all the problems that you must handle. Number them according to the order in which you think they need to be handled. Suggest a solution for each.

  • _____ Sharp rocks can be seen dead ahead.

  • _____ There is a gaping hole in the hull and some water is rushing in.

  • _____ You fear that hostile natives may inhabit this area of the coast.

  • _____ The food supplies are in the hold, which is fast filling with water.

  • _____ The crew members are unhappy and are arguing among themselves.

  • _____ One of the ship's cannons has broken loose and is careening across the deck.

  • _____ A woman on board is about to give birth.

  • _____ A small fire has broken out in the ship's kitchen.

  • _____ One of the ship's masts has been broken by the storm and has fallen, pinning a crew member, perhaps breaking both of his legs.

  • _____ Some of the colonists are trying to break into the powder magazine containing all of the ship's weapons and gunpowder.

  • _____ A passenger is demanding that he and his scientific records be put ashore in the ship's boat.

  • _____ A crew member has somehow managed to get drunk and is singing in his hammock.

3. _Approaching problems involving differing, conflicting, and opposing points of view:_ Understanding, accommodating, and relating to the ideas and opinions of others is a major problem of cooperation. It is also the foundation of understanding conflict of all kinds. Problem-solving exercises of

this type involve the student in actively trying to identify the likely opinions of others. Examples of this type of exercise include the following:

- **The Telephone:** Think about how people in the nineteenth century felt about the invention of the telephone. Think about the impact that the first telephones might have had on different people's lives. By just after the turn of the century there were only a few hundred telephones even in the very largest cities. But even then, people were beginning to see the change that a telephone network was going to bring. Write down a few sentences each about the views of the people that follow. Then, we will assign roles in groups and discuss what our feelings would have been if we had lived at the turn of the century.

  Opinion of the owner of the telegraph company

  Opinion of a messenger boy whose job might be threatened

  Opinion of a New York businessman

  Opinion of a New York housewife

  Opinion of a conservative, country minister

- **Programming:** Pretend that you are the programming director for a major television network. You are considering the eight o'clock Monday night slot, where this program will be up against established shows that have had good ratings. You are considering a long-running comedy program that has been revamped after being canceled by another network (as the ratings reached an all-time low); a new comedy with a star who once had a hit drama series but may not have comedic ability; a show aimed at teen and young-adult viewers and starring several young, unknown actors; a news program presenting controversial issues and public opinion; and a hard-hitting action show with an up-and-coming African American star and lots of violence. What would be the views of:

  The conservative network president

  The president of a fast-food chain that is a big sponsor

  The head of an organization of concerned parents

  A 16-year-old boy

  A 12-year-old girl

  4. *Approaching problems that stress possible alternative solutions:* This kind of task begins with a problem that has several plausible solutions, none of which can ever be absolutely identified as the single correct one. The basic question the problem solver must ask is, "What is the impact of each iden-

tified?" For example, the teacher might begin with a serious contemporary problem like drugs, gangs, pollution, prejudice, or terrorism and suggest, or have students suggest, several of the partial solutions that have been articulated by social scientists and politicians. The students would then try to think hypothetically about what positive and negative impact each of these solutions would have if implemented.

5. *Approaching problems involving identifying aims, goals, and objectives:* The focus in this type of problem is on identifying the purposes which people might conceivably have. It sometimes involves looking on our own aims as well. The basic strategy uses analogies, stories, and situational scenarios. The problem solver has to examine the wants, needs, and hopes of the people involved in the particular setting. In each case the key problem is to identify the major aims, goals, and purposes that the individual or group is pursuing in this situation. This kind of problem focus should help students become more purpose-oriented and help them to know the reasons they are doing things.

Examples include tasks such as the following:

- Identify the central aims, goals, and objectives of each of the main characters in a children's book or story (e.g., *Treasure Island, The 7 Dancing Princesses*).

- What are the main goals and objectives of Alcaida?

- What are the main goals of the school rules?

- What were the aims, goals, and purposes of African Americans during the civil rights movement?

6. *Approaching problems that emphasize identifying advantages, disadvantages, and unique and interesting features:* In this type of problem solving, the problem is an assertion or an idea to be examined. The purpose in the problem-solving process is for the students to be able to see all of the possible advantages and problems or disadvantages that the implementation of that assertion would bring. A secondary purpose is to have them analyze the unique and interesting features of this assertion. The teacher might want to begin by having students show agreement by hand signals or standing up. A few examples of such assertions are

- Students should volunteer when they know the answer.

- There should be a law that all containers and print materials be recyclable and that users recycle such containers.

- Abraham Lincoln should have issued the Emancipation Proclamation immediately when the southern states seceded.

- People ought to be able to do whatever they want to with property that they own.

INCORPORATING THINKING AND LEARNING SKILLS INTO THE SOCIAL STUDIES

Problem solving and decision making are the core of good social studies teaching. Only if students are mentally engaged in the classroom are they going to learn. The major thrust of the social studies is to develop the ability of students to think and learn for themselves. If they can do that, then they are ready for any body of knowledge and facts about any social studies topic. If they cannot think, then each topic and each encounter with content requires the teacher to present and guide them through, and the student is always a dependent learner. People who need such guidance are not going to be the kind of citizens that democracy absolutely requires to survive.

LOOKING BACK

There is increasing concern over the development of thinking in the social studies. If the major goal of teaching is to help children to become independent learners, then there has to be a real emphasis on the development of the ability to think and to solve problems.

Obtaining, understanding, and remembering information are among the thinking skills that are important to social studies learning. Generally, children can learn to relate new information to previous knowledge, to identify the patterns and relationships of information and ideas, and to identify purposes for learning. They can be aided in learning to remember through planned repetitions of information accompanied by appropriate feedback. Thinking skills can be taught through modeling by the teacher, through carefully planned discussions, and through guided practice.

Problem-solving skill is the most essential thinking ability in the social studies. Problem solving is an important part of the inquiry process. The use of alternative problem-solving strategies can be taught directly through structured activities. Among these strategies, the following are useful as models:

- Identifying all the factors related to the problem
- Prioritizing
- Looking for different points of view
- Looking for alternative solutions
- Examining and defining the real purposes and goals
- Examining the advantages, disadvantages, and interesting features of proposed solutions

SELF-TEST

1. What does the term *schema* mean and how does it relate to thinking?

2. What is meant by the expression, story map?

3. Can you identify and describe some different types of problem-solving tasks?

REFERENCES

NCSS Task Force on Early Childhood/Elementary Social Studies. (1989). Social studies for early childhood and elementary school children—preparing for the 21st century. *Social Education,* 53 (January), 14–23.

NCSS Task Force on Scope and Sequence. (1984). In search of a scope and sequence in the social studies. *Social Education,* 48 (April), 249–262.

Task Force of the National Commission on the Social Studies in the Schools. (1989). *Charting a course: Social studies for the 21st century.* Washington, DC: The National Commission on the Social Studies in the Schools.

SUGGESTED READING

Eeds, M., and Wells, D. (1991). Talking, thinking and cooperative learning: Lessons learned from listening to children talk about books. *Social Education,* 55 (February), 134–137.

Fair, J., and Kachaturoff, G. (1988). Teaching thinking: Another try. *The Social Studies,* 79 (March/April), 64–69.

O'Reilly, K. (1991). The Commission Report on critical thinking: A defense. *Social Education,* 55 (September), 298–300.

Sewell, A. M., Fuller, S., Murphy, R. C., and Funnell, B. H. (2002). Creative problem solving: A means to authentic and purposeful social studies. *The Social Studies,* 93(4) (July/August), 176–179.

von Eschenbach, J., and Ragsdale, C. (1989). The integration of elementary social studies and mathematics through experiential learning. *The Social Studies,* 80 (November/December), 225–228.

9 Character Education and Development of Attitudes, Values, and Appreciation

LOOKING AHEAD

Social studies is about becoming citizens. It is about becoming the best people we can be, understanding the world that we live in, and getting along with others. All of this means that a major focus of the social studies has to be on character and values. This chapter focuses on the social studies teacher's role in character education, the development of values, and the cultivation of positive attitudes. While values education and character education will always be controversial, the necessity of effective democratic values and character education elements in the social studies program cannot be denied. Teachers want their students to develop high moral character. We want children to grow in what is sometimes called "civic virtue," which is the central element of good citizenship. Both high moral character and civic virtue require strong positive values and attitudes.

Character education and values education are not quite the same thing. Character education is a broad, overreaching phenomena aimed at developing a personal code of behavior based on doing what is right rather than serving one's own self interests. That code predisposes how an individual will act in any situation. Character education does involve developing a values system, though character is based on a values system.

The word *value*, on the other hand, may be defined in various ways. Value can be used to refer to the relative *worth* of a person, material goods, services, or ideas. When we talk about *value* education, though, we are referring to what in life is important. Our values are the principles or standards of quality we use in making all our decisions. Our values shape our attitudes toward actions, people, and things. They also direct our aspirations and ambitions.

As teachers we need an understanding of the ways that personal values are in the process of being shaped during the elementary school years. It is equally important that we think about our own roles and responsibilities in this process.

Character and personal values and attitudes are critical attributes of school success or failure. They influence whether students do their work and how well they do it, how children behave in any setting, and interpersonal relationships. Teachers deal with these values constantly. They want students to feel positive toward school; to strive to do their best work; to have certain kinds of ambitions for themselves; to be fair and friendly in dealing with other students; and to be honest, industrious, loyal, and so on. On the other hand, there is a delicate balance between values and ways of teaching and dealing with values that are acceptable and appropriate and those that are not. In American public schools, for example, it is inappropriate to teach religious values or to advocate a religion; but religious values are not the only ones that are inappropriate. There is a point at which dealing with political situations or teaching about loving one's country becomes indoctrination. There is even a point when teaching what are thought of as *family values* may be in conflict with what is taught at home.

This chapter focuses on values and attitudes and the ways that teachers can deal positively with them in elementary school. It takes the position that a problems approach offers the most acceptable way of dealing with values issues because this approach enables the children to make their own decisions, but to do so on a solid basis.

Teachers deal with student value systems constantly. They want students to feel positive toward school; to strive to do their best work; to have certain kinds of ambitions for themselves; to be fair and friendly in dealing with other students; and to be honest, industrious, loyal, and so on. While teachers are concerned about the whole child and his or her character, they are limited in that there is a delicate balance between appropriate and inappropriate teaching of values. There are values that are acceptable and appropriate and those that are not. In American public schools, for example, it is inappropriate to teach religious values or to advocate a religion. Teachers have to be careful in dealing with political situations, not to advocate a party or candidate. Even teaching about democratic principles or loving one's country can easily become indoctrination. There is even a point when teaching what are thought of as *family values* may be in conflict with what is taught at home.

This chapter focuses on character education and on values and attitudes, and attempts to present ways to deal positive developmental practices in elementary school. It takes the position that a problems approach offers the most acceptable way of dealing with character development and values issues because this approach enables children to make their own decisions and to do so on a solid basis of their own research evidence.

CAN YOU? DO YOU?

Can You

- Explain why character education is so important for today's schools.
- Describe your own values and tell how they were formed?
- Identify or describe some specific decision-making skills?
- Think of some activities in which children could have experiences in determining alternatives?

Do You

- Know what character education is?
- Know what should be taught about values and how it should be taught?
- Understand why it may be necessary to deal with values related to living in a pluralistic society in school?
- Understand different ways of teaching about values?

FOCUS ACTIVITY

Following is a list of 20 different descriptions of children. Most of these descriptions identify both a desirable and an undesirable quality. If you were given the choice of having children in your class who fit 10, no more or less, of the 20 descriptions, which 10 would you choose? Use the list as the basis of discussion. You might also like to generate additional descriptions.

- _____ A child of average abilities whom you can trust
- _____ A child who is brilliant but who often tells untruths
- _____ A child who is hard working but slow in his or her work
- _____ A child who is respectful and polite but has severe learning disabilities
- _____ A child who is high-achieving but rebellious
- _____ A child who always does his or her homework but asks bothersome questions

- _____ A child who is a leader but often challenges your authority

- _____ A child who always has an excuse for failing to do the right thing

- _____ A child who gets along well with others but seldom contributes much

- _____ A child who volunteers for every task or job but needs constant supervision

- _____ A child who has to be coaxed to volunteer but works independently

- _____ A child who constantly talks out in class but is usually on task

- _____ A child who constantly whines and complains but does good work

- _____ A child who takes advantage of others whenever it serves his or her ends but always acts respectful toward authority

- _____ A child who is always a winner and will do anything to win

- _____ A child who is very messy but seems to always do his or her best

- _____ A child who is a tattler and who does everything to make the teacher like him or her

- _____ A child who is emotionally needy and whom other children seem to dislike

- _____ A child who always follows the rules of every activity but cannot deal with ambiguities or situations where there are no rules

- _____ A child who is always copying the work of others and cheating in other ways but who has great ability when he or she does the work

CHARACTER EDUCATION AND CITIZENSHIP

Over the last decade there has been increasing support for programs and approaches in school that will develop children's character early on. In November of 1996, the National Council for the Social Studies approved a report by its Task Force on Character Education. The thunderous message of that report, "Fostering Civic Virtue: Character Education in the Social Studies" (1997) was that social studies teachers have a "clear responsibility and duty to refocus their classrooms on the teaching of character and civic virtue." The report made strong statements about fostering moral and civic virtue in school environments, which are themselves models of the core values and principles being taught to young people. Teachers are reminded that they have a responsibility to be role models. The report also points out the need for schools to have dialogue with community members over the values that schools will teach. Similar statements have been issued by the organization of state social studies supervisors (CS4, 2000) and the organization of secondary school principals (Harned, 1999).

LOOKING AT CHARACTER EDUCATION AND VALUES FROM A WORLDVIEW PERSPECTIVE

The goals of character education include establishing life patterns and personal codes of behavior that include qualities such as integrity, belief in self and others, responsibility, and honor. Character itself has a strong relationship to how individuals view the world and their values. What individuals feel to be important or even worthwhile has impact upon character too, as does how they view the importance of themselves and others.

Particularly during childhood, an individual's values and worldview are developing and changing. The family and school, as well as other formal and informal social structures, help shape and form the individual's worldview and his or her interwoven values, attitudes, and appreciations. In a democratic society we want children to grow in their reasoned commitment to such democratic principles as majority rule, equal opportunity, individual rights, the rule of law, freedom of speech, and religious freedom.

Every society tries to shape the values of the young. Those who personally care about an individual child—and hopefully this includes parents, teachers, and a lot of others—want that child to grow up with the very best set of values possible. But not everyone agrees about just what that set is or about how it needs to be developed.

Parents and other family members present the child with their perspective, often a complex one. Various social groups attempt to exert pressure as well, having what is termed as a conserving influence. Conserving influences in any culture are those which transmit, maintain, and preserve that culture as it is. Religious, political, and social groups pressure the child to accept and believe in the values upon which the groups themselves are based. Schools also exert their own conserving influence. It should go almost without saying that the influence of any of these forces is not always unified. (Nor is it always positive.)

DECISION-MAKING SKILLS IN RELATION TO VALUES

One goal of character education is to develop children's abilities to make decisions based on democratic principles and sound moral values. There is nothing new about this. It was implicit in the education of young Roman citizens in the ancient Roman Republic. In modern times, two generations of social studies teachers have praised and quoted Shirley Engle's eloquent advocacy of the belief that *decision making is the heart of the social studies* (Engle, 1960). Making decisions involves value judgment calls. Engle pointed out that evaluation skills are needed throughout life. People constantly have to decide not only what is the right thing to do, but what is the best thing to do, what they want to do and what they have to do. Evaluation skills are always difficult because of dilemmas and conflicts and because there is often doubt about evaluational criteria and questions such as relevance, truth and accuracy, suitability, importance, utility, greatness, potential, goodness, beauty, quality, effort, or even quantity.

We make judgments and decisions on the basis of what we hold to be important, sensible, good, and worthwhile. However, the essential evaluation skills that teachers need to develop in children build from awareness and reasoning (the essential thinking skills discussed in Chapter 8). To develop this awareness, students need to be given frequent and significant opportunities to make decisions. They need to learn how and when to question what they see and hear. Teachers need to model how such decisions are made.

Children need to learn to determine when and how they should make decisions. They need to be able to distinguish different kinds of situations requiring decisions.

- Sometimes decisions have to be made on the basis of some single criterion and sometimes it is necessary to weigh and consider several criteria.

- Sometimes the difference between right and wrong is clear-cut, but more often the decision is not so clear.

- Some decisions have to be made with only partial information.

- Some judgment calls are easy and some are difficult because of conflicts in how we feel.

- Often we have to make holistic judgments based on experience.

- Some decisions are made on purely personal bases, solely on what serves one's own ends, personal ambitions, or feelings and emotions.

- Some decisions should be made altruistically with the good of one's self sacrificed for the good of others or of the group.

Values are involved in determining what alternatives are actually available (what the options actually are) in a given decision-demanding situation. Values also are the basis for making choices among the available alternatives (What course of action should be pursued? What solution is the best "fit" to existing conditions? What alternative offers the most advantages or fewest disadvantages? and Which choice is most dangerous or most safe?) Values even influence how we deal with evidence (distinguishing fact from speculation, conclusion from opinion, fantasy from reality, truth from falsehood, etc.), determining relevance, determining adequacy of evidence, projecting a trend, and making personal decisions or determination of ultimate courses to take (e.g., defining justice or morality in a particular situation). Teachers who are trying to help children become more responsible as well as more effective problem solvers have many opportunities in the social studies to give children experiences and practice that develop evaluation skills. Following are examples in each of the skill areas.

Determining Alternatives

- On a map, have children determine alternative routes to a single location or alternative destinations which will fill a particular need for the crew of a ship (political safety during a war, water before the crew dies of thirst, etc.).

- Have children hold class contests for such things as favorite historical character, favorite book, ideal vacation spot, best place to live, and so on. Have a nomination process and then choose advocates.

- Have children nominate possible sites for real and hypothetical projects, field trips, and so on.

- Even young children can suggest menus, ingredients, activities, etc., for social events and cultural celebrations.

- Do brainstorming activities where children have a specific number of responses to something (e.g., ten best reasons for, ways to interpret music through movement, etc.).

- Include nominating (favorite, best, etc.) as a regular part of daily activities.

- As children read about people's actions, stop and ask what else these people could have done that would have been honest and right.

Choosing among Alternatives

- Give children alternatives from which to choose as a regular activity. (These can be very real decisions that have impact on them and what they do.) Help them to understand the consequence and the implications of particular choices.

- Talk about the reasonableness of different explanations and theories. (The alternatives available to different people in history, the school, the home, etc., and their possible reasoning in making the decisions that they did.)

- Give three or four alternative titles for stories and let children choose among them and explain their reasoning.

- Let children vote for favorites among short series of stories, television shows, movies, and so on.

- In studying history and geography, give children brief real or made-up biography-character summaries of several different people. Then have them choose the best person for such things as an arctic expedition, a Safari, a rescue mission, a delegation to take a particular message to the president, and so on.

Distinguishing Fact from Speculation, Conclusion from Opinion, Fantasy from Reality, and Truth from Falsehood

- Give children a series of statements and let them try to identify which statements are fact and which are opinion.

- Give children a series of untrue statements about some topic they have been studying and have them tell why the statements are untrue.

- Have children identify fantastic elements in stories, television shows, movies, and so on.

- Bring in a magician who will talk about the ways that magicians fool people.

- Show a picture and let the children make a series of statements about the picture. As each statement is made, have the other children determine if the statement is actually true or if it is speculation, conclusion, or opinion.

Determining Relevance

- Give children a statement that makes an assertion or hypothesis. Then present them with a series of other statements of fact and opinion. With each of these, have the children decide if the statement is relevant.

- Write a question on the board. Have children scan a paragraph and volunteer to read any statements that are relevant to the question.

- Give children a proverb, truism, or superstition. Follow it with a collection of action statements and facts. Let the children classify the actions and facts as relevant or not. (They should be able to reach the conclusion that a fact may be relevant and supportive without proving the original statement to be true.)

Determining the Adequacy of Evidence

- Give children a series of arguments or reasons and then ask them to judge if a case has been made.

- Give students a series of "If A and B, then C" statements. Have them determine which ones they accept and which ones they do not.

- Give children a series of assertions. Ask them to tell what it would take by way of evidence for them to accept the truth of each one.

- Tell students a preposterous story about a well-known historical person. Make it so farfetched that they cannot believe it. When they start expressing their disbelief, have them try to tell why they do not believe. (Two of my favorites are stories I weave around the characters of George Washington and Christopher Columbus. In the Washington story, I build a tale that it was not George Washington but an exact look-alike who turned up at Mt. Vernon who became the first president. With Columbus, I make the claim that it was really a woman masquerading as a man who made the voyages.)

Projecting a Trend

- Give students a series of events and have them predict the event(s) that will follow.

- Describe a series of events and have students give the trend a name.

- Have students do a relevance web showing the connections among events that make the series of events a trend.

Defining Justice for Particular Instances

- Read stories with a moral to children and let them verbalize their own views of what the moral is.

- Provide a series of open-ended scenarios and problems and ask the children to tell what they think would be the right thing to do in these situations.

- Read some examples of actions of courts and governments and ask the children to decide if the action taken was fair.

WHAT VALUES DO WE WANT TO TEACH?

The place of values in the classroom is controversial. Whether teachers should teach values is not really the point. Nearly everyone concedes that teachers have to deal with values. Opinions differ, though, about what values should be taught and how we should teach them. Teaching a particular religious or political viewpoint, how to vote in an election, or what constitutes acceptable reading or entertainment are certainly questionable.

There are, however, at least three areas where it seems important that the schools take an active and effective role in developing children's beliefs. These are:

- Values related to living in a democracy

- Values implicit within a multicultural society

- Values that relate to school success and to the functional classroom

The main purpose of the social studies is to help children develop as good citizens. Character education is at least implied in the goal of civic virtue. While few would take issue with the importance of good citizenship or the development of character, there is controversy over what these terms mean and about the methods that can and should be used.

Emotional charges of indoctrination can be levied easily and words such as *nationalism* can be intoned with either positive or negative meanings.

Though a broad spectrum of viewpoints exists, there seem to be at least six areas of values where teachers need to work in order for the democracy to continue to exist.

- The need for participation

- The worth of and rights of the individual

- The rule of the majority and the rights of the minority

- Personal responsibility

- Respect for law and authority and for other people

- Equality and justice

The goals of character education in relation to these values can be developed in a number of ways. Teachers need to develop classrooms that are moral communities, where fairness, trust, caring, and taking responsibility are both expectations and norms.

History is an important part of the development of these values and intrinsic to character education. Classrooms which are themselves moral communities should promote greater awareness in children of what has happened in the past and what is happening now related to their own country and others. Knowledge of the reasons that governments exist, the principles and purposes upon which they were founded, and the events leading up to their present state is essential for understanding the present and for preparing for the future. Simply looking at the founding of this country and others and studying history in general, of course, are part of an established educational tradition. But to build democratic values, an active learning approach is needed. Children can be given responsibility, can make decisions, and can develop their own views in relation to what has happened in the past. Teachers can hold mock elections and mock trials and they can use opinionnaires and polls in the classroom. They can set up classroom governments, and look at questions of human rights and individual and corporate responsibility in current events. Even so simple a thing as playing games and sports can become occasion to talk about the importance of rules, personal responsibility, and concern for the rights of others. Things that teachers do to help individuals gain acceptance, success, and confidence are all an important part of citizenship education in a democracy.

Values Implicit within a Multicultural Society

One of the terms that has received a lot of attention in recent years is *multicultural education.* Multicultural education is a definitive attempt to make students more aware of the distinguishing differences and unifying similarities among various cultures and ethnic groups in the world. It is not simply education of a particular nature designed for minority groups. Part of its outcome should be helping students to value themselves and others. Multicultural education is directly tied to our democratic values, the principle of equality, the pluralistic nature of our society, and the concept of the global village. Multicultural education is aimed at the eradication of racism, classism, discrimination, sexism, prejudice, and ethnocentrism.

There are many reasons for moving to greater emphasis on multicultural education in the social studies. Among them are the following ideas:

- We live in a pluralistic society, a global village.

- Almost without exception, cultural groups have a history of prejudice and discrimination.

- There is a natural tendency among human beings to distrust people who are different and to hold them at arm's length.

- It is generally believed that the more people know about another culture, the more positive they will feel about it.

- Women, a number of ethnic groups and racial groups, and numerous cultures have been largely ignored or misrepresented in curriculum materials in the past.

Multicultural education works on several basic assumptions and beliefs. For example, there are some generally held beliefs about the nature of various cultural, ethnic, and racial groups in the world. One of them is that members of every cultural and ethnic group have been and are productive and resourceful and, therefore, have made substantial contributions to world civilization. Another is that no sex and no race or cultural or ethnic group is innately superior or inferior to any other. Such assumptions become important teachings in multicultural education, as do assumptions about people. The latter include the belief that historic injustices and discrimination are not reasons for present personal guilt or retribution and neither are they cause for the continuation of prejudice into the future. An important realization that is part of this assumption system is that everyone has prejudices and biases.

Finally, multicultural education is based on some major educational assumptions. The chief among these is that ethnocentrism, racism, and provincialism are going to continue to thrive without the kind of strong positive effort of multicultural education. These assumptions have led to the development of a variety of goals for multicultural education. Typical of such goals is the following set.

Students will develop

• Understanding of cultural diversity within our society and diversity within culture groups

• The ability to communicate with other culture groups both to resolve conflict and to improve relationships

• Attitudes, values, and behavior that are supportive of ethnic and cultural diversity

• Pride in their cultural heritage

• Knowledge, appreciation, and understanding of other cultures both in this country and throughout the world

• A sense of the history of both their own culture and those of others

The most significant tool of multicultural education is knowledge. Knowing about one's own and other cultures, viewing others through undistorted pictures of their strengths and accomplishments, is essential to appreciation. Naturally, it follows that increased positive, mutually beneficial contact with people of other groups (e.g., other cultures, races, religions, sex) is going to promote mutual understanding and appreciation.

Values That Relate to School Success and to the Functional Classroom

Values relating to being good students have implications for both the present and future lives of children. The success of the school experience is based on the student's doing his or her own work, giving his or her best effort, staying on task, completing work and doing it on time, getting along with people, always trying, always participating, not bothering others, obeying the rules, doing what the teacher says, and other related behaviors. These, in turn, are based on values such as: (work) integrity and honesty, the work ethic (the view that success ought to come from work and indeed will result if you work hard), the high value of achievement, the importance of honest effort, the importance of (and belief in) the essential code of fairness, justice, and equality governing individuals and (to an acceptable extent) societal behavior, concern for others, and complying with and having respect for authority.

The fact is that schools function on such values. The classroom can only "work" if most of these values are, at least in some measure, broadly accepted. The same is true of most workplaces and of the entire society. A teacher has to have control and be the authority. The school must be a place to work and grow in ability to do work.

Essentially these values are taught in a number of ways, not the least of which are traditional expectations that children bring to the first day of school. Children come to school expecting to have to behave in certain ways and with a set of pre-formed notions about what teachers are and how they are supposed to be treated. Schools continue this development through the personal classroom expectations of teachers, through the development of patterns and habits of behavior, through constant and consistent practice, through setting and making clear sets of school and classroom rules, through involving children in the rule-making and decision-making process, and through the development in the students themselves of a rationale for order and good work that continues throughout the school years.

HOW DO WE DEVELOP VALUES?

Those who attempt to develop and/or alter values and beliefs including character educators use a number of different approaches. Some of these approaches utilize questionable propaganda techniques, even to the point that they appear to be nothing less than types of indoctrination. A teacher should have ethical concerns about such approaches even when motivated by unselfish caring and concern. Other approaches, at first glance, seem unlikely to have any influence at all. However, the teacher should realize that any single approach can be used ineffectively as well as effectively. Ryan (2000) has pointed out that talk about character education is easier than doing it. He outlines six methods which he calls the six "E's" of character education: example, explanation, exhortation (praise and pep talks), ethos (ethical environment), experience, and expectation of excellence. The six "E's" are one way of conceptualizing how we go about teaching value-laden material. However, I have found the following five basic categories of methodology to be more useful.

1. *Teaching values through pronouncements, rules, and warnings:* Many times adults simply tell young people what to believe. This may occur very openly or it may be much more subtle. In school, for example, it is common to begin by giving children a set of classroom rules. There may or may not be discussion of these rules, but the fact is that the children are told that these rules have to be obeyed. The rules tell them what is right, what is wrong, what is good, what to admire, and so on. Values are also taught very directly when certain behaviors are expected in children. Teachers, parents, and other adults imply what is good and bad by the be-

haviors that they demand or expect. Values are taught directly through home and school rules, requirements, and individual and group orders and statements. The teacher says, "Stand up straight! Do your homework! Work carefully and neatly!" The teacher wants and expects work to be on time and complete. The headings have to all be alike. Paper and writing utensils have to meet certain standards. Children are to be quiet except when the adult wants them to talk. All of these actions imply compliance with authority, responsibility, taking pride in work, and other attributes that constitute at least part of being good. The pronouncements are often supported with consequences.

Young people vary in the extent to which they may be influenced by this way of teaching. They are not as likely to believe something that contradicts values they have learned earlier, especially strongly entrenched beliefs. Nonetheless, a constant and unvarying repetition of the same message or of the same expectations has a conditioning effect. For instance, when children are quieted whenever they speak out in class, when they are required to sit in the same seat every day, or when at the same hour and on the same cue they are required to get out a particular book and turn to a prearranged page, they grow to believe that this is the way things are supposed to be. When behavioral expectations are accompanied by a consistently applied punishment and reward system, over time behavior and beliefs fall into line. Some systems of classroom management are based on this approach.

2. *Teaching values through examples and models:* Children like heroes and they want to be like their heroes. Their heroes include people they know, people they see in television and movies, and people they read about or hear about. Characters in nearly every story children encounter serve as models for children. Children are watching characters from history, from school reading books and library books, from comic books, and from television and movies every day as models. Even toys such as Barbie dolls and Hot Wheels, which are advertised for children, become models of ideals. When used in school, the modeling approach involves getting children to look at figures in stories and history as the kind of people that they should aspire to be. As a way of teaching values, modeling involves making children more aware of people, of accomplishment and principle, and makes children feel more positive toward these people.

Teachers often model values unconsciously. They show who and what they think highly of or, conversely, do not think highly of by their emotional reactions. They share personal heroes, preferences among activities, approval and disapproval of the actions of people and other qualities with emotional signals that communicate in infectious ways to children. We also should not ignore the fact that the teachers become models themselves. As they work with their students, these children grow to like and admire different qualities that they see in their teachers. Teachers, for children, are often models of fairness, of a caring personality, of intelligence, of dress, and so on.

Teachers may also unconsciously or consciously be using a modeling approach when they hold students up for praise or when they display students' work. They are saying to the children that this is the way I want you to be.

The most obvious use of modeling in the social studies involves identifying heroes in history, heroes from real life today, and heroes from fiction or from radio, motion pictures, or television. Teachers do this by reading to children, by telling stories, by encouraging discussion, and by having children read. Teachers who use this approach most effectively present desirable heroes in exciting ways and bring out the most admirable qualities of these heroes.

Among the major plusses for this approach is that it makes school more interesting and positive and may even make the teacher seem more aware of the real world in which the children live. Schools tend to ignore the many positive characters in television shows and in movies, and this is one place where this set of child-selected experiences can be brought to good use. Folk tales are rich in heroes and can provide a way of helping children to see qualities that are admirable while examining cultural values and beliefs. Most children's fiction involves protagonists who represent the good versus antagonists who are perceived as bad.

A major danger of the modeling approach with real-life heroes is that real people all have weaknesses, shortcomings, and even vices. Whenever we deal with heroes we risk later disillusionment. Children find out that some of the stories that they learned as "truth," stories that even their teachers thought were true, are merely legends and are probably not true at all. The George Washington stories about throwing the dollar across the Potomac and chopping down the cherry tree are prime examples. Even worse, children may discover that the heroes they thought were perfect have made bad mistakes, shown prejudice or other very negative emotions, or been unfair or even dishonest. It is often difficult to maintain admiration for what heroes have stood for when their imperfections and humanity are revealed. Disillusionment with a hero may also mean rejection of the positive values he or she represents.

The problem is that there are no infallible heroes. This may be an argument, at least, for reliance on mythical and fictional heroes. These kinds of models have a distinct advantage. Their lives are limited to the stories in which they appear. Hidden flaws cannot be discovered outside that context. But the advantage is also a limitation. Most story heroes lack depth, and because of this they do not always seem real enough to serve as models. The best solution seems to be to continue with a combination of historical and fictional heroes, teaching children to admire the positive aspects of their heroes while recognizing shortcomings and weaknesses.

3. *Teaching values through stories with morals or lessons:* Another way of approaching morals, values, and worldviews is through stories and examples that speak directly to particular values. A story is told with a lesson

embedded in it. Typically, the stories show how to behave or how not to obey in situations where a decision has to be made. Often in these stories right behaviors and actions are rewarded and, of course, wrong behaviors bring undesirable consequences.

Fables and parables have been used to teach right and wrong for thousands of years. This approach is most effective when the listener or reader is provoked to think by the story and then through discussion and thought discovers the lesson embedded in the story. Obviously, the lesson in the story can be too difficult to figure out or too obvious. When either is true, the approach is not very successful. It also fails if a lesson runs contrary to the existing worldview of the audience and when the story seems to be an attempt to force a belief that they do not want to accept. The story approach offers a lot of possibilities for the teacher. Most importantly, stories have plots, characters, and settings—all factors that make them both interesting to listen to or read and, at the same time, memorable.

Nonfiction or fiction stories provide a way to look at different cultures, different times, and different beliefs. Every folk story tells a great deal about the culture from which it came. It shows what those people believed and, more importantly, what they thought was worth teaching or passing along to the younger generation.

Stories offer opportunity for discussion and thinking, for questions, for focusing on alternatives, and for comparison both with other stories and with personal experiences. Students can learn through dramatizing experiences with stories, through looking at character motivation, through examining alternative outcomes and beginnings, and through looking at the author's viewpoint, for example.

4. *Teaching values through examining personal actions of self and others:* One of the ways that teachers can help children to develop their values is to give them experiences where they can become more reflective and analytical about what they do themselves and what they see. The teacher needs to get children to examine more carefully the occurrences of everyday life, how they acted and felt in particular situations, and the reasons behind these feelings. This kind of values analysis involves looking carefully and sequentially at the details of what happened, making special note of behavior, then looking at the causes or reasons contributing to that behavior as well as the outcomes of it. The analysis does not end there. The next step is to speculate about alternative possible behaviors and consider what might have been more reasonable, moral or right, and effective in the situation. There must be constant reminders of what the principle people involved did and did not know at the time.

One of the outcomes of this approach is that it gets students to look at their own lives instead of just two-dimensional characters in media, storybooks, and history. The teacher may begin with autobiographical anecdotes or description of events in the classroom that the students have experienced. The autobiographical stories serve as models to provoke examples from the students and as one way of communicating the real humanity of the teacher. Often the stories point out times when the teacher did not act in the best way. If the teacher can share an embarrassing moment, it may have a releasing effect on the students. The shared class experiences need to be carefully selected, however, and developed as a group effort. The teacher should not be using the approach as a way of criticizing or scolding students. Rather, it should be an honest joint exploration of an event that was not exactly satisfactory in its outcome. Used well, the approach also has a bonding effect for the class.

Usually the approach goes through a series of definitive steps beginning with a narrative description of the situation, which is then discussed from the standpoint of identifying the central issue, concern, or problem. This last may require considerable time because it is critical to really get a clear vision of the heart of the matter. The next step is to look at all sides of the matter, examining the most minute detail and looking for things that may appear trivial, but, upon examination, are critical. This is essentially an information gathering stage. That information is then examined and sifted to remove the clutter of irrelevant or unimportant observations that are not needed for judgment. The final stages take the students through tentative judgments that are evaluated and appraised before final assessments are made.

5. *Teaching values through problem solving:* Many of the approaches to effective teaching that have been developed in recent years have involved problem solving. They begin with dilemmas or conflicts where decisions are demanded and ask the learner to make a judgment and then explain it. Both the moral reasoning approach, which involves moral dilemmas, and clarification approaches are essentially of this type.

Moral reasoning approaches, popularized by Lawrence Kohlberg (1984, 1985), involve the development of a sense of justice through a series of progressive stages. The basis of Kohlberg's approach is that individuals can be guided and accelerated in these stages, developing their reasoning ability by thinking about a series of dilemmas in which there are no clearcut right and good actions to take. In essence, the individual has to choose between alternatives where it is a matter of determining the "lesser of evils." An example of such a dilemma follows:

> In the 1840s, a boy who was traveling by wagon train to Oregon becomes the head of his family when his parents sicken and die. Other families in the wagon train are too much occupied with their own survival problems to try to take all these children under their wings, so the boy is pretty much on his own. Soon, the boy and his brothers and sisters are the last wagon in the train, struggling just to keep up. Because the wagon train has been slowed by a series of difficulties, the food supply for the boy's family soon begins to run out. One day, the boy sights a herd of deer crossing

the trail in back of the wagon train. If he stops to hunt, the wagon train will move on without his family and the winter may close down on them in the mountains. If he does not hunt, he and his brothers and sisters may starve. Should he have his own family make camp while he goes after the deer or simply try to keep up with the rest of the wagons?

If they are shown dilemmas such as the one described here, students can soon develop the ability to create their own in a guided discussion format. The dilemmas themselves, which can be designed to fit the age level and to relate to content being studied, should create involving points of departure for discussions of moral values. The essential position of the Kohlbergian research is that the development of moral reasoning occurs through exposure to such dilemmas and that growth is both irreversible and important in influencing moral behavior.

Values analysis approaches are designed to help students become clearer about why they act and think as they do. The essential view is that people should reflect their values in the way they act, but they do not always do so. The reason they do not is that they do not see what implications their belief systems have for their lives. The approach confronts students with decisions that simply have to be reasoned out or clarified. Teacher questions that probe the reasons for feelings and decisions are at the heart of this technique. The student is often confronted with open-ended situations where the question of what the meaning is becomes most important. Students may be asked to set priorities, choose from among alternatives, and examine choices. The overall concerns are, "What do you choose and prize?" and "How would you act?"

Problem related approaches can be adapted for use with practically any topic or theme under study. They allow the student to examine questions of right and wrong as well as other values in the past, in other cultures, in hypothetical and fictional settings, in current events, and in their own lives.

LOOKING BACK

Character education involves the development of moral and civic virtue. This means that teachers need to be involved in developing the value systems of their students. Values have a close relationship to our personal worldview. They have an impact on decision-making ability and especially on every aspect of evaluation. Teachers should expose children to many types of values-based, decision-making activities including those in which children determine alternatives, those in which they choose alternatives, those in which they are required to distinguish fact from speculation, conclusion from opinion, fantasy from reality, and truth from falsehood, those in which they determine relevance or adequacy of evidence, and those in which they project trends.

In the social studies, teachers need to be most concerned with values related to living in a democracy, values implicit within a multicultural society, and those values related to school success and successful functioning of the classroom. Teachers develop values through a variety of approaches, including direct teaching, modeling, moral stories and lessons, and examination of personal actions and the actions of others.

SELF-TEST

1. What is meant by the term *character education?*

2. Why is there a need for multicultural education?

3. Why are values so often taught very directly?

4. What are some different ways of modeling values?

5. What are some stories that you know that teach values?

6. Under what conditions is a problem-solving approach to teaching values effective?

REFERENCES

CS4. (2000). Character education and the social studies: A position statement for the Council for State Social Studies Specialists. Available on the web at http://www.cssss.org/character_education_position_paper.html.

Engle, S. H. (1960). Decision making: The heart of the social studies. *Social Education,* 24 (November), 301.

Harned, P. (1999). Leading the effort to teach character in the schools. *NAASP Bulletin,* 83 (October), 25–32.

Kohlberg, L. (1985). *The Meaning and Measurement of Moral Development.* Worcester, MA: Clark University.

Kohlberg, L. (1984). *Essays on Moral Development: Vol. 2. The Psychology of Moral Development.* New York: Harper and Row.

NCSS Task Force on Character Education. (1997). Fostering civic virtue: Character education in the social studies. *Social Education,* 61 (April/May), 225–227.

Ryan, K. (2000). The six e's of character education: Practical ways to bring moral instruction to life for your students. Available on the web at http://www.sed-mac66.bu.edu/CharacterEd/6Es.html.

SUGGESTED READING

Lockwood, A. L. (1991). Character education: The ten percent solution. *Social Education*, 55 (April/May), 246–248.

McArthur, J. R. (2002). The why, what, and how of teaching children social skills. *The Social Studies*, 93(4) (August), 183–95.

Nucci, L. (1997). Moral development and character formation. In Walberg, H. J. and Haertel, G. D. (Eds.), *Psychology and educational practice*. Berkeley, CA: MacCar-chan, 127–157.

Otten, E. H. (2000). Character education. ERIC Digest. Bloomington, IN: ERIC Clearinghouse for Social Studies/ Social Science Education. Available on the web at http://www.ed.gov/databases/ERIC_Digest/ed444932.html.

Richburg, R. W., and Nelson, B. J. (1990). Using a historical incident to focus on value information. *The Social Studies*, 81 (March/April), 80–83.

10 Using Simulation Games and Other Types of Drama in the Social Studies

LOOKING AHEAD

Teaching aims at "impact." We want to make the learning environment so powerful that students remember what goes on there as well as the information and skills. Several factors contribute to the impact of teaching, including: (1) The ability and interest of the learner; (2) Previous background knowledge and experience; (3) How well particular teaching/learning experiences are understood; (4) The amount of practice or repetitions; (5) Student perceptions of the importance of learning; (6) The degree to which students feel or do not feel safe, secure, and accepted; and (7) The particular senses and intelligences involved in the learning experience. However, even though all of these are important, teachers who think about the dramatic effect of activities and of the pacing of the school day are more likely to do high impact teaching. If the way that we teach creates dramatic excitement and sometimes suspense, what we teach will be remembered. School experience that is truly educational will intellectually and emotionally involve students, commanding both interest and response. If it does not, it will have little or no positive impact on how students learn, think, and feel about people, places, and events. When we think of drama in the classroom we need to think first of the dramatic impact of the entire school experience. Whether children are engaged in reading, writing, and listening, drill and practice activity, project work, learning games, or discussion activity, dramatic pacing qualities are present. We have to consider interest span, the tension created by deadlines, and the suspense of waiting for a discovery to occur. The main focus of this chapter is on the very broad range of actual dramatic techniques available to the social studies teacher. Learning to use some of the varied types should enable a teacher to make the classroom come alive.

This chapter examines the uses for drama. It attempts to show how problem solving is a natural and intrinsic element of drama and how dramatic techniques can be a vitalizing and energizing force to social studies. The chapter offers explanations and examples of a wide variety of dramatic techniques. The examples can serve as models for activity development for a variety of topics and levels.

CAN YOU? DO YOU?

Can You

- Tell how the teacher is a *stagecrafter*?
- Tell how drama is a problem-solving activity?
- Identify several reasons for using dramatic activities?
- Describe several different forms of mock trials?
- Tell stories and get students to tell stories in ways that are meaningful for the learning context?

Do You

- Know what *dramatic tension* is?
- Know how to use a variety of dramatic techniques in the social studies?
- Know the difference between role play and sociodrama?
- Know what a guided fantasy is and the purposes of this technique?
- Know what an *in-basket* game is?

FOCUS ACTIVITY

In small groups, generate a list of remembered powerful quotes from speeches and writings of historic figures. Here are just a few examples:

"I have a dream."–Martin Luther King, Jr.

"This day shall go down in infamy."–Franklin Delano Roosevelt

"We hold these truths to be self evident."–Thomas Jefferson

"Ain't I a woman?"–Sojourner Truth

"Four score and seven years ago, our forefathers set forth on this continent a new nation, conceived in liberty and dedicated to the proposition that all men are created equal."–Abraham Lincoln

"Give me your tired, your poor, your huddled masses yearning to breathe free. . . ."–Emma Lazarus

Repeat each quote several times going round the group with each person trying to express the quote as dramatically and differently as possible. Discuss the meaning of each quote, and the nuances that the different ways of stating the quote added.

What does this say about how we learn from dramatic and eloquent figures in history and what we can learn from using drama in teaching?

THE IMPORTANCE OF DRAMA IN THE SOCIAL STUDIES

The longest running show in the world is not *Cats* or *Les Mis* or *Phantom*. It is not *My Fair Lady* or *Hamlet* or even *The Mouse Trap*. In fact it is an ever changing piece of theater that is acted out thousands of times daily on more stages than all the great plays put together. For any of its thousands of performances, this show is done at only a fraction of production costs of a Broadway play. I am speaking, of course, of the show that is staged daily in classrooms everywhere, a piece of theater that can be filled with dramatic tension; is rich in plot and character; and is couched in suspense, comedic genius, and pathos. It is a show in which teachers everywhere have the opportunity to plan, write, direct, and produce. When they are at their best, teachers co-star in the drama. I say "at their best, they co-star" because the very best teacher dramatists make the students the real stars.

Every classroom, every school day, every lesson is a dramatic experience. If the teacher does the job of stagecraft well, the classroom experience is going to be interesting, exciting, and eventful, a memorable time filled with just the right level of plot and suspense, an opportunity for some very unusual learning. If the teacher has no flare for the dramatic, then the classroom is likely to be a somewhat lifeless and unexciting place where only routine learning occurs.

Drama is more than putting on a play, more than a category of techniques that teachers can use in the social studies. Drama is a way of looking at the entire learning thrust of the classroom. That thrust is the product of the emotional atmosphere, the teaching style and range of the instructor, and the kinds of activities in which students are engaged. When dramatic tension is the focus of the classroom, then there is a positively charged atmosphere that can be felt. This kind of tension is the distinguishing feature in the very best classrooms regardless of the teacher's style. It is an almost visible glow of anticipation on student's faces. It is evidenced in the way students come into the room, in what happens when class is begun, in how small groups and large groups are handled, in the things that contribute to order and management, in the kinds of assignments that are made and how and when they are made, and in when and how oral reading is done.

The dramatic tension of the classroom is as much a part of little mysteries, surprises, and suspense that teachers plan as it is of role plays and staged productions. The teacher promises a surprise. A mysterious visitor is coming. A kindergarten class, for example, can build excitement for several March days over the strange visits of an invisible leprechaun who leaves activity materials and green tracks (made of construction paper) whenever the class leaves the room. Such mysteries create curiosity through the asking of provocative questions, provision of problems to solve, and supplying of interesting anecdotal descriptions. What happened to the Roanoke colonists? Was Booth aided in his assassination of Lincoln by Washington insiders? What happened to Hitler or to Meriwether Lewis? What can be done to preserve the ozone, the rain forests, and the various endangered animals? The questions could go on and on.

Teachers are always performers in the drama of the classroom, but their roles and the ways they play them vary. There are teachers who are wonderfully dramatic solo performers, good storytellers, and powerful mood setters. There are others who develop their own dramatic flare best while interacting with their students. Some have a way of evoking passion and excitement and curiosity in a class while remaining quietly in the background. Others seem to be mostly organizers and catalysts to unleash the impassioned thoughts and feelings of the student. You can be a good teacher without being a ham, but not without enthusiasm and a flare for lighting the flame in others.

Mostly, those teachers who create the dramatic atmosphere are stage managers. They provide students with a dramatic vision of history, of culture, and of human relationships. They allow them to experience and to become involved in the conflicts and controversies, the personalities and plottings—in effect, the drama—implicit in the very name *social studies*. They make students aware of the dramatic moments of the past and of the present, the elements of conflict, climax, comedy, and tragedy; plot or story; suspense and resolution; setting, character, and dialogue. As stage managers, teachers can also utilize a number of dramatic techniques that get children involved, provoke curiosity and give reason for research, develop a sense of event sequence, develop skills of oral and written expression, and develop sensitivity to the feelings and ideas of others. The use of drama as a teaching approach makes the social studies come alive. Most importantly, drama can stimulate research and often give purpose and meaning to gathering and studying data.

Only when the perspective of drama is understood is a teacher really going to be able to use the spectrum of dramatic techniques purposefully and effectively. Dramatic techniques are almost always involving. In almost every type, a variety of problem-solving opportunities occur. Fortunately for teachers, there are variations of drama that can be done with almost any ability level and require amounts of time varying from a few minutes to weeks. The amount of teacher centeredness and control also varies and children can be moved slowly from dependence toward independence in planning and carrying out dramatic activities. Over the next few pages, about a dozen different dramatic techniques will be described with examples.

SIMULATION GAMES

Perhaps the most familiar of the social studies dramatic techniques, for those who know the literature of the field, is *simulation gaming*. Simulation games have become part of the culture. Fantasy simulations are played out recreationally by young people worldwide and there are many well-known computer games that are described as simulations. Many popular board games, including the perennial favorite, "Monopoly," have elements of simulation gaming in them.

Essentially, simulation games are structured decision-making activities in which students assume roles and then solve problems. Participants are given problem scenarios and additional information related to the problem and their roles. Their job is to come to the decision points in the game and then make the best choice among the options available. Decisions and actions of students playing the games are limited by sets of restrictive rules. These rules make simulations more patterned than other role-play activities. The decisions often result in consequences and, more often than not, at least some chance is involved in those consequences. The problem scenario itself, which serves as the beginning point and the heart of the games, may be based on some very real current or historical situation or on a hypothetical one.

Like any school activity, simulation games used as a teaching technique should be more than just for fun. Both the choice of games and the way that the gaming activities are conducted is critical. There are several important considerations in choosing and playing such games at any level. Perhaps the most critical of these is that the game should serve an important curricular purpose. Let me put that textbook type phrase into understandable language: When children play these games they should be learning something. The games should help them understand better. Once that is the prime consideration, other concerns follow logically. The students ought to be aware of and understand what they are doing. The game should be one that students truly enjoy and they will immerse themselves in the issues and the content. The best games provoke questions, reading, and research. All of these considerations should make teachers aware that how the teacher sets up the game and follows through after the dramatic game playing is complete are critical to using simulation activities effectively. These are often referred to as briefing and debriefing, and few simulations have much meaning or learning value without them.

Samples of Simulation Games

At the elementary level, simulation games need to be relatively simple. The amount of reading required in order to play the game is a factor that needs to be controlled to fit the abilities of the particular group of children. It is usually advantageous to use games that can be played in one day (from about 10 minutes in the early grades to just under an hour in upper elementary and middle school), depending on the attention span and involvement level of the students. This reduces the possibility of students continuing the game in unsupervised settings. Another factor that the teacher may want to consider is the ability of the children to work independently. This factor is the all important one if a game is played with less than full teacher control. Several different games are presented here. Each is a model that can be duplicated with similar information for many different units.

GAME 1: THE PRESIDENT'S CABINET

(A real information simulation)

MR. PRESIDENT, WHOM WILL YOU CHOOSE?

The president's cabinet helps in the decision making and directs the day-to-day operations of the executive branch of the government. While the first president had only five members in the cabinet, more recent presidents have had far larger cabinets. Following is a list of some of the various cabinet offices held over the years. Which five of these do you think Washington would have had on his first cabinet?

State	Commerce	Housing and Urban Development
Labor	Defense	Transportation
Energy	Justice	Attorney General
Education	War	Health and Human Services
Interior	Treasury	Health, Education, and Welfare
Navy	Agriculture	Postmaster General

President George Washington had the same problem as every other president when it came to selecting the people to help him take on the job of chief executive. Who should he ask to serve on his cabinet and in what jobs should he place them? Because his cabinet had only five members, the choices, even among the people that Washington had known and worked with, were many. Following is the list of Washington's cabinet offices and brief descriptions of some people who might have been considered.

███████████████████████████████████

MR. PRESIDENT, CHOOSE WHO WILL SERVE!

Pretend that you are George Washington and make your choices and placements for your cabinet. Before you begin, you will need to answer one question. In choosing a cabinet, Mr. President, which factors do you think are more important? To help you answer this question, nine of the factors Washington might have considered are identified on the following list. Rank order the factors (plus one factor of your own) to get your mindset for making your final selections among the 10 finalists for your cabinet:

- _____   Represent all regions of the country on the cabinet.

- _____   Choose the people who are best qualified for the jobs.

- _____   Represent the small states as well as the large states.

- _____   Select friends who are loyal and true to you.

- _____   Favor people who have great political influence.

- _____   Have people with the most experience in government.

- _____   Reward those who gave outstanding military service.

- _____   Have people who have opinions and views similar to your own.

- _____   Include people who have outstanding accomplishments.

- _____   Other _____

Actual Offices of Washington's Cabinet

State	War
Treasury	Postmaster General
Attorney General	

Potential Cabinet Members
(The teacher may want to assign each of the people under consideration as roles to students and let them try to make a case for themselves for a particular cabinet post.)

1. Boston bookseller; forced to flee Boston in disguise in 1774; Revolutionary War general; served as an artillery officer with Washington's army; developed a reputation for being able to move equipment and supplies quickly; known as sound, solid, and dependable.

2. Revolutionary War general; served with distinction and bravery; considered a strong, brilliant leader in battle who men would die for; fought guerilla-type warfare from the swamps of his native state for a considerable period of time while British were in control of the area.

3. Strong-minded, clear speaking champion of individual rights; opposed to a central government that is too strong; extensive experience in dealing with other nations; took a leadership role in Congress during the Revolution.

4. Supporter of a strong national government and a strong executive branch (may even want a king rather than a president); Revolutionary War officer of Washington's personal staff and strong supporter of Washington; good organizer and thorough planner; wants to establish a national bank and be sure that the new nation has a strong economic base.

5. Supporter of strong central government; southerner from a powerful state; lawyer by occupation; took a leadership role in the approval of the U.S. Constitution; keen observer and careful record keeper.

6. Elder statesman with ambassadorial experience; had a strong role in both the Declaration of Independence and the U.S. Constitution; extremely well liked; inventive and scientifically curious; writes extremely well and has many publications.

7. Outspoken critic of the U.S. Constitution and defender of states' rights; spirited public speaker whose words caused many to support the Revolution; experienced as a state governor and a long time member of a state legislature; has a real vision for the future.

8. Lawyer from a powerful northern state; took a key role in the effort to gain separation from England and helped in the writing of the Declaration of Independence; considered uncompromising, unyielding but a man of principle; advocate of a strong central government.

9. Boston merchant; Harvard graduate; served in the Revolution, first as a captain and later as a colonel; strong supporter of the U.S. Constitution; first Commissioner of the U.S. Treasury, 1785–1789.

10. Virginia lawyer; aide de camp to Washington; governor of Virginia; member of Congress; attended Constitutional Convention but refused to sign; urged the ratification of the Constitution on the grounds that the union was necessary.

The students may want to compare their choices to Washington's and know the names of the people who were candidates. This is one case where it is really not so important that their choices line up with the first president's.

Actual Selections (First Term)

State	Thomas Jefferson (3)
Treasury	Alexander Hamilton (4)
War	Henry Knox (1)
Attorney General	Edmund Randolph (10)
Postmaster General	Samuel Osgood (9)

Not Chosen by Washington

Francis Marion (2)	Patrick Henry (7)
James Madison (5)	John Adams (8)
Benjamin Franklin (6)	

GAME 2: WHO WILL GO WITH THE KING'S ENVOY?

(A real and hypothetical information simulation with one decision)

The people do not have to be real for simulations and the situations can be more general.

It is the fourteenth century. The English King is sending you as his envoy to the court of the King of France. You are to pick a party of five to go with you on the journey and to work with you at that court. Although there is currently peace between your country and France, it is an uneasy peace. There has been a series of wars spanning over half a century. Even recently, the two nations have been tottering on the brink of war. Your job is to make sure the peace continues so the King can fight wars in Scotland and Wales. You obviously want to pick the five people who can best help you. As ambassador your task will be to keep things smoothed over, avoiding war if that is possible. You also are to find out as much about what France is planning as you can.

SIR WILLIAM OF DOBRET speaks French fluently and has spent some time at the French court. He is a capable knight of thirty-five who rides well, has a reputation as a swordsman, and has battle experience. He is from a noble family of French descent and knows the people and the geography of the area well. He has never been disloyal to your King, but his loyalty has not really been put to the test, and there is a widely held belief that he is more French than English.

ROWAN OF LOGANSBY is a trusted friend and a seasoned fighter of unquestioned loyalty. He is a free man and a commoner, but his family has served your own for four generations. At twenty-nine he is the best man with a longbow you have ever seen. He speaks a little French and has a good ear. Unusual for one of his class, he reads and writes. He is a blunt-speaking, hot-tempered Englishman through and through.

BERTRAND DORSETT is a clerk in the king's court. He is a source of knowledge about everyone and everything. He makes it his business to know. A young man in his early twenties, he is very ambitious, but he is loyal to none but himself. As a clerk he has mastered both Latin and French, and he speaks, reads, and writes fluently. He is an intriguer who will learn all of the ins and outs of the French court. He is very anxious for advancement.

THE COUNT OF EDWINGHAM is an experienced diplomat of 50 who is somewhat resentful of you because he feels that he should have been selected as the ambassador. He is an old campaigner, still fit for battle. He has served in the French court in the past and knows many influential members of the French nobility. He speaks the language well and is totally loyal to your King.

SIR GEOFFREY OF COURAN is not the type to love battle, loving the life at court and especially gifted as a minstrel. In his early thirties, he has managed to avoid serving in most of the constant wars. He has an ability to charm men and women alike and he is especially adept at smoothing ruffled feathers and calming those who are angry. The King is particularly fond of him because of his wit, his charm, and his ability to sing and play the lute. Since he sings and speaks French as well as English, his skill as a minstrel will make him popular at the French court.

JOHN FITZHUGH has been very helpful to the English King in identifying plots against the crown and helping identify agents of other kings. He is second to none in his skill at espionage, having a devious mind himself. He is a secretive, careful, and very thorough kind of man who likes to work behind the scenes. He can speak French with a variety of dialects and pass as a native. He is also a master of disguise. It is said that his father was a French knight and his mother the young widow of an English merchant.

HENRY OF SELFIELD is one of the most successful merchants in England. His ships have been trading at important ports in Europe for twenty years. He is neither a soldier nor a courtier and is not a member of the nobility, but he speaks several languages, including French, and knows the importance of commerce to the future of England. He has been of great help to the king in financing some of his military campaigns.

LADY JANE SELRIDGE is a cousin of the Queen and highly thought of in the English court. She is witty, charming, an excellent hostess, and speaks flawless French. She knows all of the intrigues of most of the royal courts of Europe and would offer the added advantage of having access to the talk of the ladies of the court.

GAME 3: WHAT DO WE NEED IN OUR NEIGHBORHOOD?

(A speculative information simulation, with many decisions)

Pretend that you are planning a new neighborhood with a shopping center. There is room for only 10 businesses in the shopping center but there are spots for four other businesses at other locations in the neighborhood. It is important to know that you and your family, as well as other people in the neighborhood, may have to travel a long way to get those services and goods not offered in your community. So, be very careful as you choose the 14 different types of goods and services you want. You also want to take care as to where the businesses are located within the community. Be very thoughtful as you place them on the map so that each business is at exactly the right spot. Here is a list of potential businesses

Auto Supply Store	Bakery	Bank
Barber Shop	Beauty Salon	Bicycle Shop
Bookstore	Bowling Alley	Candy Store
China Shop	Clothing Store	Convenience Store
Craft Store	Delicatessen	Department Store
Dentist	Doctor's Office	Drug Store
Dry Cleaner	Eye Doctor	Fabric and Sewing Store
Fast-Food Restaurant	Flower Shop	Furniture Store
Garden Supply Store and Plant Nursery	Grocery Store	Hardware Store
Hospital	Ice Cream Store	Jewelry Store
Laundry	Library	Miniature Golf
Music Store	Pet Store	Post Office
Produce Market	Restaurant	Service Station
Shoe Store	Skating Rink	Souvenir Shop
Toy Store	Variety Store	Veterinarian
Video Store	Video Game Arcade	Zoo

WHAT DO WE NEED IN OUR NEIGHBORHOOD?

GAME 4: ESTABLISHING A COLONY

(An in-basket simulation)

In-basket games are prioritizing activities. They are based on the notion that quite often, life choices require us to decide what we must do first and what can be put off or done later. In-basket games begin with a list of activities or jobs that a single individual must do. The central question is, "In what order should these jobs be done?"

In this in-basket game, you are the leader of a group of colonists who have come to the new world during the seventeenth century. You have sighted the coast and sailed along it for several days, finally dropping anchor in a quiet cove. There is a likely area for a colony just ashore and a small river flows into the sea here. The area does not appear to have any permanent settlements, but you have seen natives peering at your ship from shore. You have no idea whether they are friendly or hostile.

You do not own your ship, but have hired the ship along with the services of its crusty old sea captain who wants to hurry you off his ship, so that he can return home to take on other cargos. A number of tasks face you. The following is a list of some of them.

- _____ Send scouting parties to explore the surrounding area to be sure that the best possible site for a colony was chosen.

- _____ Find fresh water to replenish the ship's stores.

- _____ Send a group to try to meet with the natives who have been seen looking out from the shore.

- _____ Hold a meeting of all the colonists to decide on the rules of government for the new colony.

- _____ Land all passengers from the ship.

- _____ Pay the captain what is still owed him for the voyage.

- _____ Draft a letter to the patrons of the colony telling of your safe arrival and suggesting what you will do now.

- _____ Determine your exact location and how far your colony is from other new world colonies.

- _____ Build a stockade for defense.

- _____ Start building shelters for the colonists.

- _____ Plant crops.

- _____ Send out a hunting party to find fresh meat.

- _____ Disembark all passengers.

- _____ Unload all supplies.

- _____ Plant the flag of your country on the shore claiming the land for your sovereign.

- _____ Hold a Thanksgiving celebration.

GAME 5: NUCLEAR WASTE DISPOSAL

(A single-choice decision simulation based on vested interest)

For this game you will need a large map of the United States and one of the world. The scenario is that there is a need to dispose of certain waste products from nuclear reactors and other sources. These waste products are radio-active. Children are divided into five groups, one representing the Congressional Committee that will be making the recommendation and the others representing various potential sites. The Congressional Committee and the four area groups meet as groups first to plan strategy. Then the Congressional Committee listens and asks questions while each group makes its case indicating why its area should not be chosen. Then the groups all meet separately again, the Congressional Committee to make its final decision and the area groups to come up with a contingency plan in case their area is the one chosen. This plan may include a set of safety recommendations, recommendations regarding specific site priorities, and some recommendations about how the amount of nuclear waste might be controlled (recycled, etc.).

Congressional Committee
The committee is made up of seven members of congress, one from each of the regions being considered and three from unspecified other areas of the country. A chairperson and a secretary are appointed. The chairperson should be an uncommitted individual. It is the job of the chairperson to keep the hearings flowing smoothly and to present the final recommendations of the Congressional Committee. The four options that the committee is considering are the following:

1. Burial of the waste in sealed containers in a southwestern state that has a small population.

2. Burial of the waste in sealed containers in a southeastern state relatively close to the majority of the facilities producing the waste. There is, of course, danger of spills and contamination whenever radioactive materials are moved.

3. Disposal of the nuclear waste by putting it in sealed waterproof containers that are then taken out to sea and placed on the ocean floor in a specified site, away from major shipping lanes or ocean currents.

4. Disposal in airtight sealed containers at a specific site in a mountainous area in a northwestern state with a low population.

Group 1: Representatives of a Southwestern State
They feel that their state does not get much, if any, benefit from the plants producing the nuclear waste. Neither does it profit from the products, which are largely military in nature. This state is one of the few areas of the country where pollution has not yet become a problem and they wish it to remain that way. They also point out that their state has many Native Americans in it and that putting the waste disposal site there would be yet another blow of oppression and discrimination against that population.

Group 2: Representatives of a Southeastern State
Their state has a potential high population growth as part of the sunbelt. They feel that as a producer of nuclear products for the nation that their

population is already exposed to enough danger. They also know that their population density already far exceeds that of the two western states.

Group 3: Representatives of a Coastal State

There is great fear in this state that no containers can be designed that can withstand the sea over time. If the waste is disposed of in this manner, it is believed that eventually leakages and seepage will bring about further damage to coastal plant and animal life and pollute the coasts themselves. This area already has one of the biggest pollution problems in the nation.

Group 4: Representatives of a Low Population Northwestern State

The severe weather of the mountainous region and the difficulty of burying anything in the rocky area make the container problem a serious one. Falling rocks or cold weather could damage a container very quickly and a nuclear leak problem would then exist. This is a nearly pollution free area and the population is very independent and wishes to stay that way. They also feel that the creation of this waste is not their problem, and that the people who benefit from the nuclear energy produced should be the people who have the waste product disposal site.

Advantages and Benefits, Problems and Limitations of Simulation Games

The strength of simulation games is that they generate intellectual engagement, involvement, and interest. Students become impassioned about the games. That very quality also means that simulation games can really stimulate students to do some meaningful research, meaningful because they want to do it and because, for once, they feel some purpose for that research.

The major emphasis in simulation games on problem solving and decision making is another important plus. Simulations offer perhaps the best vehicle available for practicing problem solving. One of the reasons for claiming this is that, although the emotional stakes and commitment may be high, the consequences that come from decisions are only vicarious ones. This allows students to practice their problem-solving skills in relative safety. Carefully conducted debriefing sessions can really strengthen the development of problem solving. Such sessions are both analytic and reflective.

The downside of simulation gaming cannot be ignored. There is no denying that games can be very time-consuming in the classroom. They often take time away that could be spent in acquiring factual knowledge. For the teacher whose concern is more slanted to how much content students learn, this does pose a distinctive disadvantage. Simulation games also may require a good deal of preparation time on the part of the teacher.

Paradoxically, the major problem of games, though, is what most game advocates consider to be their greatest strength, the emotionally involved commitment of students. Simulations can be very competitive and, in some games, may also develop and encourage undesirable values. Some feel that simulation experiences do not develop a spirit of cooperation and working together. The way that students throw themselves into some games may also cause some unwanted carryover into relationships among students. If this danger is to be avoided, game debriefing has to include a definite and convincing closing down of all phases and aspects of roles that students have taken during the game play time.

MOCK TRIALS

The activity of the courtroom offers many possibilities for drama. Because the justice system is so integrally important to understanding democracy and the democratic process, various kinds of dramatic activities can be built around the legal process. This can be useful in helping students understand the constitution and the legal system as well as the various conflicts and controversies that have been and continue to be important issues. Understanding the legal system seems nearly as important as understanding the democratic process itself and developing the knowledge and attitudes needed to participate. Most people will be involved in the legal system several times in their lives, and the more students learn about the law and the courts and how they operate, the better prepared they will be to deal with these legal encounters throughout life.

By far the most used dramatic activity related to the legal process is the mock trial. Mock trials enable students to reexamine history and to look at questions of right and wrong as they relate to the law and the legal system. Mock trials can take numerous forms and be developed with varying thoroughness and detail depending on such factors as the teaching purpose, the ability level of the students, and the time available. There are at least nine forms of mock trials.

1. Re-creation of real trials from the past: We attempt to reenact the trial as it took place. The more thoroughly we research it and the more preparation we do, the more completely this can be done. Because of the court record-keeping system, almost exact reenactments are even possible if desired. With elementary and middle school children, of course, giving the broad picture of what happened is more likely to be more comprehensible.

2. Staging trials from the past with open verdicts: This type of mock trial is similar to the first in all but one respect: the verdict can be changed. In fact we want to see if a jury of students is going to come to the same decision that was reached at the original trial. When comparisons are made, the question is always going to be why the verdict was the same or different.

3. Hypothetical trials of historical and contemporary figures who have never stood trial: With this type of trial, the students' sense of justice and fairness or even their natural curiosity is served, as well as their biases.

Trials of historical characters like Oswald, Hitler, and Custer have been the subject of speculative movies and novels. The question is, what kind of evidence and testimony might have been given if the figure went to trial. Figures from centuries ago, such as Attila the Hun, Brutus, King John of England, Jack the Ripper, or Ivan the Terrible, might be tried. More recent figures, such as Richard Nixon or Harry Truman (the atom bomb), also give insight.

4. Creating cases to retest a landmark decision of the Supreme Court: The emphasis is on discussing the issues and the particular circumstances of the original case and then attempting through discussion to come up with a parallel case that might cause the Supreme Court to offer a modern opinion.

5. Trials related to current controversies and issues: The cases come right out of the newspapers and news broadcasts, and relatives and friends have information and opinions. The issues of current events become relevant and important to young learners as they try to make their own case.

6. Reenactment of trials suggested in fictional books: Trials are a popular subject in fiction. Having children develop the detail to enact one of these trials can help comprehension and test their creativity.

7. Fantasy trials of story and book characters: Moral themes are almost universal in children's fiction. Putting a fairy tale character like Jack or the Wolf on trial can be a delightful learning experience. The advantage is that children are very familiar with the story line and the characters. The trial gives them a new perspective on the events of the story.

8. Creation of a new crime scenario and then staging the trial: This is a totally creative experience in which the children create a crime, a victim, witnesses and clues, and an accused perpetrator of the crime. The teacher can exercise some control by a discussion in which specifications regarding the nature of the crime are carefully drawn.

9. Development of a classroom court to try discipline offenders: Several systems, ranging from very simple to very elaborate, may be used to put members of the class on trial for breaking the classroom rules. The major benefit of the exercise is that children develop clearer, more meaningful ideas about such issues as reasonable doubt, the relationship of punishment to crime, and punishment as a deterrent to crime. The technique has been used successfully by some teachers as part of their classroom management plan.

Trial-Related Activities

There are various activities that can help children learn about the legal system. Role playing a crime with various witnesses giving independent accounts of what they saw can teach children that people see and remember events differently. Visits to law school mock trials or to one of the mock trial competitive programs put on at the high school or visiting a courtroom can be real learning experiences if carefully planned. Classroom visits by attorneys, judges, and police officers are also profitable if such guests can relate to the children. Students can examine laws and go through the process of debate and enactment of a particular law. They can go through structured writing exercises to write trial briefs.

DRAMA THROUGH READING: GUIDED FANTASY, CLASS ACTION DRAMA, READERS' THEATER, AND DRAMATIC READING

The dramatic power and eloquence of the printed word can be used to create images and suspense when read aloud. Here are two techniques in which the teacher does the reading and two in which the students are the readers.

Guided Fantasies

Guided fantasies, also called visualizations, are dramas in which even the most shy children can participate because they require no acting, only good listening concentration and sensory imagination. The students are asked to sit with their eyes closed and to envision as vividly as they can a particular scene as it is described by a reader. If some of the students are really expressive readers, they can be involved in this capacity as well as being listeners. This is especially true in the upper grades.

When the fantasy is read, a special kind of listening needs to occur. The teacher wants the children to get the feel of what it is like to be in another time, another place, or another time in another place. She wants them to be able to see it in their minds, to smell the smells, to hear the sounds. What she wants, in short, is a very imaginative sensory kind of listening, the kind that involves the students and makes them want to interact with and know more about what is being described.

The readings need to be fairly short, certainly within the concentration span of students. They need to be very descriptive, sensory, and specifically detailed to the point of being graphic. The scenes that they describe should, of course, be relevant to the curriculum. They should help students envision the settings, the culture, and the sequence of events. In essence, you want them to smell the smoke of the battlefield, the stench of the prisons, the perfume of the flowers, and the aromas of the feast spread before the king. You want them to almost hear the sounds of the royal court, the noises of battle and of the marketplace, and the voices and clatter that fill the city and the streets. In their minds' eyes, you want them to see as clearly as they can the panorama and the detail of everything.

The scenes described can be historical or contemporary. What is important is the amount of imagery they create, so it is important to get the students involved. Step out of the story to tell them to breathe in the smells and ask them what they are smelling. See if they can add detail to the vision. Reread short segments of the description that are particularly strong in the images they create. Pictures and objects and things to touch, hear, and even smell, can be examined to add to the intensity of the sensory experience and to increase input into the discussion from students.

Guided fantasies can describe a range of times from the distant past to the events in the news today. Newspaper and Internet accounts can be used. Since guided fantasies may be just too stressful and powerful, teachers have to be careful what they choose to use with elementary children. For example, you would not want to use the radio account of the destruction of the Hindenburg or the contemporary accounts of the killings at Columbine or the World Trade Center attack. But you could use descriptions of opening events at the Olympics, a World Fair, or description of life in a historic mansion.

As a follow-up activity, the guided fantasy can be reenacted as a pantomime. Through pantomiming the event while the fantasy is read aloud, students can intensify the visualization and express the images they have seen in their minds.

EXAMPLE: THE TORNADO OPENING

(Something like the first paragraph here needs to be standard to establish the kind of mood and attitude desired. Children might be seated in a circle or perhaps on the floor so that there is a sense of closeness in the group. At its best, the technique allows the listener to totally immerse him- or herself into the images being created and suspend disbelief in their reality.)

Close your eyes and let your mind go blank for a minute. Now I want you to begin to see a picture in your mind. Try to make this picture as clear and as filled with vivid detail as you possibly can.

It has been an uneventful April day in the town of Xenia in central Ohio. It is a quiet kind of old-fashioned town most days. This part of Ohio is fairly flat and you can see from one end of town to the other. The carhops at the local drive-in rootbeer stand are taking orders. Along with other girls and boys, you are waiting for a ride in front of the school. The air seems strange, kind of heavy and oppressive, and there is a quietness in the air that does not seem normal even by the standards of a midwestern American town. Though it is not raining, dark clouds are hanging low and daylight seems to be going early.

Something catches your eye. Off to the southwest, a huge darker cloud has formed and seems to be revolving. In minutes, it is funnel shaped. You have been listening to radio weather, and you know that conditions are dangerously right here in the "tornado alley," so you have no doubt. That cloud is now a tornado! And this one looks like a bad one headed right into town.

You run back into the school screaming, "Tornado! Twister coming and coming fast!" Looking out the window of the school, you and other students and teachers can now see with horror a terrible fearsome twisting cloud only a few hundred yards away. Everyone hits the floor in terror as the tornado slams into the building with screaming force. Crashing, banging, and grating sounds fill the air along with the screams of terrified people. It is raining rocks, slabs of concrete, tree limbs, bricks, and great chunks of earth that have been ripped from the ground. Daggers of broken glass twirl through the air everywhere. The huge beams of the school are falling everywhere.

The tornado funnel moves across the town at 40 miles per hour, leaving a trail of destruction and rubble. Wood frame houses are crushed or swept from their foundations. Huge old trees are torn from the earth and hurled in the air. The air is filled with objects, from furniture to cars and trucks, all now being hurled with monstrous force.

The black twisting tornado hits the rear of a train moving through town. Several train cars are thrown from the tracks across the main street where they crash into the red brick post office, a museum, and a restaurant.

Finally, the destructive tornado passes. Thirty-three people have been left dead and hundreds injured. Over 1,300 buildings have been destroyed. Of course, you don't find this out until later. For now, you can only see the awful damage everywhere. You and the rest are left dazed and unbelieving, but you feel lucky to have survived.

(Based on accounts of the destructive tornado that swept the Midwest on April 3, 1974)

Class Action Dramas

A class action story is one that is read aloud. Students listen for particular words or phrases. When they hear them, they have to quickly respond in a prescribed way. You may have done these little stories and called them by a different name or had no name for them at all. What they involve, more than anything else, is listening skills. But there is drama in them, too, or at least opportunity for expressive fun. Students have to listen carefully to the story as it is read. The required words and actions usually involve only rudimentary drama and generally even the shyest child will participate in most roles.

The results are usually fun and funny. The stories themselves may include stereotypes and may even contain misinformation. The stories may also contain blatant exaggerations. Often the responses ideas are made to look ridiculous. The stories can provoke solid discussion of issues and values.

For some words and phrases, a response may come from a single individual. For others, a group within the class may be asked to respond. In many cases though, the entire class may be required to react when a key word is read. Scripts can be adapted from historical events or from books and can even be written as class projects. The first job after writing the story and determining the key words and the responses is to assign the roles within the group. It is usually good to rehearse responses before doing the entire story. The story should be read with as much excitement and expression as possible, but the rate has to be regulated to allow everyone to see, hear, and participate in the responses. Here is an example based on a familiar version of a series of historical incidents involving the famous Revolutionary War figure, Paul Revere.

PAUL REVERE'S MANY RIDES: A CLASS ACTION STORY

When the Reader Says This	You Do and Say This
The English	Shout, "The British are coming!"
Paul Revere or Paul	Pretend to jump on a horse and ride.
Tea	Raise a pretend cup and pretend to drink while saying, "Mm, good!"
Taxes	Shout, "No taxation without representation!"
American(s)	Whistle the first line of "Yankee Doodle."
Horse	Shout, "Get your dogs, cats, and chickens off the road!"
Boston	Shout, "Is that where they invented baked beans?"
Philadelphia	Shout, "Is that where they invented cream cheese?"
Ride, Rode, Riding or Ridden	Make the sound of a horse.
Lexington/Concord	Shout, "BANG! BANG!"

The **English** wanted to **tax** everything in its **American** colonies, and **Paul Revere** and his friends in **Boston** didn't like it one bit. First the **English** put a **tax** on everything the **Americans** printed. Then the **English** wanted to **tax tea,** and glass, and paper. The **Americans** protested so strongly that the **English** took back all the **taxes,** all, that is, but the **tax** on **tea.** The **Americans** liked their **tea** but they refused to pay the **English tax.** One night **Paul Re-**

vere and some other **Americans** dressed up as Indians and boarded three **English tea** ships in **Boston** Harbor. They threw all the **tea** into **Boston** Harbor. Afterwards, **Paul** jumped on his **horse** and **rode** to tell other **Americans** in Massachusetts, Connecticut, and in **Philadelphia,** Pennsylvania. For the next year, **Paul Revere** kept an eye on the **English** soldiers who were now all over **Boston.** He **rode** his **horse** from **Boston** to **Philadelphia,** all the time carrying messages about what the **English** were doing. One night, a friend of **Paul Revere's** found out that the **English** soldiers were going to march to the towns of **Lexington and Concord** to capture guns and ammunition that the **Americans** had stored. The **English** also wanted to take two **American** leaders, Samuel Adams and John Hancock. **Paul Revere** and others were sent to warn the **Americans** in **Lexington and Concord.** So off **rode Paul** on his **horse.** Before he even got to **Lexington** he was almost stopped by two **English** officers, but **Paul** got away and woke up Hancock and Adams. **Paul** and two others started out on their **horses, riding** toward **Concord,** warning farmers along the way. But the **Americans** were stopped by **English** soldiers who took their **horses. Paul** had to walk back to **Lexington,** where he met the **American** leaders, Adams and Hancock, just getting in their carriage to leave. **Paul rode** out with them but had to walk back to save a trunk full of secret papers that they had left behind. **Paul** walked back to **Lexington** to find it full of **American** farmers armed with muskets. In fact **Paul** was just carrying the trunk out when the **English** troops arrived and he heard the sound of gunfire. So **Paul Revere** actually heard what was later called, "The shot heard round the world."

Readers' Theater

Readers' theater involves turning a story that is written in narrative form into a play. A group of students read the story and then plan together how to alter it so that it can be read as a play. The focus is on the drama planning process. The students have to think out how they can change the way that the story is told. They have to develop a thorough understanding of the characters; a feel for the setting; and a mental map of the purpose, themes, and the plot line or sequence. They literally rewrite the story, putting in dialogue to cover narrative passages. They are made to think about what character would be most likely to relate the information and how it can be fitted in as conversation or as monologue. Of course, one of the natural tendencies is to fall back on the device of a narrator, but ideally the use of this voice should be prohibited altogether or kept at a minimum.

Because the focus of dialogue is human interaction and monologue is really a way of revealing inner thoughts, dreams, and concerns, this technique has a lot to offer to the social studies. Of course, some stories are better suited than others. Stories that place a lot of emphasis on character, those that are written in the first person, and those that are already rich in dialogue usually take less adaptation. For social studies content purposes, folk tales, biographical episodes (such as those in the books of Jean Fritz), historical fiction (such as *Nettie Goes South*), and stories which emphasize culture and human relationships (such as *Ming Lo Moves the Mountain* or *Frog and Toad are Friends*) are most useful.

After the story is planned and usually rewritten, the students can try reading through it different ways, running through it several times. This can allow different people to express themselves in the roles and allow rewriting and rethinking different parts of the story.

Dramatic Reading

There is a wealth of short dramatic material that children can read expressively. These can be fun and either funny or serious, depending on the material. The trick is finding and/or adapting (which most often means cutting down to a reasonable length). For adaptable or abstractable material, popular descriptive histories and historical fiction are good sources. Good material can also be found in popular history and geography magazines such as *National Geographic, Smithsonian, Cobblestone,* and others. It is also productive fun for students to prepare their own readings as creative-writing assignments and creative reporting exercises.

The teacher needs to set it up so that more than one student reads the material aloud. That way, they can begin to envision the range of expressive possibilities. Seven types of readings are briefly discussed here: brags, cliff-hangers, character monologues, in-role reports, first person poems, expressive poems about human feelings, and historical poems

1. Brags

Brags are comic devices. They are humorous partially because boasting is considered inappropriate behavior in mainstream society and partially because of the use of exaggeration that is implicit in all bragging. In reality, most children's social interactions are filled with boasting claims from the stereotyped, "My father can beat your father up!" to the "dares" that are so common to youth society and on to the name dropping of adults. Brags involve strength, ability, status, possessions, and relationships. Bragging has become and continues to be an art form in some societies (including that of frontier America).

Written brags make excellent oral reading devices. They invite competition and imitation. They make excellent models for creative writing, and they can incorporate a great deal of knowledge of a culture. Here are two brags, one from a fictitious inventor the other from a real one. They might be used in a unit on invention and discovery or one dealing with a period of history where invention was a major theme. Have the students read these to see who can read most expressively. Then have them write their own scientist brags.

PROFESSOR IMA CHEENIUS

Of course, *I* am the greatest inventor of all time! *My* inventions will one day be household words. Why, *I* have inventions in process right now that will make life easier for everyone, save energy, repair the ozone, cure cancer, get us to other planets, make clothes and shoes and cars that will never wear out, and solve the energy shortage. And here is my little secret—*I* am inventing an engine that will run entirely on polluted air. Too much for you! Well, try this! I am going to invent instant water to save the world from water shortage. All you need to do is add water. Can you believe how clever I am? I just don't know what I'll come up with next, maybe chewless gum or a math pill that helps children get their math homework done twice as quickly! Why, next to me, Edison was a bulb head and Newton was a fig cookie. Bell was a ding-a-ling and Marconi was pasta. And, just between you and me, I think Franklin flew a few too many kites in the lightning. I am just *so* clever!

GEORGE WASHINGTON CARVER BRAG

I am George Washington Carver. I am a modest man, so it's hard for me to brag. I worked my way through high school and was the first Black student ever to attend Simpson College in Iowa. I worked as a janitor there 'til I got my degree in agricultural science, then went back and got a masters degree. You think that's tough to do now; it was a thousand times tougher for a Black man in the 1800s. But I was a worker and a man who looked, looked close at things. I once said that "When I talk to the little flower, or the little peanut they will give up their secrets." And they did just that to me too.

Another thing I said was that "Ninety-nine percent of the failures come from people who are in the habit of making up excuses." And that I never did. In 1897, Booker T. Washington asked me to come to Tuskegee. I was there for 50 years. I invented 325 products from peanuts alone and 228 from sweet potatoes. My inventions would fill a large hall. I created synthetic rubber, synthetic marble, vanishing cream, wood filler, mucilage, rubbing oils, instant coffee, insulating board, linoleum, creosote, bleach— why it would hard to name something that I couldn't create a version of. I even taught the poor Black farmers to rotate their crops and restore the worn out land.

Now this part you really are not going to believe. Most of my inventions I just gave away. I wanted people to benefit, not to make a lot of money for myself. I told people, "God gave my ideas to me, How can I sell them to somebody else." In fact, in 1940, I gave my life savings to the establishment of a research foundation at Tuskegee.

But I did get my honors. Simpson College gave me an honorary doctorate in 1928. I became an honorary member of the Royal Society of Arts in

London and received the Spingarn Medal from the NAACP. In 1939, President Roosevelt even gave me a medal for saving the southern agriculture.

---

2. Cliffhangers

Cliffhangers are readings in which the central characters are depicted in impossible situations, dire straits from which it may seem impossible that they can ever extract themselves. I like to design these as problem-solving readings. After they have been read aloud a few times to try alternate expressions, have the students try to suggest ways out of these truly solution-defying situations. Generally, the decisions do not involve moral dilemmas so much as insurmountable difficulties. They can really test the students' problem-solving thinking to the limit. One thing that these discussions can teach is, when faced with many impossible problems, one has to look at them individually *and* together, often beginning with the initial task of identifying the least impossible one to solve.

THE SEA CAPTAIN EXPLORER

There I am. My ship has run aground in totally uncharted waters. There is a gaping hole in the hull and even if it were fixed, there seems to be no way to get this heavy ship back out into the water. Speaking of water, there isn't any, and thirst is a terrible killer at sea. The stores are in short supply and we've been eating wormy ship's biscuits for a week. The crew, which is made up of the worst cutthroats that ever signed sailing papers, has been grumbling and refusing to take orders. The sailors are beginning to plan a mutiny, and some pretty nasty looking types are starting to edge toward me with cutlasses and belaying pins in their hands. Out of the jungle-like growth just a few hundred yards away, a large group of hostile looking natives, wicked looking spears at the ready, are moving toward the beached ship and me. Out to sea and moving toward us, I can see a fierce seasonal storm, the kind that can pick my poor ship up and break it entirely on the rocks. It is coming fast. The only path of retreat is the sea, which will soon be stormy. But that may not be the worst part. Out on the bay, I can see a half dozen black fins slicing through the water. What are you going to do?

THE NEW COUNTRY EXPLORER

There I am, climbing the mountain trail where no Englishman has gone before. The mountains tower all around me, and the only trails are those made by animals. A single misstep along a narrow ledge and I go crashing down through underbrush and scrub trees, hitting every rock as I go. Desperately grabbing at trees and rocks, I try to break my fall, finally sliding to a stop only inches from a 200-foot drop-off. Badly bruised and shaken, I try to struggle to my feet only to find one leg twisted grotesquely underneath my body. For a moment there is no feeling at all in the leg. Then the pain hits me with a jolt and, in a cold sweat, I nearly pass out. Just then, I hear a snarling growling noise. The hair on my neck stands on end as a giant brown and gray grizzly bear rises on its hind legs not more than a hundred feet away. Pitifully, I struggle to drag myself away. Suddenly, there is a whizzing sound and an arrow thuds, quivering in a tree trunk a few feet away. I look up to see a party of dreaded Blackfeet warriors with bows drawn on the ledge above me. It is at that exact moment that I hear the warning rattle of the rattlesnake at my feet. So, what are you going to do?

---

3. Character Monologues

Character monologues are readings that reveal the history, philosophy, or plans of an individual. Shakespeare's plays are filled with them, Caesar, Hamlet, and so on. Browning's poetry as well as the writings of people like Dickens, Poe, and Twain contain other examples. Children's books, from humorous treatments such as Sid Fleischman's McBroom series of tall tales and Judith Viorst's Alexander stories to serious historical fiction is rich in usable material. In addition, there are many usable primary resource materials, particularly letters, diaries, and newspaper accounts. Generally, first person writing is best, but individual examples should be judged on their own merit. Whatever the examples used, they should help children get a feel for the person and his or her cultural context and value system.

4. In-Role Reports

In-role reports represent one device that can be used to get the students to write their own dramatic reading. In-role reports bring a refreshing change from standard student reports. It has been common practice for decades for students to copy reports directly out of an encyclopedia or some other reference and then read with little comprehension what they have copied. With in-role reports, students take a character role and give the report from the perspective of that character. Characters may be real or created. Students have to pick a point in time for the character and report as if they knew nothing from that point on. For example, someone taking the role of Lincoln on the first of April, 1865, would know nothing about the assassination and might even end the report by describing plans to see *An American Cousin* when it plays at Ford's Theater. The point of these reports is to get into the feelings or perceptions of the characters involved.

5. First Person Poems

Poetry is one of the most personal forms of writing. It expresses feelings in their most essential form. Poetry is also designed for oral display by its very nature. A number of kinds of poems are excellent material for dramatic and expressive reading. *First person poems* are especially useful and, when their subjects are historical and geographic characters, may even be a very different type of in-role report because they are more likely to express feelings than facts. Humor poems as well as more serious poems can be really superior first person dramatic devices. Most are lively, relatively short, and very intense.

6. Historical Poems

Historical poems, particularly narrative ones, bring a certain epic quality to the past, conveying pageantry and drama as well as presenting a picture that conveys strong emotions, ideals, and values. They can be segmented or performed as plays, and acted out as they are read aloud by a series of readers.

ROLE PLAYS AND OTHER STRUCTURED DRAMA TECHNIQUES

Role Plays Structured

Structured role plays are dramatic activities in which character information and a scenario are provided to the participants. Some device is used so that the sequence of the drama is controlled, more or less, by the teacher.

EXAMPLE OF STRUCTURED ROLE PLAY

Create two groups of six to eight students each, the Rollercoasters and the Merry-Go-Rounds. Other students can be observers or the activity can be duplicated if space and control variables are favorable.

Scenario: The Rollercoasters and the Merry-Go-Rounds live in neighboring villages, but their cultures are very different and neither knows much about the other. The Rollercoasters have decided to invite the Merry-Go-Rounds to a big Getting-to-Know-You Party. The fact that no one in either village speaks the other's language causes some problems, but the invitation is finally sent and understood. There are some differences in culture, however, that may cause the people of the two villages to believe about what one can and cannot do.

Only the Rollercoasters know the following:

- You honor your people by always letting your guests eat first.
- The most honored people (your guests) are always served apples.
- Your teachers have taught you always to wear something blue.
- You must give a gift to a guest.
- During a meal it is impolite to talk or stand, but just before and after the meal, everyone shouts, "Yeow!" very loudly several times.

Only the Merry-Go-Rounds know the following:

- It is impolite to start eating before your hosts take a bite.

- Apples are a forbidden and profane food. Any of your people who eat apples are thrown out of the tribe.

- Blue is a sacred color of the sky and sea, to be worn only by the most holy person in the village. When anyone else wears blue it is a terrible wicked thing.

- It is rude to take gifts from a host.

- When one is a guest, a good Merry-Go-Round does everything he or she can to please the hosts.

- One is silent before and after meals, but, while eating, a polite guest shouts, "Gooba!" and jumps up and turns around after every bite.

The role-play event involves the party. It can be played two ways, either with the two cultures able to speak to one another or with both ignorant of the other's language. The role play can be suspended at any moment with a "freeze" signal for discussion of questions about the nature or culture or about the culture clash that is occurring. The obvious problem for the role play to resolve is, how can the different cultures resolve their differences?

Sociodramas

Sociodramas involve acting out the solutions to problems. The major difference between role play and sociodrama is that in sociodrama you are yourself. The essential problem situation begins, "If you were in this situation, what would you do and what would you say?" Quite often the problems are essentially of the sort that children themselves encounter, such as someone wanting to copy their homework, seeing someone cheating or stealing, meeting someone new, relating to someone who is very old, getting directions when lost, giving "how to" directions, making a complaint in a store, or going to the principal about an unfair rule. But children may be projected into a situation in which they are asked how they would act in parent or career situations if they were involved.

Children's Theater

Schotick and Walsko (1997) have described a structured approach they call children's theater which they use to teach economic concepts. The term may be somewhat confusing since "children's theater" has long been the term to describe scripted dramas of any type done for a juvenile audience, but the idea itself is a useful one. Basically, they describe a method in which a story is presented to the audience in play form with the audience being asked to interact with the actors, usually answering specific questions as the play develops. It is in some ways very like the notion of interactional drama described later in this chapter. However, the high structure of the approach makes it worth noting here.

ART- AND STORY-RELATED DRAMATIC TECHNIQUES

There are any number of techniques which specifically utilize art and literature. They not only develop cultural appreciation and expose children to exceptional examples but show the relationship of the arts to culture and to history. A few ideas are given here as examples.

Picture Pantomimes

Picture pantomimes require prints of paintings showing historical or legendary events or people in action in cultural settings. Children look at the painting and isolate and focus on two or three motions they see that they can do in sequence. They then do these motions and each person's response is discussed, at the same time drawing out the meaning and explanations of the paintings.

Story Play

Story play is a technique in which stories are acted out without pre-written scripts. The story line, at least to begin with, is a familiar one. The children have a solid understanding of "how the story goes." This is either because the story is an extremely familiar one or because the teacher has taken them through the reading or the telling of the story a sufficient number of times to give them a good sense of who and where in the story the characters are and where the plot line goes. The children then plan how to play the story and then act it out based on their plan. The actual dialogue is improvised as they go. The children can do the story as it is written, experiment with different endings or different twists on the plot, or try putting the story in different contexts (doing parodies such as a modern version of "Cinderella" called "Successerella," based on economic problems, for example).

Usually these story plays are done not for an audience but for the experience of doing them. Children delight in having these videotaped or in doing a radio drama on audio tape. They also can profit from the opportunity these dramas afford for experimenting, redoing the same stories, using different students in the same roles, treating closed-ended stories as though they were open-ended, and so on.

One device that can be incorporated into these story plays is story cards. In essence, the teacher or the students in the planning process create a storyboard of the story. Each story card on the storyboard represents an advancement of the plot, a different scene or an event in the sequence of the story. For example, the first card from "The Brave Little Tailor" might read, "While working in his shop, the Little Tailor swats at some irritating flies, killing seven of them; and is so proud of his feat that he goes out to seek his fortune." All of the story cards are then put in a stack on the chalk ledge and revealed one at a time as the story play is enacted. This gives students a better metacognitive map of the sequence of the story. It keeps the drama moving, too, and when the students themselves are in on the planning of these stories, they learn about sequencing and writing a story. This enables them to develop a sense of the importance of sequence in any chain of events.

Story cards allow students to plan and create new endings as well. Most importantly, they give the children an experience in drama that can be the basis of discussion. After the children become familiar with using the story cards as a way of developing and pacing the drama, they can use them to develop entirely new story dramatizations. A sixth-grade class created and dramatized the following story using their own story cards, creating various endings each time they played it out.

1. The expedition was alert for any sign of danger as the horses moved at a slow trot along the dusty trail.

2. The explorers were looking for a route that would lead them to the Pacific Ocean.

3. From the dense undergrowth, the captain of the expedition felt hostile eyes watching his small party.

4. In a small glen, a spring bubbled up out of the rocks and there the party stopped for a refreshing drink.

5. The captain felt rather than heard the footsteps on the path behind them and turned to see a large party of armed natives moving toward him.

6. The small party of explorers was helpless to do anything but follow the natives back through the undergrowth.

7. The walls of the strange city loomed high in front of the party, catching the explorers by surprise.

8. Where the explorers had been expecting primitive natives, they found a people who were far advanced in every way.

9. The explorers were led into the magnificent halls of the king's palace.

REENACTMENT

Hobbyist reenactment groups across the country work yearly at staging authentic Civil War and Revolutionary War battles. In various historic sites, local preservationists and employees go through the motions of living and working as early settlers as a part of the attempt to show visitors what life was like. Various plays and other performance pieces are staged at various times by theater groups. When teachers have children participate in any form of reenactment, they find that the children can become very motivated to do the needed research. That purposeful research aimed at doing an authentic and accurate job in a reenactment role can be, defensibly, one of the most invaluable experiences students ever have.

The adult reenactment groups create at least one misconception about reenactments—that they are something that young children cannot do. This is, of course, far from correct. What is true is that the kind of reenactments that children can do is altogether different.

The general guidelines for any reenactment begin with the selection of some event that will put the children in touch with the historical and cultural world heritage. The event should be one that children can reproduce with *some* faithfulness to history, but it should also be one with an internal sequence that is simple enough for the students to follow. Another consideration also might be that the event should be one that they can reenact without doing any violence to one another. (Battle scenes, so popular with reenactment hobbyists, are almost always excluded by this consideration.) The event should be one in which the sequence of actions by participants can be researched and reproduced.

Among the events that reenact well with young children are ceremonies and cultural rituals (greetings of two people, home entry rituals, tea ceremonies, a military group from a particular period setting up a camp, etc.), historic document development, and exchanges and land sales (the Louisiana Purchase, the Purchase of Manhattan, etc.), and parades and celebrations (women parade for the vote, labor movement picket lines, etc.). Once the event is selected, the students need to do basic research, identify the sequence of events, and then plan how they are going to replay the event. If possible, I like to go through the reenactment in the early stages of the research and then again after the research is complete. It gives the teacher and the students a better sense both of what they know to begin with and of what they have learned. It also gives some ideas about the kind of questions that need to be answered in the research. During the planning period, the teacher needs to help children discuss the meaning of what they are doing as well as the things that they cannot accurately or fully portray.

INTERACTIONAL DRAMA

Interactional drama involves an outsider or outsiders playing out a scenario from a historical context in front of the children. The actors, usually in costume, play in such a way that they draw the children into the dialogue, either by asking direct questions or asking the students about what they think (in such a way that they solicit both opinions and viewpoints). The dramas are not scripted and are usually open-ended, leaving the children the job of solving problems and conflicts the actors have brought to them.

Though interactional drama usually involves no role taking by the children, the success of the technique depends on *suspended disbelief,* the ability of students to think and act as though what is happening is real instead of just pretend. Suspended disbelief is what enables anyone to enjoy a play, a movie, or a television program, thinking of the characters as real people instead of as actors playing people. To make this happen in interactional drama, older classes especially may need to be coached beforehand. Convincing actors who stay in role and know their material are essential. It may be helpful but not essential to use actors who are not recognized by the class.

It may be best if the historical persons who visit the classroom for these dramas are not famous figures. In general, famous characters are more difficult for the children to believe, especially if the children already have a physical image of how the person looks in mind. Ordinary people or less well-known historical personages are easier to impersonate. There are a number of ways that the visitors can work:

- *Interview:* The visitor gives an introduction of him or herself and then answers children's questions. The actor really has to have a good background on the character to do this, and the children will do better if prepared so that they can ask better questions.

- *Storytelling:* The visitor, in-role, tells stories about his or her life.

- *Eavesdropping:* The visitors have a conversation staged so that the children seem to be overhearing something they were not meant to hear. (There may be a "freeze" signal that causes the actors to seem to become statues while the teacher and the students talk about what has been said.)

- *Recruitment:* The different actors, taking different sides, try to get the children to side with them.

- *Confrontation:* The actors are set up to have a conflict. One of the characters wins the sympathy of the children and gets them to help defend him or her against the adversary.

Following are a few sample scenarios that indicate some of the kinds that might be used for interactional dramas:

- The time frame we want to take the children to is September, 1776. Two revolutionary figures enter, arguing. One says that Washington's situation is so hopeless that he ought to retreat from Long Island, burning New York City behind him so the British cannot quarter there for the winter. The other argues that this is too drastic because it would destroy a lot of American property and leave many people homeless.

The other replies that two thirds of the property in New York belongs to Tories anyhow. Both try to recruit the children to their side.

• Two people dressed in turn-of-the-century garb enter, arguing. One thinks that women should be given the vote. The other is convinced that this is the wrong thing to do. The two (I prefer for them both to be women) try to recruit the children to their view, limiting themselves to arguments of the period.

• A young man (or woman) dressed in ancient garb sneaks into the room looking frightened and wary. He claims that he is a Roman slave and that his master was killed in his home during the night. Because the murderer cannot be identified, Roman law says that all the slaves of the household can be executed. He asks the children to hide him. After he hides, a burly Roman enters looking for the runaway slave. He tries to get the children to reveal the hiding place. When the young man is found, the teacher convinces the Roman officer that they should debate the law right there in the classroom before he is allowed to take the young man away. (It is admitted in the debate that the circumstances of the death indicate that a much stronger man than this youth and probably an assassin from outside the house committed the crime.)

DRAMA UNITS

Entire units of studies can have a dramatic focus. One approach is what Fulwer and McGuire (1997) call "Storypath." It utilizes a story line as the effective organizer for a study. A story scenario is the point of departure, with students creating roles for themselves consistent with that scenario. Discussion and art work allow students to elaborate the scenario. As events unfold in the scenario, the children construct meaning for themselves. They obviously are stakeholders in the story line and because of that they have both character sympathy and a real need to solve the problems in the evolving plot line. Social interactions and involvement are natural. The technique is highly adaptable and may be used to create "neighborhoods" for stories set in any culture or period of time.

STORY TELLING

Story telling is experiencing a worldwide revival. Throughout human history, story tellers have passed on the culture, created and preserved heroes, and passed on the history. Story tellers were often both the best historians and the foremost entertainers of bygone times.

I include story telling as a dramatic technique not because professional story tellers are consummate actors, but because every good teacher that I have ever known was something of a story teller. Story makes the past come alive and humanizes other people, no matter how different their culture or the geography of where they live.

Both teachers and students learn and benefit from becoming better story tellers. Telling a story to an appreciative audience is extremely satisfying. More importantly, a story provides a context in which information is given meaning and may be remembered. There are really only three steps in becoming a story teller: learning to choose a story that is worth telling and fits your purposes; learning how to learn a story; and learning how to tell a story (Turner, 1994). Choosing a story may be as easy as contacting the school librarian. Simply find a story that you like, that teaches something important, that is simple, suspenseful, exciting, and/or funny. Learning a story comes more easily once you learn how to "map" it out into a sequence of incidents and master a style of practice that fits you.

Telling a story well—now that is the difficult part. I have four hints:

1. Know your story so well that you don't have to concentrate your attention on what comes next, in fact so well that you can change it and add material to it. If you do forget something, don't "double back." Either add what you lost later, make up stuff to cover, or forget it all.

2. Work on expression, putting a lot of emotion and change in your voice.

3. Involve your audience by asking questions in the story, getting them to do stuff, pretending that each one is a character, etc.

4. Keep the story simple and direct and human.

EFFECTIVE USE OF DRAMA

Drama in the social studies can produce the kind of memorable Camelot moments that students will carry with them throughout their lives. It can help develop the research drive in lifetime students and make research purposeful and important to even marginal ones. It can make the classroom an exciting place to be, and can help students remember historical and cultural concepts and facts that they would otherwise forget. It can teach about social interactions and develop self concepts in a way that traditional "lecture, read, and recite" social studies can never do. However, dramatic activities used without instructional purposefulness can be a waste of time. In fact drama can become disturbing. The difference lies in the way the teacher handles drama.

If drama is to be effective in the social studies, the teacher has to first feel comfortable with it. He or she must be attracted to dramatic techniques and feel very positive about his or her potential to make the entire classroom a more exciting and interesting place. Teachers should avoid using techniques that make them feel they are losing control of the classroom.

Because dramatic techniques require high student involvement and sometimes include student planning and student leading in different directions, they may do just that. Teachers also need to feel that what they are doing with drama is solid and purposeful. Drama cannot be used as a mere time filler or entertainment. It has to have curricular importance and value. The teacher has to feel that and has to communicate that effectively to the students and usually to parents and the rest of the school as well.

Drama requires preparation. If there is a first rule of effective use of drama in the classroom, it is, "Be prepared!" The teacher has to know what he or she is about, find the right material, plan and structure the dramatic activity, and lead the students through planning and rehearsal and up to the dramatic enactment moment. The plan and the material cannot be developed along the way. The teacher who shoots from the hip with drama is likely to fall flat or, worse, waste a lot of valuable learning time.

Drama only works in a conducive atmosphere. That atmosphere is one that is open and experimental and charged with exciting stimuli. It also offers emotional security so that children feel safe psychologically. To take the kind of personal risks that drama demands, children have to be sure that their peers will not be ridiculing or demeaning them for their efforts. No child wants to appear to be foolish or ridiculous. Paradoxically, some children will act silly on purpose to avoid looking silly while trying to be serious. The safe conducive atmosphere for drama comes only with a series of positive experiences in which the teacher slowly edges the class toward dramatic expression that involves more risk taking.

LOOKING BACK

Teaching is stagecraft, and teachers who have a stronger sense of the drama of the classroom are going to add suspense and excitement to their teaching. They create a dramatic atmosphere and give children visions of history, of geography, of culture, of government, and of society that are vivid, interesting, and memorable.

Simulation games involve students in usually competitive ways and combine elements from games and role play. Though there are many types of simulation games, the ones most suited for social studies are those which can be understood and played by children within a short period of time. Simulation games are most effective when played with a definite learning purpose and when children understand that purpose.

Mock trial activities range from re-creation of historic trials to invented trials of fantasy characters. One form of mock trial even involves invention of everything from the crime to the witnesses.

Among the many other forms of drama that can be used in social studies instruction are guided fantasy, readers' theater, various types of dramatic reading, class action dramas, story play, sociodrama, and role play. Drama can even be the focus of entire units. Even if other forms of drama are not used, certainly all teachers and many students can become story tellers and, by doing so, make social studies more memorable and more involving. Drama activities of all types become memorable experiences themselves, and that experience can provide the basis for learning new concepts and information.

Increasing attention has been paid recently to two forms of drama requiring background research. Historical reenactments involve studying past events in detail and trying to re-create them. In interactional drama, actors, in-role, attempt to draw children into a problem discussion related to issues and events of some historic period.

SELF-TEST

1. What is a simulation game?

2. Set up an in-basket game for one of the following three individuals:

    • The Abbot of a Medieval Monastery under attack by Vikings

    • A wagon master of a wagon train traveling to Oregon in the 1850s

    • The chief of a village in Africa that is in fear of being raided by slavers in the 1700s

3. Describe three types of mock trials.

4. What is *readers' theater*?

5. What is the point of class action stories?

6. Why is humor used in so many of the dramatic techniques?

7. What is the difference between role play and sociodrama?

8. What is story play?

9. What are some ways in which a teacher or student can become a better story teller?

10. What purposes do different dramatic activities serve in the social studies?

REFERENCES

Fulwer, B. E., and McGuire, M. E. (1997). Storypath: Powerful social studies instruction in the primary grades. *Social Studies and the Young Learner,* 9 (January/February), 4–7.

Shotick, J. A., and Walsko, G. (1997). Using children's theater to teach economics. *Social Studies and the Young Learner,* 9 (January/February), 11–13.

Turner, T. N. (1994). Storytelling—it's never going to be easy. *Tennessee Education,* 24 (Spring), 5–10.

SUGGESTED READING

Chilcoat, G. (1989). The melodrama and the American slave experience. *The Social Studies,* 80 (November/December), 225–239.

Freiberg, H. J. (2002). Essential skills for new teachers. *Educational Leadership,* 59(6) (March), 56–60.

Gonzalez, J. B., and Regan, F. S. (1995). Getting started in cultural diversity: Dramatizing a story. *Stage of the Art,* 7(8) (Fall), 12–16.

Simpson, J., Herring, J., and Klein, D. A. (2002). Developing creative curriculum: A model for preservice teacher training in drama education. *Stage of the Art,* 14(3) (Spring), 1–4.

Turner, T. N. (1990). *Stand Up and Cheer.* Glenview, IL: Scott Foresman.

Turner, T. N. (1979). Variations on a theme: Three simulations based on the fallout shelter model. *The Social Studies,* 70 (November/December), 281–285.

Whaley, C. (2002). Meeting the diverse needs of children through storytelling. *Young Children,* 57(2) (March), 31–34.

Index